JEAN RENOIR

•

André Bazin

Edited with an Introduction by
FRANÇOIS TRUFFAUT

•

Translated from the French by
W. W. HALSEY II *and* WILLIAM H. SIMON

A TOUCHSTONE BOOK
Published by Simon & Schuster, Inc.
NEW YORK

A
L202a £3.95

CONTENTS

●

Introduction

by François Truffaut

●

No one should expect me to introduce this book with caution, detachment, or equanimity. André Bazin and Jean Renoir have meant too much to me for me to be able to speak of them dispassionately. Thus it is quite natural that I should feel that *Jean Renoir* by André Bazin is the *best* book on the cinema, written by the *best* critic, about the *best* director.

André Bazin died at forty on November 11, 1958. More than a critic, he was a "writer of the cinema," striving to describe films rather than to judge them. Bazin's essays on Bresson, Chaplin, Rossellini, Buñuel, von Stroheim, and Fellini, as well as his masterful little book on Welles,* have been translated throughout the world. His death interrupted his two most interesting projects: this book on the work of Jean Renoir and a short film on Romanesque churches.

A contributor to *L'Ecran Français*, *L'Esprit*, *Le Parisien Libéré*, *Télérama* (then called *Radio-Cinéma-Télévision*), and *L'Observateur*, Bazin profoundly influenced the film makers of the "New Wave," starting with those whom he brought together at *Cahiers du Cinéma* and who had just begun to make films when he passed away after ten years of illness. Thus it was not fortuitous that the filmography of Renoir's work reprinted at the end of this book was put together under Bazin's direction by

* *Orson Welles*. Edition le Chavanne, 1957.

Jacques Doniol-Valcroze, Claude de Givray, Jean-Luc Godard, Jacques Rivette, Eric Rohmer, and myself in 1957, and completed and updated by Claude Beylie, Jean Douchet, Michel Delahaye, Jean Kress, and Louis Marcorelles in 1971.

André Bazin, whose health deteriorated year after year, found the strength to look at films and to comment on them until his last day. The day before his death he wrote one of his best essays—the long analysis of *The Crime of M. Lange**—having watched the film on television from his bed.

Renoir's work excited Bazin more than any other. He was working on this study of his favorite director when he died. His fragmentary manuscript has been reconstructed and completed by his friends with the assistance of his wife, Janine Bazin.

I am responsible for the final organization of the work, for its division into ten-chapters approximating the chronological development of Renoir's work. Obviously Bazin would have done it differently if he had had time. I think he intended to devote a chapter to the themes treated by Renoir, another to his work with actors, another to the adaptation of novels.

In one of his last letters, Bazin wrote me:

"I am circling around Renoir by reading the life of Augustus, the novels of Zola: *La Bête Humaine* and *Nana*, Maupassant . . . I will eventually have to approach him more directly, but I am now at a point where I know either too much or not enough. Too much to be satisfied with approximations, not yet enough to fill in all the variables of his equations" (July 7, 1958).

I am not far from thinking that the work of Jean Renoir is the work of an infallible film maker. To be less extravagant, I will say that Renoir's work has always been guided by a philosophy of life which expresses itself with the aid of something much like a trade secret: *sympathy*. It is thanks to this sympathy that Renoir has succeeded in creating the most alive films

* Those of Renoir's films which were commercially distributed in the United States are referred to here by their American titles. The dates are those of the original release. American and French titles, as well as the American release dates of the French films, are given in the filmography at the end of the book. Translators' note.

in the history of the cinema, films which still breathe forty years after they were made.

André Bazin, whom his friends remember as an extraordinary man full of joyous goodwill and intelligence, found himself in complete sympathy with the work of Renoir, with his thirty films all of which revolve around the famous sentence from *The Rules of the Game* (spoken by Renoir himself in the role of Octave): "You see, in this world, there is one awful thing, and that is that everyone has his reasons."

If this beautiful book by André Bazin is unfinished, consider it unfinished in the manner of *A Day in the Country*, which is to say that it is sufficient to itself and, even in its fragmentary state, the finest portrait of Jean Renoir ever written.

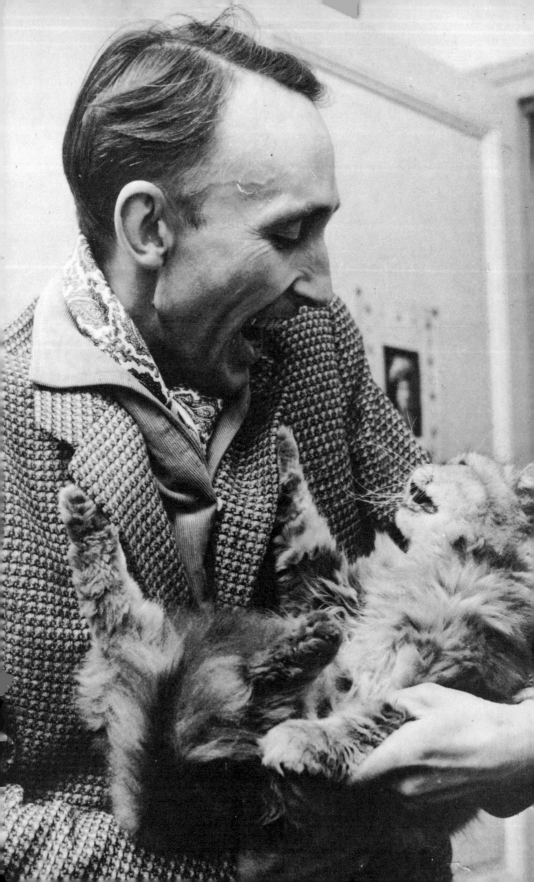

André Bazin's Little Beret
by Jean Renoir

●

The more I travel through life, the more I am convinced that masks are proliferating. I have difficulty finding a woman whose face looks as it really is. Our age is the triumph of make-up. And not only for faces, but, more important, for the mind as well.

The modern world is founded on the ever increasing production of material goods. One must keep producing or die. But this process is like the labor of Sisyphus. Forgetting Lavoisier's dictum, "In nature nothing is created, nothing is lost; everything is transformed," we convince ourselves that our earthly machines will succeed in catching up with eternity. But to maintain the level of production on which our daily bread depends, we must ever renew and expand our enterprises.

One prefers that this process be peaceful, but events have a way of getting out of hand. This is an age of violence, and it is likely to become even more so. Still, we do everything we can to conduct our operation peacefully, to conquer by persuasion. And thus, the cancer of our society: advertising.

Occasionally in such troubled times, men or women come forth to dedicate themselves to helping us reestablish a sense of reality. Bazin was such a man.

I loved him because he belonged to the Middle Ages. I have a passion for the Middle Ages, just as I have a distrust for the

André Bazin (1957)

Renaissance. That movement, which laid the foundations of industrial society, is ultimately responsible for the atomic bomb.

The frail figure of Bazin, withered with sickness, was like Pascal's "thinking reed."* For me, he was the incarnation of one of the saints in the Cathedral of Chartres who project a luminous and magical vision through their stained-glass representations. I would have liked to visit Chartres with Bazin. I regret that I never had the chance. This enthusiast of the cinema was as much at home in a medieval chapel as he was in front of a screen on the Champs-Elysées.

Clothes looked different on Bazin. They were the same clothes one saw on other people, but on him they lost their contemporary appearance. The anachronism of his outward appearance was neither a protest nor a revolt, nor least of all, an aesthetic declaration. It was involuntary. It identified him as an aristocrat before he opened his mouth, and he was not even aware of it.

His little beret perfectly suited the frail figure of the reformer of the French cinema. I will never forget it.

The sickness which gnawed at Bazin vanquished his spirit before he was able to finish this book. François Truffaut and others of his friends undertook to complete it. Theirs are names which, to my mind, figure prominently in the history of the cinema. I would be falsely modest if I did not express my deep gratitude to them. I do not know if I deserve this honor, but I hasten to accept it. This moment is a beautiful gift from Bazin. It is not the first, or the last: great men do not die.

At the thought of Bazin who dedicated this book to me and of his disciples who completed it, I feel a very gentle pride. My feeling is that of a man who has just been given a firm handshake by someone he admires greatly.

March 18, 1971

* "Man is but a reed, the most feeble thing in nature; but he is a thinking reed. The entire universe need not arm itself to crush him. A vapor, a drop of water, suffice to kill him. But if the universe were to crush him, man would still be more noble than that which killed him, because he knows that he dies and the advantage which the universe has over him; the universe knows nothing of this." Blaise Pascal, *Pensées*. Trans.

PART ONE

Catherine Hessling and Werner Krauss in *Nana*

CHAPTER ONE

THE SILENT FILMS

•

In a remarkable article published in *Le Point* in 1938 Jean Renoir looked back on his days as a silent film director a decade earlier. He emphasized his admiration for the American cinema of the 1920s, but said that his real desire to make movies was born the day that a showing of *Le Brasier Ardent** taught him that a film of quality could be produced somewhere other than Hollywood. This first conversion was followed, like Pascal's, by another, more profound and radical vision when Renoir saw von Stroheim's *Foolish Wives*. "This film astounded me," Renoir recalled. "I must have seen it at least ten times. Destroying my most cherished notions, it made me realize how wrong I had been. Instead of idly criticizing the public's supposed lack of sophistication, I sensed that I should try to reach it through the projection of authentic images in the tradition of French realism."†

Renoir sought to cultivate the realism, the authenticity, which he had found in the popular American productions and in von Stroheim's work through the proper direction of his

---

* A 1923 film made in France by the Russian émigré actor-director Ivan Mosjoukine. Trans.

† The famous *Le Point* article is reproduced *in extenso* in Part II. François Truffaut.

Catherine Hessling in *Une Vie sans Joie*

Nana

actors. "I was beginning to realize," he said, "that the movement of a scrubwoman, of a vegetable vendor or of a girl combing her hair before a mirror frequently had superb plastic value. I decided to make a study of French gesture as reflected in my father's paintings."

Renoir's silent work is dominated by his principal actress, Catherine Hessling. It was to set off her extraordinary personality that he made *Une Fille sans Joie* (produced and written by Renoir, directed by Albert Dieudonné), *La Fille de l'Eau, Nana, Charleston*, and *La Petite Marchande d'Allumettes*.

One cannot help but wonder how much of the credit for Jean Renoir's work belongs to this woman, who was both his wife and his favorite actress. It is true that this remarkable doll-faced girl with the charcoal circles under her great bright eyes, and the imperfect but strangely articulated body reminiscent of the figures in certain Impressionist paintings, was an extraordinary incarnation of femininity. She was a curious creature, at once mechanical and living, ethereal and sensuous. But it seems to me that Renoir saw her less as a director than as a painter. Enchanted by the unique beauty of her body and her face, he worried less about directing the *actress* in her dramatic role than he did about photographing the *woman* from every possible angle. This more or less conscious aim is clearly discernible, for example, in *Charleston*, whose thin and whimsical scenario is little more than a pretext for an incoherent but charming exhibition of Catherine Hessling.

It is possible, then, that this actress helped Jean Renoir to the self-discovery which is essential to his art at the same time that she slowed his passage from the simple photographing of actors to true movie making. In any case, it is with good reason that in the same article in *Le Point* Renoir set three films apart from the rest of his silent work: *Nana, La Petite Marchande d'Allumettes*, and *Tire au Flanc*.

It is common to consider *La Petite Marchande d'Allumettes* as a fairy tale and to classify it as a work of the French avant-garde. But if this judgment is correct historically, it is hardly so from an aesthetic point of view. More precisely, *La Petite*

Catherine Hessling in *La Petite Marchande d'Allumettes*

Marchande d'Allumettes represents an intrusion of Renoir's realism into the themes and techniques of the avant-garde. The source of the still radiant charm of this little film is apparent today: it is the very realism of Renoir's fantasy. It is not Andersen's tale but Renoir's fascination with technical effects—the almost sensual pleasure he derives from the originality of his fantastic images—which is the basis for the film's poetry. While normally one goes to great lengths to hide technical effects, to camouflage photographically the imperfection of sets and makeup, Renoir does not hesitate to reveal in close-up and sharp focus the actor beneath the wooden soldier's mask or the actress playing the porcelain doll. He goes so far as to emphasize the tricks of perspective and the differences in scale between the actors and the miniatures to draw on these incongruities as material for his imagery.

And the protagonists of the tale—Karen, the handsome officer, and the Hussar of Death—are not simply caricatures meant to terrify or reassure us. They assert themselves with an intimate clarity which endows them with a poignant human appeal. From this Scandinavian fairy tale, Renoir has made a tender and sensual, bittersweet poetic fantasy in which even Death becomes a friend and acquaintance.

Unlike *La Petite Marchande d'Allumettes*, *Tire au Flanc* is considered one of the light-hearted concessions to commercialism which Renoir was forced to make from time to time. For example, René Jeanne and Charles Ford wrote in their *Histoire du Cinéma:* "In these declining years of the silent cinema one finds Renoir's name on *Tire au Flanc* ("Goldbrick"), a film no better than any of the other military comedies scattered through French film history." One would like to believe that these historians, unable to see the film again, were betrayed by their memories, for *Tire au Flanc* is much different from the others of its genre. And Renoir is perfectly justified in recalling it fondly: "I had the good fortune in this film," he wrote, "to introduce Michel Simon, who was already the great actor he is today. And I remember the collaboration with the dancer Pomiès, who was to die soon thereafter, as a pleasant episode in my career. Making this partly tragic, partly whimsical burlesque, with no clear relation to the play it was taken from, gave me great satisfaction."

Made rapidly with minimal resources, *Tire au Flanc* really bears only superficial resemblance to the traditional military comedies. A little attention and sensitivity enable one to share the obvious pleasure that Renoir derived from his successful effort to transcend the conventions of the genre imposed upon him. *Tire au Flanc* owes more to Mack Sennett and to von Stroheim than it does to Mouézy-Eon.* And one can see today in its juxtaposition of comedy and tragedy, of fantasy and cruelty, the beginnings of Renoir's quest for the *drame gai* which was to culminate ten years later in *The Rules of the Game.*

This quality stands out in many of Renoir's silent films—

---

* A. Mouézy-Eon was the author of several highly popular, though quite conventional farces, one of which was the source of Renoir's film. Trans.

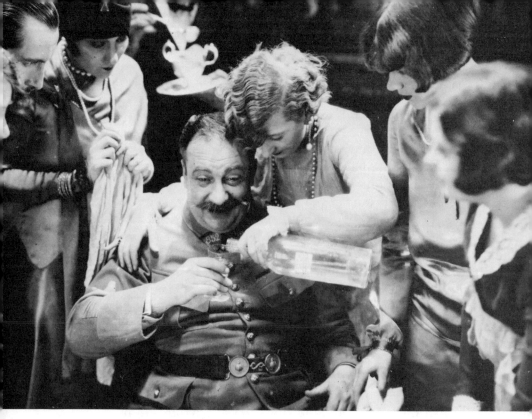

Félix Oudard in *Tire au Flanc*

Félix Oudard and Georges Pomiès in *Tire au Flanc*

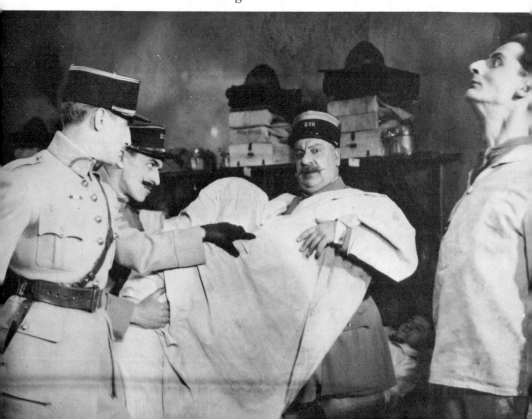

not only in *Nana*, *La Petite Marchande d'Allumettes*, and *Tire au Flanc*, but even in the films reputed to be thoroughly commercial, such as *Le Bled*. It was on these films that Renoir served his technical apprenticeship. The importance he accorded to photographic style and, above all, to the choice of lenses is apparent in *La Petite Marchande d'Allumettes*, and perhaps even more so in *Le Bled*. This latter film is a technical absurdity from beginning to end: although many of the scenes were conceived with important elements in the background, Renoir insisted on using fast lenses, which gave a very soft image and virtually no background clarity. These results led him later to take the opposite tack, requiring his cameramen to take all their shots with one deep-focus lens. Renoir only barely emerged from this period of technical groping with *Boudu Saved from Drowning* in 1932.

The early films also give the impression that in the silent period Renoir had not yet found reliable guidelines for his editing; the shots follow one another with no logical or dramatic coherence. He was still preoccupied with his performers and not yet able to subordinate acting to the demands of storytelling on film. I do not believe that there is a single pan shot in either *Nana* or *Le Bled*, although this device would become crucial to all his sound films. On the other hand, he developed in these early films a considerable prowess for lengthy deep dolly shots, which is scarcely apparent at all in *The Rules of the Game*. In his subsequent work Renoir's fundamental preoccupation became the widening of the screen—already deepened by the lenses—through lateral reframing. To this end panning and lateral dollying became his two main camera techniques.

The themes which Renoir developed in his sound works were also present in rough and sketchy form in the silent films. There is, for example, the theme of mechanical toys in *La Petite Marchande d'Allumettes* or the hunt in *Le Bled*, which we find so brilliantly handled in *The Rules of the Game*.

In considering Jean Renoir's work in the years preceding 1930, then, we must fight the critical prejudice that would have us believe that with the exception of *Nana* and possibly *La Pe-*

tite Marchande d'Allumettes the creator of *The Rules of the Game* made only clumsy and insignificant films in his early period. For even the worst of these films is full of a charm which testifies to the genius of its creator. And one can see in all of them the first tentative, but spirited and ambitious, efforts of a nimble talent groping for the course it would find several years later in *La Chienne*.

Which is to say, in sound! For it must be admitted that while his silent films foreshadowed what was to come, there is no comparison between even the best of the silents and the worst of the sound films. Unlike René Clair, who perfected his style in 1927 with *The Italian Straw Hat* and confirmed it with *Les Deux Timides*, Renoir is decidedly a sound director.

Renoir's silent work is irrevocably marked by an unfinished and expectant quality, as if he had been waiting for the technical discovery that would liberate his visions. With his adaptation to sound, Renoir established himself as a man of the future. He welcomed technological advance because it helped him achieve the realism he had sought since his first half-conscious experiments in the silent era.

CHAPTER TWO

THE FIRST TALKING FILMS

●

On Purge Bébé (1931)

"My first talking film was sort of a test. People didn't trust me, so I had to prove myself. I managed to get a job directing *On Purge Bébé*, based on Georges Feydeau's play. This film is not much, but I shot it in only four days.* Even so, it is more than 2,000 meters long.† It cost the producer less than 200,000 francs, and earned more than a million. . . . It was the age of bad sound. The props and the sets were arranged around the mike with an unbelievable naïveté. These practices annoyed me, and to show how dissatisfied I was I decided to record the flushing of a toilet."‡

Renoir's first sound film is famous for the flushing toilet and for the debut of Fernandel. Having only seen it in negative and on a Movieola, I can say little except that it has the least cutting of any of Renoir's films. There are just a few shots per

* Questioned recently, Jean Renoir said six days, which doesn't really alter the point. (Notes not otherwise attributed are by Bazin. Trans.)
† Nevertheless, the existing negative is only five and a half reels long, or 1,675 meters. (If the original was 2,000 meters, it must have been about 1 hour and 10 minutes long. The existing copy runs about an hour. See page 156. Trans.)
‡ One also sees and hears a chamber pot shattering on the floor.

reel and only half a dozen close-ups, including that of the chamber pot. Most of it was shot within the three walls of a stage set. And the film was completed after six days of preparation, four days of shooting, and six of editing. Less than two weeks later it opened at the Aubert-Palace, and by the end of the first week it had earned back its entire cost.

La Chienne (1931)

The film opens with a prologue introducing the work and its characters. A gendarme appears and intones, "You are going to see an allegorical drama, etc., etc." Guignol* arrives, thrashes the gendarme, and insists that the film has no message and will not teach anyone anything at all.

M. Legrand appears at the beginning as a model employee. He is a cashier in a small hosiery company. Bored at a small party given in honor of the boss by the employees, he nonetheless refuses to follow his colleagues to a brothel. On his way home he encounters a drunk, Dédé, beating his mistress, Lulu. He intervenes and takes the young woman home in a taxi. Lulu promises to write him.

At home he accidentally makes some noise and awakens his wife, Adèle, who castigates him and invokes the memory of her first husband, Sergeant Godard. M. Legrand waits for the storm to pass and turns to his paintings. M. Legrand is a Sunday painter.

M. Legrand has set Lulu up in a small Montmartre apartment. He visits her during the day while Lulu saves her nights for Dédé. But Dédé becomes more and more demanding. He is angry that Lulu cannot get more money out of Legrand, whom they both believe to be quite wealthy. One day, Dédé takes Legrand's canvasses (which the poor man has brought to Lulu's

---

* Guignol is a stock character of the French puppet theater. A colorful figure, he is good-humored and clever, and while sometimes duped, he is never bested. Trans.

Jany Marèze and Georges Flammand in *La Chienne*

Michel Simon in *La Chienne*

place in response to his wife's nagging) and makes the rounds
of the art galleries. He passes the paintings off as the work of an
American woman, Clara Wood. At Walstein's an art critic
named Langelard sees possibilities in the work of this primitive
woman artist.

Clara Wood's career is launched with a reception at Walstein's. The atmosphere is rather decadent, and Langelard paws
Clara/Lulu with a practiced hand. Walstein suggests that Clara
begin immediately to paint a portrait of one of his customers.
She refuses (and with good reason!), but Dédé convinces her to
try to string the customer along and get some money out of him.
(The customer is played by Jean Gehret.)

While passing by the gallery, Legrand sees one of his paintings on display and realizes that Lulu is selling them. He does
not hold this against her, and this revelation has no consequence
later in the scenario. It is perhaps one of the more improbable
elements of the script.

To "help" Lulu/Clara, whose demands for money (for her
Dédé) are increasing, Legrand has filched his wife's savings
from under a pile of linen. One night in the street he runs into
his wife's old husband, Sergeant Godard, who has not died after
all but has taken on the identity of a dead man in order to escape
Adèle. Sergeant Godard first tries to blackmail Legrand by
threatening to reappear to reclaim his wife(!), but Legrand has
another idea. He suggests to Sergeant Godard that he come and
rob his "widow" that night at eleven o'clock. It is a trap designed to lead to a confrontation between the sergeant and Adèle
and allow Legrand to regain his freedom. The trap works perfectly, and taking advantage of the confusion, Legrand flees
with his suitcase to Lulu's. But Lulu, not expecting him, is
bedded down with Dédé. Legrand discovers them and retreats
in dismay. A violent scene ensues between Dédé and Lulu: she,
completely in love and not giving a damn about anything; he,
caring only about Legrand's bankroll.

The next morning Lulu is reading in bed when Legrand returns, ready to forgive. He tells her that he understands that she
is at the mercy of this evil man . . . But Lulu abuses him. It is

Dédé she loves, and as for Legrand, he has been had: "You never looked at yourself in the mirror . . . ," she says. Beside himself with anguish, Legrand takes a letter opener and strikes Lulu until she is dead.

Outside a singer in the street sings, "Be true, O my unknown beauty . . ."

Dédé returns by car. He enters the building, and the concierge yells at him for failing to say hello. A minute later he hurries out again, pale and upset, and in view of everyone gets back in his car and drives off. Naturally it is he who is suspected of the crime. He is arrested a little later in a café.

The witnesses assemble at the inquest. Walstein tries to take advantage of the occasion to talk Lulu's mother into turning over to him any canvasses Lulu might have left with her. Legrand is completely exonerated. Dédé, clumsy in his denials and intolerably cocky, is of course indicted.

Legrand is fired from the hosiery company when 2,500 francs is found to be missing from his books. Obviously, it is money that he has embezzled to give to Lulu.

The trial: the witnesses (the concierge, the colonel of Dédé's regiment . . .); the summation interrupted by Dédé to proclaim that all this is pointles blather and that he did not kill Lulu (his lawyer: "It is suicide"). Dédé is condemned to death.

Epilogue: Legrand, dirty and ragged, opens car doors in front of the art galleries on the Avenue Matignon. Another derelict does him out of a tip. It is Sergeant Godard. They both laugh as the customer carries off Legrand's self-portrait in his car.

The photography in *La Chienne* already shows a marked attempt at depth of field identical to that of *Boudu Saved from Drowning*. The sets are designed to emphasize the deep focus. The window of the house opens on a narrow courtyard, and through the windows of the neighboring apartments we see a woman doing housework, a child practicing scales on the piano. Inside Legrand's apartment, too, the staging is organized around actions which move from foreground to background as the characters go from one room to another.

The cutting in the great scene where Legrand discovers that Lulu is sleeping with Dédé somewhat foreshadows the editing at the end of *The Crime of M. Lange*. The camera is first behind Legrand, picking up the bed through the door. Then it jumps to the exterior of the house and observes the scene through the curtains in the window. There is a deliberate attempt here to use a frame within the frame to underline the importance of all that lies beyond the limits of the screen.

The sets are admirably realistic, notably Legrand's apartment, and particularly the kitchen. Lulu's rooms are strikingly detailed (the porcelain bibelots). The importance of the street is emphasized by the realistic set, which is defined and concretized by sharp details (the slope) and by pictorial effects such as reflections in shop windows or automobile mirrors. The street's importance is also underlined by the simultaneously recorded sound.

The sound track of *La Chienne* is consistently excellent thanks to the on-location recording. The atmospheric noises are fantastic because they are real. For example, the romantic dialogue between Legrand and Lulu beneath her apartment is accompanied by the loud rushing of water in the gutter. On the other hand, the street singer's song was clearly recorded in the studio. Even in the scenes consisting completely of dialogue, which were shot in the studio, the sound is realistic. When a character walks away, we feel him walking away: this is no technical effect.

In *La Chienne* the dialogue and the direction of the actors reach the sublime. Difficult to define, the style seems to be the simultaneous expression of the greatest fantasy and the greatest realism. We have the impression that the dialogues were partially improvised to fit each actor's style.

At the core of this realism there is a feeling of passivity. For example, when the art merchant Walstein, sitting in the waiting room at the court, asks Lulu's mother if the girl has left any paintings or drawings, the old woman remains stubbornly silent and expressionless. This is a realism of manners, not of psychology. Psychological realism is never complete realism. Realism works in relation to the freedom of the *mise en scène.**

Night at the Crossroads (1932)

André Bazin left no writings on this film. See the note by Jean-Luc Godard in the Filmography. F.T.

* Strictly speaking, *mise en scène* refers to the material organization of a stage or film production: the choice of sets, the lighting, the positioning and the direction of actors. Bazin frequently uses it in a broader sense to suggest the translation of an idea or story into visual or cinematic terms. Trans.

Pierre Renoir (standing with glass) as Inspector Maigret in *Night at the Crossroads*

Boudu Saved from Drowning (1932)

One of the most paradoxically appealing aspects of Jean Renoir's work is that everything in it is so casual. He is the only film maker in the world who can afford to treat the cinema with such apparent offhandedness. It took Renoir to muster the audacity to film Gorki on the banks of the Marne or to handle the casting as he did on *The Rules of the Game*, in which almost all the actors, except the servants, are so marvelously out of their usual characters. If one had to describe the art of Renoir in a word, one could define it as an aesthetic of discrepancy. *Boudu Saved from Drowning* is no exception: in this film the scenario is tangential to the subject; the casting, incidental to the characters; and the plot, oblique to the situation. Only the découpage* is to the point, for it is the editing which directs the dance with diabolical cleverness and which shapes the contradictory elements in this aesthetic universe into a coherent style.

I would not go so far as to say that the best moments in *Boudu* are those which are most false. But while the pinnacles of

* *Découpage* has a variety of meanings and cannot always be translated by the English "editing." It may mean simply "shooting script" or "continuity"; it may mean the *process* of breaking down an event into separate visual "shots"; it may refer to the style inherent in the conception of these shots; it may mean simply the "techniques" used to record the shots on film. Bazin writes at one point, for example, "*découpage*, which is to say, framing and camera movement . . ." (*Qu'est-ce que le cinéma?* Vol. II, p. 57). More frequently, however, he uses the term as he does here, in its abstract sense, to refer to the entire operation of translating an idea into cinematic terms. (For a detailed discussion of the French concept of *découpage*, see Nöel Burch, *Praxis du cinéma*, Gallimard 1969.)

The French term which most closely approximates "editing" is *montage*, the organization of separate bits of film. It is important to note, however, that *montage* has a special, usually negative, meaning for Bazin. As a rule, he uses it only to describe editing in which shots are juxtaposed in such a way that they mean more together than they do separately (a shot of people emerging from a subway followed by a shot of a herd of sheep, for example, as in the opening sequence of *Modern Times*). To the extent that this technique fragments the essential continuity of reality and imposes upon it a meaning which is not necessarily its own, Bazin disapproves. Trans.

Sévérine Lezinska, Graudval, Michel Simon, and Marcelle Haina in
Boudu

Renoir's work are often remarkable for the sureness and realism
of their tone, they also sometimes owe their dazzling impact to
carefully contrived dramatic disharmonies.

One of the best scenes in *Boudu Saved from Drowning*, the
suicide attempt from the Pont des Arts, was made in total de-
fiance of the logic of the scene. The crowd of unpaid extras gathered on the bridge and the river banks was not there to witness
a tragedy. They came to watch a movie being made, and they
were in good humor. Far from asking them to feign the emotion
which verisimilitude would demand, Renoir seems to have encouraged them in their light-hearted curiosity. The film does
not for a moment convince us that the crowd is interested in

Boudu. Some of the spectators turn around to get a better look at the cameraman, much as in the earliest newsreels when people had not yet grown accustomed to the camera. And, as if he felt the falseness of the acting were not sufficiently apparent, Renoir had some rapid shots taken from behind the crowd, which leave no doubt of its lack of emotion.

This incongruity is reinforced by the fact that Renoir is one of the masters of photographic realism, the heir of the traditions of the naturalistic novel and its contemporary, Impressionist painting. A fraction of these "mistakes" would condemn any other director. But they are an integral part of the style of Jean Renoir, often the best part of it. For Renoir, what is important is not the dramatic value of a scene. Drama, action—in the theatrical or novelistic sense of the terms—are for him only pretexts for the essential, and the essential is everywhere in what is visible, everywhere in the very substance of the cinema. Of course, drama is necessary—that is what we go to the movies to see—but the story can get along easily by itself. It is sufficient to sketch just enough of it so that the audience has the satisfaction of understanding. That done, the real film remains to be made: characters, objects, light, all must be arranged in the story like colors in a drawing, without being directly subordinated to it. At times the very interest of the finished product may be in the fact that the colors do not fit neatly within the contours of the drawing. The effects Renoir creates out of this overlapping seem all the more subtle because he knows how to stay within the lines beautifully when he wants to.

Let us return to *Boudu Saved from Drowning*. Boudu throws himself into the water without knowing why. Because he was hot? Because he has lost his dog? Because he didn't like the looks of a cop? What difference does it make? Boudu throws himself into the river. That is all you need to know. You would perhaps like some shots to show you *how* Boudu tries to drown himself. That would be sadistic. *You* don't want to try, so let him handle it by himself, and be satisfied with being told about it. You would do better to look at the Pont des Arts (which seems to be made of match sticks and which sags under the weight of the crowd) and the fishermen along the banks of the Seine who are yelling because all the commotion is scaring the fish.

Besides, isn't all the distraction which the camera imposes on you the greatest possible measure of fidelity to the action, because it makes you behave as Boudu himself would act if it were you who had jumped into the water?

The discrepancy between dramatic content and its visual presentation, then, is the principal medium of Renoir's irony.

MANUSCRIPT NOTES

1. Function of music in *Boudu*. Essentially an erotic indicator: sometimes foreboding (for example, the barrel organ in the street), sometimes suggestive (when Anne-Marie hums, when Lestingois picks out "Les Fleurs du Jardin . . ." on the piano), sometimes triumphant and symbolic (the military horn in the engraving on the wall over Mme. Lestingois's bed). You could say that whenever we hear music in *Boudu* we know that someone is aroused. ("quelqu'un bande")

2. *Boudu's* charm lies in its glorification of vulgarity. It portrays the most blatant lubricity in a civilized and nonchalant manner. *Boudu* is a magnificently obscene film.

3. Everything that an actor can be in a film, Michel Simon is in *Boudu*. Everything!

Chotard et Cie. (1933)

Chotard is a wealthy grocer in a small town in the South of France. In his home he rules with an iron hand. His daughter has two suitors, a police constable and a poet, neither of whom suits Chotard in the least. In the course of a masked ball at the town hall, the poet, Julien, carries her off. Chotard resigns himself to having an artist for a son-in-law.

The result is even more disastrous than he feared. The poet, calmly and obliviously, makes a complete mess of his father-in-law's business. The exasperated Chotard throws him out.

Julien packs his bags and goes. However, while he is waiting for the train, the newspapers announce that he has won the Prix Goncourt. Thunderstruck, Chotard retrieves his son-in-law at the station. Reconciliation. Chotard is delighted by the situation, but he sees it through the eyes of a merchant. Literature, he thinks, can be more profitable than the grocery business. He shuts up his son-in-law in a tower, commanding him to produce twenty pages a day, ten novels a year. The young man gets sick of confinement and revolts.

Chotard's business is going to ruin because everyone is reading novels and poetry.

Julien spells out the moral of the affair for his father-in-law: each man must fulfill his own destiny. Chotard will put his business back in order, and the poet will write only when he is inspired.

Chotard et Cie. has the appearance of a rough draft for *Boudu* made after the fact. It is pleasant enough, but betrays its theatrical origins more than Renoir's other films. The acting style is not unified, and Georges Pomiès (the poet) in particular seems not to fit in with the rest of the cast.

The film is enjoyable all the same for its imaginative details and for all that Renoir added of his own to Roger Ferdinand's play, although it must be said that the final result makes the play itself appear even worse than it is.

The film seems to have been made very quickly. I did not notice any scenes shot outside the studio, but I enjoyed some amusing formal effects: a long and complex dolly shot at the beginning presenting Chotard's store and his apartment, and an analogous shot at the end. On the other hand, in many other shots the actors play face to the camera, as in the theater, probably a consequence of the very tight shooting schedule.

Madame Bovary (1934)

To our knowledge, André Bazin wrote nothing on *Madame Bovary* besides a few references in the chapter "The French Renoir." See the note by Eric Rohmer in the Filmography. F.T.

Valentine Tessier and Robert Le Vigan in *Madame Bovary*

CHAPTER THREE

THE ERA OF THE POPULAR FRONT

●

Toni (1934)

Having presented *Toni* to film clubs two or three times since the war, I thought I knew it rather well. However, I was surprised by the film when I saw it again recently. Judgments of movies evolve particularly rapidly, just as the cinema itself develops at an accelerated pace. Five years in the history of the cinema is easily the equivalent of a generation in literature. This accounts for the need never to rely on memories and to revise one's opinions periodically. This rule applies particularly to *Toni*, one of the key films in Jean Renoir's work. I say "key," but the picture is more. It is a veritable chain of keys.

Toni is certainly not the best or the most perfectly constructed of Renior's prewar films. Quite frankly, it is unusually rich in defects. But it is perhaps, along with *The Rules of the Game*, the most interesting, and in any case, the film in which Renoir pushed his personal and cinematic quest the farthest.

I say "personal" because the moral thrust of *The Rules of the Game* and of Renoir's later films is already fairly explicit in *Toni*, at least insofar as "those famous relationships between man and woman" (Dalio in *The Rules of the Game*) are concerned. Furthermore, if *Toni* prefigures *The Rules of the Game*, *The Rules of the Game* is reminiscent of *Toni*. In both films

Pierre Renoir during the shooting of *Toni*.

Renoir has in mind the famous dialogue between Dalio and Toutain after their scrap at the château: "You read in the papers from time to time that an Italian worker has run off with the wife of a Polish laborer and that the affair has ended in knife play. I didn't think such things were possible, but, my friend, they are . . ."

But *Toni* seems even more impressive in view of the subsequent development of cinematic realism. In a piece written at the time of the revival of the film, Renoir pointed out the similarities between the aesthetic implications of *Toni* and those of the Italian neorealist films of the post–World War II era. He emphasized the contrast between his own cinematic predilections and the type of cinematography that was in vogue in 1934. Contradicting the generally accepted tenets of the day, he was laying the foundation for what was to become neorealism ten years later. Renoir's role in the genesis of the Italian school of film making can hardly be disputed, given the fact that the first major neorealist work, *Ossessione* (1942), was made by a former assistant and great admirer of Renoir, Luchino Visconti.

The fact that Toni foreshadowed the Italian movement is little understood and for the most part forgotten, perhaps even by Renoir himself, for French realism was to evolve entirely apart from developments in Italy. The postwar realists found their inspiration in the naturalist romanticism and the highly stylized social mythology which had characterized the French school from 1936 to 1939.

But before the advent of the "black realism" popularized by Marcel Carné and his scenarist Jacques Prévert, *Toni* gave witness to the contradictions which the cinema was going to have to sort out. These contradictions account for the weaknesses in the movie, but also for its interest and charm.

Reacting against the theatrical and literary conventions which characterized the cinema of the day, Renoir took his scenario from a news item about a criminal case and the details of the case he gleaned from the files of a police commissioner in the South of France. We can recognize now what came to be a typical neorealist approach. He situated his story in a real region near Martigues and filmed it on location using local people, notably Italian workers, to fill out his cast. But at the same time that he treated his social and natural setting with unusual realism, it is clear that Renoir was preoccupied only with the essence of the matter—which is to say the morality of the individual relationships—and references to the facts of the case serve more than anything as an excuse to dispense with psychological realism. These days when one writes a scenario based on an actual case, he feels it necessary to create psychological veri-similitude, reorganizing reality in accordance with a precon-ceived logic of the interaction of character and event. In 1934 the public was less demanding, and the film maker was more free. Perhaps at the time Renoir had the impression that he was being faithful to reality, but in fact he was using it as arbitrarily as Corneille used Roman history to justify his tragedies. What stands out when we see the movie today is an unintended dia-lectic between the raw documentary reality, presented without regard for psychological verisimilitude, and the moral truth, also achieved without reference to psychology. The film switches continually from one to the other through characters who are totally unrealistic in terms of personality, having only social and ethical import. This disregard, or even scorn, for psychology will appear to audiences brought up on the psychological films of our day (cf. Aurenche and Bost*) to be old-fashioned and awkward. I, on the other hand, find in Renoir's approach the freshness of an inspiration which has not yet dominated or cam-ouflaged the fertile contradictions of its raw materials, notably, the contradictions which can exist between realism and truth.

Later Renoir will bear witness to the reality prewar France with greater dexterity and will succeed admirably in fusing moral statement and social observation so that each sheds light on the other. If the message is conveyed equally well by the Italian coal workers in *Toni*, the typesetters in *The Crime of M. Lange*, the soldiers in *Grand Illusion*, the *petits bourgeois* of *A Day in the Country*, and the *grands bourgeois* or the aristocrats in *The Rules of the Game*, it is precisely because through all his social metamorphoses Renoir was interested only in the same sets of morals and because social realism was for him only a means of experiencing and demonstrating the permanence of man and his questions. Renoir is a moralist.

---

* Jean Aurenche and Pierre Bost wrote practically all of Claude Autant-Lara's scenarios after 1943, notably *Le Diable au Corps*. They also wrote *Forbidden Games* for René Clément. Trans.

The Crime of M. Lange (1935)

Amédée Lange, an employee in a commercial publishing house, is exploited, as is the rest of the personnel, by the ignoble Batala, the devious president of the fly-by-night enterprise. But Lange is blind to the evil-doing of his charming boss, first of all because of his naïve idealism and also because his mind is elsewhere. He spends his nights writing "Arizona Jim," the silly tale of a western hero whom Lange has dreamed up. He is so preoccupied that he fails to notice the advances made to him by Valentine, the kind owner of the laundry on the first floor of the building where he lives.

One day Batala, on the verge of bankruptcy, takes flight, having seduced Estelle, the innocent fiancée of the concierge's son. But his train goes off the tracks, and Batala is thought to have been killed in the wreck. In fact, however, he has taken the vestments and assumed the identity of a priest who was traveling with him. With the president presumed dead, the debt-ridden publishing house reverts to the principal creditor, who, having nothing to lose, accepts the suggestion of the employees that the firm be launched as a cooperative. Soundly administered, the company enjoys a brilliant success with its new publications, largely thanks to "Arizona Jim." Everyone is happy: the financial backer; the workers; the son of the concierge, who has pardoned Estelle; and Lange, who can give his imagination free rein in further literary exploits and who has finally begun to appreciate the charms of Valentine.

It is at this point that the despicable Batala returns to break up the party and to claim his rights of ownership in the newly revived publishing firm. Lange is destroyed: Batala is going to ruin the little communal paradise won through the friendship and solidarity of all. But since it was the false death of Batala which permitted the utopia in the first place, the only solution is to kill him for real. So, mechanically, naïvely, Lange shoots his former boss.

This scenario is presented in the form of a flashback after

a brief prologue which shows us Lange and Valentine hiding out in a country inn at the Belgian border after the crime. But their descriptions have been broadcast, and Lange is recognized by a guest at the inn. So while Lange is resting, Valentine takes it upon herself to explain the case to those who would turn him in. This improvised popular jury will decide their fate. Indications are that they will decide in favor of acquittal and help the couple to cross the border.

The Crime of M. Lange was made in a rather peculiar historical and political atmosphere, which explains in part the general spirit of the film. Shooting started in October 1935, on the eve of the elections of the Popular Front, and the men present at its execution, as at its conception, were to a certain degree touched by the same social idealism which moved the statesmen and politicians of the day. In this sense The Crime of M. Lange can be seen as a film à thèse: against evil bosses and capitalist exploiters, and for the workers, solidarity, and collectivism. Beyond this social message, Renoir and Prévert would go so far as to willingly excuse Lange's crime on the grounds that he had freed the earth of an irredeemably pernicious man protected by the ill-conceived laws of an imperfect society.

At the outset the film was based on an idea of Jean Castanier, the Spanish painter and set designer. It was originally to be titled "Sur la Cour" ("Overlooking the Courtyard"), a title perhaps less commercial, but more expressive of the spirit of the work than the one eventually chosen. Then, after Renoir had completed the first script (which was rather different from the final version), the producer suggested that Jacques Prévert, whose name would guarantee the interest of the distributor, collaborate on the film. So the story was rewritten with new dialogue by the author of Dîner de Tête. It is, of course, impossible to evaluate how much influence Renoir retained in this collaboration, where the marks of both men are evident.*

The Crime of M. Lange was made rapidly (in a month), with a small crew and at a relatively small cost (one million

* The reader will find in Part II an early scenario for The Crime of M. Lange, written before the arrival of Prévert. F.T.

francs). These conditions probably explain certain technical shortcomings in the film, but they may also account for some of its virtues.

The film was released at the end of January 1936 and was fairly well received by the critics. Most of the writers recognized (although perhaps without emphasizing it sufficiently) the novelty of the subject matter and above all the tone of work, whose intelligence and aims were so different from most French productions of the day. Roger Leenhardt wrote in *L'Esprit*:

> The interest of *The Crime of M. Lange* lies beyond technique and cinema *per se*: it is in the profound meaning of the film and the message of its authors. The film is all the more remarkable because it owes its spiritual style to the harmonious collaboration of its director (Renoir) and its adapter and dialogue-writer (J. Prévert), two names frequently mentioned in these pages, two uncompromising temperaments. . . . In short, Prévert has brought his sprightly, mordant wit to Renoir, who lent, in turn, the depth and resonance of his authentic romanticism to Prévert's imagination, which is more clever than creative. The result is a stunning spectacle, uneven, moving, and terribly nonconformist. . . . The direction, while touched with genius, still includes some of Renoir's usual awkwardness. Oh, those zigzagging pan shots! Are they due to a mistake or simply a lack of money? Or to Renoir's mania for improvisation, for inspiration on the sets?

It is worth noting that in January 1936 Renoir was known in the fledgling criticism of the era only as the director of a single sound film of any consequence (*Boudu* had not been considered "serious"), and Prévert had but *L'Affaire Est dans le Sac*. But it was the age when the poet with anarchist-communist tendencies reigned at the Deux-Magots (the Café de Flore would not eclipse the Deux-Magots until much later). *The Crime of M. Lange* was conceived in the little world of the film intelligentsia of the Left Bank, which during the prewar years seemed more or less in opposition to its counterpart along the Champs-

Elysées on the Right Bank. Perhaps more than any other of Renoir's works, it was a film made by friends, for friends.

An "imperfect" film, *The Crime of M. Lange* is nonetheless one of Renoir's most beautiful works and one of the most representative of his genius and talents. Personally, I would not rank it far from *The Rules of the Game*, for which it is a rather detailed outline. In any case it is, along with the sublime *A Day in the Country*, one of the most "charming" of Renoir's films.

As Roger Leenhardt pointed out, in assessing this "charm" it is important to take into account the somewhat paradoxical collaboration of Prévert. This collaboration produced one of the best, if not *the* best, dialogue of French prewar cinema. All of Prévert's qualities are there without any of his excesses, these having been tempered by Renoir's unflagging efforts to ensure that none of his actors would be asked to say anything out of keeping with his character. One has the impression that the original verbal creations of the writer have been adapted to fit the actors, even, if necessary, during the shooting. To be sure, the dialogue is considerably more obtrusive in *M. Lange* than in Renoir's other films. It often asks you to listen to it for its own sake. But this phenomenon is not necessarily a flaw, when the dialogue is so delightful.

Without slighting Prévert, it is easier to see the undeniably original contribution which Renoir made to the film.

It is curious to note that most of the critics at the time of *M. Lange*'s release (including Leenhardt himself) reproached Renoir for his complicated and awkward camera work, failing to see both the need for so much movement and the rigor inherent in it. Since the film's release, of course, much has been made of the use of depth of field. And this technique is indeed important here, just as it is important in all of Renoir's prewar sound films. Two illustrations in particular from *The Crime of M. Lange* come to mind: the taxi scene and the opening of the window in the middle of a wall covered by a great painted advertisement. But depth of field in *M. Lange* is subordinated to a more general structural conception of the film, which must be

DIAGRAM OF THE MAIN SET FOR *THE CRIME OF M. LANGE*

BATALA'S OFFICE

FOUNTAIN WHERE BATALA DIES

COMPOSING ROOM

STAIRWAY TO SECOND FLOOR

CONCENTRIC STONES

LAUNDRY

GARBAGE CANS

CONCIERGE'S APARTMENT

ENTRANCE FROM THE STREET

•••• LANGE'S ROUTE (THE CAMERA FOLLOWS HIM THROUGH THE WINDOWS)

– – – MOVEMENT OF THE CAMERA

defined in order to better understand the movements of the camera. For such a definition, we must begin with the set (see diagram).

Let us recall that the original scenario was called "On the Courtyard." The general idea of the film is to bring together around this courtyard a certain number of characters and activities and to depict the little community, this chance product of urban geography, in an almost *unanimiste** vein. There are those who both live and work on the courtyard: the concierges, the washerwoman, and Lange himself; and those who only enter the courtyard when they come to work: the typographers, the women who work for Valentine, etc. With the exception of a few "exterior" scenes, we know this community only in relation to the courtyard and the activities which center around it.

This dramatic concept was realized in a set, but not a set built on a series of studio stages. The set was built in its entirety in the courtyard of the Billancourt studio. In this vast complex each important part of the set (the concierge's lodge, the laundry, the big stairway, the composing room, Batala's office) occupied its actual position around the courtyard, whose center became the geometric locus for all the action. A significant detail added to this geometric conception: the concentric pattern of the paving stones in the courtyard.

Given this physical disposition of the set, it is clear that while the deep-focus shot would be the appropriate technique for action at the periphery, only the pan would be logical for action observed from the courtyard. Renoir took this concept to its logical conclusion in a stroke of genius which brilliantly synthesizes the whole spatial structure of the film: the 360-degree pan which follows Lange from Batala's office, through the workshop, down the steps and onto the stoop, continuing counterclockwise as he walks across to the right and out of the camera's line of vision, and sweeping the entire courtyard before coming full

* Unanisme was a French poetic movement of the early twentieth century which emphasized the notion of universal brotherhood and sought to invoke the greater soul of the human group, of which the particular souls of individuals were only constituents, incomplete in themselves. Trans.

circle to pick up Lange again at the fountain where he has gone to kill Batala. This stunning turn of the camera, apparently contrary to all logic, has perhaps psychological or dramatic justification (it gives an impression of dizziness, of madness, of suspense), but its real *raison d'être* is more germane to the conception of the film: it is the pure spatial expression of the entire *mise en scène*.

It is true that this sweeping shot, which is not immediately justified, could seem arbitrary or pretentious. Let us not forget, however, that Renoir has prepared us to accept it, with the scene in which the drunken concierge drags the garbage cans all *around* the courtyard. The circular movement has been inscribed in our eye, and the fact that the idea persists helps us to accept the abstraction of the 360-degre pan which is to follow.

In only one other film did Renoir explore further the possibilities of a *mise en scène* at once concentric and in deep focus. That is *The Rules of the Game*, in which he perfected the technique and used it with more rigor and finesse.

It would be impossible to separate the acting in *The Crime of M. Lange* from any consideration of its style. The actors contributed perhaps as much to the film's style as did the director. There were three distinct types of players in the cast: Renoir's nonprofessional friends (Duhamel, Grimault, Brunius); the proven actors who could be assimilated into Renoir's design because of the simplicity of their acting style or because of the affinity they shared with Renoir for the ambiance of camaraderie on the set (Florelle, René Lefèvre, Nadia Sibirskaïa, Maurice Baquet, Jean Dasté); and finally the *monstre sacré*, the superactor whose very incongruity with the rest of the group served both Renoir's desires and the sense of the movie: Jules Berry. Renoir adores this kind of genial ham actor, who is never better than when working with him. He knows how to put them at ease while at the same time giving them the necessary direction. In *The Crime of M. Lange* Berry's is a sublime creation of villainy, which for all its brilliance does not move us to hate him, so removed is that violent emotion from Renoir's work.

Florelle, Nadia Sibirskaïa (fainted), Marcel Duhamel, and Jules Berry in *The Crime of M. Lange*

What is striking about the way the film is acted is the fact that to a certain extent it was made for the pleasure of those who were working on it as much as for the appreciation of the public. It is like a finely decorated cloth so nearly as beautiful on the back as on the front that one hesitates to wear it exclusively on one side. *The Crime of M. Lange* was made for the pleasure of all, from the director to the stagehands, and particularly for the actors. This approach holds more or less true for all of Renoir's works, but seldom has it been as apparent as in this film.

La Vie Est à Nous (1936)

MANUSCRIPT NOTES

The film opens in a classroom, during a lesson on the riches of France, illustrated by sumptuous pictures. When school is dismissed, comments by the children on the poverty and misery of their parents belie the rosy picture painted in the classroom, or at least its optimistic point of view.

A second montage sequence presents the nationalist uprisings of 1934, the wealthy "two hundred families" of France, the menace of Hitler.

Next, we find ourselves in the office of Marcel Cachin, editor of *L'Humanité*. He is opening his mail, in particular three letters, the contents of which are depicted by three sketches illustrating the role of the Communist party in the defense of workers.

First sketch: the factory. A collective action is organized to fight against the tyranny of the clock, which imposes an excessively rapid pace of work, and to protest the arbitrary firing of an old worker. The administration accedes to the demands of the workers after a warning strike. The old man is rehired, the pace of work is slowed down, salaries remain constant.

Second sketch: in the country. An auction which

would have deprived a peasant of his only source of revenue is sabotaged by his Communist friends. The comrades stifle any would-be bidders and manage to buy back the peasant's stock and equipment at a ridiculously low price. The man will be able to continue working.

Third sketch: a student couple (Nadia Sibirskaïa and Julien Bertheau) is practically dying of hunger. The young man, a graduate of the Ecole Supérieure d'Electricité, looks for work, gets hired by a garage owner who exploits him, falls back into poverty, and is taken in by a militant who takes him to a meeting where he is fed and comforted. A kind of celebration is organized. The young man will handle the lighting for the affair.

Add to this a series of speeches from Marcel Cachin, Jacques Duclos, and Maurice Thorez and an apotheostic finale inspired by classic Russian montages.

The whole indicates a tremendous didactic naïveté. The scenario is terribly moralizing, but the film itself is remarkable for the sincerity of the players and the quality of their acting. Renoir achieves some curious effects by using real militants in addition to his sympathizing friends.

Two scenes to note: the auction with Léo Larive (who played Louis Jouvet's servant in *The Lower Depths* and the cook in *The Rules of the Game*) examining the horse put on the block. This scene, more cut up than the rest of the film, perhaps owes more to Jacques Becker (who collaborated on the scenario) than to Renoir. And second, the marvelous pan which starts with Nadia Sibirskaïa on her balcony, continues along the rooftops, descends to the courtyard, and comes back up to a general shot of Paris.

La Vie Est à Nous will continue to be discussed. With time it will become a more and more precious document on the spirit of 1936. For that reason it makes a worthy companion piece for *The Crime of M. Lange.*

A Day in the Country (1936)

MANUSCRIPT NOTES

"M. Dufour, a Paris hardware dealer, in the company of his mother-in-law, his wife, his daughter, and his clerk Anatole, who is also M. Dufour's future son-in-law and successor, has decided, having borrowed a carriage from his neighbor the dairy man this Sunday in the summer of 1860, to go out and commune with nature." They choose Père Poulain's* inn as a propitious spot for a picnic on the grass. Two sporty fellows on vacation see the family arrive and, moved by their own high spirits, decide to make discreet advances to the ladies of the party. After the picnic, while M. Dufour and Anatole go fishing with lines lent to them by the helpful duo, the ladies accept an invitation to go for a boatride with the two oarsmen. The mother, still attractive in spite of her years, lets herself be tempted into the bushes by her enterprising companion, while the daughter knows the pleasure of a brief but passionate embrace in the arms of her partner, a more sensitive and shy young man. Rain puts an end to the idyll.

"Years pass with Sundays as melancholy as Mondays. Anatole has married Henriette . . ." The young couple returns to spend a Sunday at the inn in Bezons. Henriette, already marked by the monotony of her new existence, encounters her erstwhile lover on the same spot where they had embraced. They scarcely have the time to tell each other of the indelible memories that each one has kept of that brief interlude, when the husband awakens from his nap. The lovers will not see each other again.

The adaptation of A Day in the Country is faithful in letter and spirit to the Maupassant story from which it is taken. The short story is in fact, with the exception of a few scenes that are more or less developed than in

* Renoir himself played the role of Poulain. F.T.

Jacques Brunius and Jeanne Marken in *A Day in the Country*

the movie, much like a synopsis of Renoir's film.

The characters of the boatmen, Henri and Rodolphe, are psychologically and dramatically a little more clear-cut in the film than in the story. The one who accompanies the mother (Jacques Brunius) is rendered a bit more comic, and the other (Georges Darnoux) is made to develop the sentimental and dramatic elements of the adventure. All that has been added is materially and psychologically justifiable, and one could even say that Renoir has improved on the story.

The love scene on the island is one of the most agonizing and most beautiful in all of cinema. It owes its stunning effectiveness to a couple of gestures and a look from Sylvia Bataille which have a wrenching emotional realism. In the space of a few frames she expresses all the disenchantment, the pathetic sadness, that follows the act of love.

Furthermore, Renoir manages to transcribe this feeling visually by use of the superb storm sequence.

The part of the story which was never filmed, which would have taken place in M. Dufour's shop, is insignificant. Thus one can say that *A Day in the Country* is a perfectly finished work.

CHAPTER FOUR

THE WAR APPROACHES

•

The Lower Depths (1936)

Louis Jouvet plays a baron ruined by gambling and women. One night he surprises Pepel, a professional thief, in his apartment. He is immediately drawn to the burglar, played by Jean Gabin. They gamble throughout the night and in the morning when the soldiers come to arrest the baron, he decides to take refuge with Pepel in an asylum for derelicts near the river.

The asylum is run by an old miser (Vladimir Sokolov), whose young wife (Suzy Prim) is Pepel's mistress. She has a younger sister whom she and her husband hope to marry to the chief of police (Gabriello) to ensure their safety.

The young girl rejects the marriage. The old man and his wife beat her. Pepel, who is in love with the girl, comes upon them and kills the miser. When the police arrive to investigate, all the tenants in the asylum side with Pepel, saying, "It is not he who killed, it is the lower depths."

Meanwhile an old man dies of an unnamed illness, a mystical, alcoholic actor hangs himself, and the baron flirts with a romantic prostitute (Jany Holt).

At the end of the story, Pepel and the girl take to the road, detouring a bit when they encounter some gendarmes. They will try to escape.

Louis Jouvet, Jany Holt, and Junie Astor in *The Lower Depths*

Jean Gabin and Suzy Prim in *The Lower Depths*

The Lower Depths is certainly not the greatest film of the man who made *The River*. It never achieves the balance of *Grand Illusion*, the sincerity of *The Crime of M. Lange*, the poetry of *A Day in the Country*, or the combination of all these qualities which marks *The Rules of the Game*. Nevertheless, with the exception of the latter film, *The Lower Depths* is perhaps the most interestingly directed of all Renoir's French films. It embodies the director's most delightful and revealing qualities.

Taken from Gorki's play, it is a curious mixture of tones and genres. From a very somber and realistic story, Renoir has come close to making a comic film. He even refuses to allow Jean Gabin to die at the end.*

The protagonists of the four or five personal adventures which cross and intermingle in the sordid dormitory are the kind of derelicts so often found in Russian novels. But in Renoir's treatment they appear curiously Franco-Russian. How can we possibly accept Jouvet as a high tsarist functionary or believe that Gabin's Parisian banter is an expression of "the restlessness of the Russian soul"?—to say nothing of taking the banks of the Marne for those of the Volga. Yet, Renoir has the gall to ask us to do precisely that!

A cardinal merit of this film is to bring together under marvelous direction Jouvet, Jany Holt, Le Vigan, Suzy Prim, Junie Astor, and Vladimir Sokolov.

This improbable game of hide-and-seek between vaudeville and tragedy, realism and parody, Gorki and Renoir, produces a work which is at the very least fascinating. Only the author of *The Rules of the Game* could so casually compel our emotion while skirting the ridiculous so closely.

* "Consider that nearly all Gabin's films, at least from *The Human Beast* to *Au-delà des Grilles*, end unhappily; usually with the violent death of the hero, which can be considered, moreover, as a more or less conscious suicide. Is it not peculiar that the commercial requirement of the 'happy ending,' which drives so many producers to weaken their 'sad' films with false resolutions, like those of Molière's comedies, does not apply to one of the most popular and sympathetic actors, one who we always hope will be happy, marry, and have many children?" André Bazin, "Jean Gabin et son destin," *Radio-Cinéma-Télévision*, October 1, 1950.

Grand Illusion (1937)

The action, which takes place in a German prison camp for officers during World War I, divides into three more or less distinct parts. It begins with a prologue in a bar near the French front, where Lieutenant Maréchal (Jean Gabin), a former mechanic who has worked his way up through the ranks, is asked to conduct the haughty, suave, and monocled Captain de Boïeldieu (Pierre Fresnay) on a mission behind enemy lines. But their plane is shot down by Commandant von Rauffenstein (Erich von Stroheim). Von Rauffenstein, an aristocrat and career officer like Boïeldieu, graciously invites the two Frenchmen to lunch before his far less courteous subordinate comes to take them to the prison.

At the camp, after the initial vexations of internment Maréchal and Boïeldieu have little to complain about. They are quickly taken in by their roommates: an actor, full of puns, a rather naïve schoolteacher, a surveyor, and the benefactor of them all, the garment maker Rosenthal (Dalio), whose sumptuous parcels from home, generously shared, provide the little company with far more agreeable nourishment than the ordinary prison fare. In spite of the differences in taste and character, largely due to differences in social position, the men develop a strong feeling of fraternity. Even the aristocrat de Boïeldieu adapts suavely to conditions in this unstratified little society. Like the others, he devotes every night to the tunnel, which the original prisoners have been digging for months and which will soon enable the little band to escape.

Meanwhile the camp has been feverishly preparing a talent show under the tolerant and amused eyes of the camp authorities. Rosenthal has had trunks full of costumes sent in for the occasion. When the trunks are opened and the first man tries on a dress, there ensues the justly famous scene in which the other prisoners suddenly stop joking, overwhelmed in spite of themselves by this pathetic simulation of femininity. Later, the show is proceeding full tilt when Maréchal silences the orchestra and

Jean Gabin and Pierre Fresnay in *Grand Illusion*

Pierre Fresnay and Erich von Stroheim in *Grand Illusion*

strides on stage to announce that Douaumont has been recaptured. The prisoners rise and sing the "Marseillaise," while the Germans, livid with anger, withdraw. His audacity will cost Maréchal a long stay in solitary confinement.

On his release his comrades console him with the news that the tunnel is finished. The escape is set for the next day. But an order arrives: the officers are to be moved to a new camp. The tunnel and all the labor spent to dig it will be wasted. Not even the English officers who take their place will be able to take advantage of it. Maréchal tries to pass on the word, but he cannot find an English officer who speaks French.

After a rapid sequence of dissolves which shows us that in the course of one or two years our heroes have been marched from camp to camp across Germany, we find Maréchal and de Boïeldieu in a disciplinary camp reserved for men who have repeatedly tried to escape. This new camp is a medieval fortress from which escape seems impossible.

The two Frenchmen are surprised to find themselves greeted by von Rauffenstein, who has suffered from a serious spinal injury and is strapped to the chin in a corset of iron and leather. The former aviator has accepted the thankless task of running the prison fortress because it permits him to continue serving his country, but he goes about it with the same aristocratic flair, the same ritual of pointless and implacable elegance, that is the rule of his class. Delighted to see de Boïeldieu again, he immediately treats him as an alter ego, a man like himself, both a noble and a career officer. Maréchal, on the other hand, appears to him as merely an unfortunate product of the French Revolution. On this point, de Boïeldieu does not agree. If he is no less committed than von Rauffenstein to the style of his class, his commitment is tempered by greater understanding because he realizes that that class is doomed. He appreciates the popular virtues of a Maréchal, and he views without bitterness the social advancement of the cosmopolitan, industrious Rosenthal, whose recently naturalized relatives today possess the historic châteaux that the de Boïeldieus could not hold on to.

Our two heroes have the pleasant surprise of finding their

generous old friend Rosenthal assigned to the same prison. The three, in spite of the difficulties posed by the fortress, start planning a new escape. A long rope of braided cloth will enable them to climb down the walls, but the guards on the ramparts are too numerous for them to hope to pass unnoticed. An incident provoked by the Russian prisoners gives de Boïeldieu an idea. With a boxful of musical pipes and the cooperation of the other prisoners, he will organize a kind of musical mutiny, which will keep the entire guard busy for at least a few minutes, during which Maréchal and Rosenthal will be able to get away unnoticed. Everything goes as planned, with de Boïeldieu, in full uniform and white gloves, insolently tootling a popular French folksong from the ramparts, to the complete stupefaction of von Rauffenstein, who is finally forced to shoot him. Mortally wounded in the stomach, de Boïeldieu dies in the arms of the German commandant.

We rejoin Maréchal and Rosenthal, haggard and exhausted, on their way to Switzerland. Rosenthal has sprained his ankle and has difficulty keeping up with Maréchal. Tired and irritable, the two begin to quarrel. They find refuge in a stable on a quiet farm, just in time to permit them to rest and restore their spirits. But the farm turns out to be inhabited by a young war widow (Dita Parlo) and her daughter. She could turn them in, but she does not. She houses them until Rosenthal's ankle heals and he regains his strength. Little by little, a romance develops between Maréchal and the blond Elsa, a love transcending the absurdity of the war. But they must leave, tearing themselves away from this peace. It too is illusory.

They continue to walk. We see Maréchal and Rosenthal somewhere in the mountains, nearly covered with snow. A German patrol spots them. A soldier raises his rifle to fire. A comrade stops him: "Forget it. They're in Switzerland."

The print of *Grand Illusion* shown in 1958 is a complete version, reconstructed by Renoir and Charles Spaak (his co-scenarist) using a negative seized by the Germans and recovered in Munich by the Americans. In the course of commercial dis-

tribution nearly all of the prints originally in circulation had
been mutilated.

The principal cuts were made in 1946 for a reissue, which
provoked some controversy. The film was criticized, notably by
Georges Altman, for being too kind to the Germans and for suggesting at least a trace of anti-Semitism. Only the mentality
which prevailed in the days following the Liberation can explain these judgments, so contrary to the spirit of the film, especially considering that a few references to Rosenthal's race and
part of the love scenes between Maréchal and Elsa had already
been cut. In any case, in 1946 the message of *Grand Illusion*
could not yet be thoroughly understood (or reunderstood). The
triumph of the film when it was next reissued, in 1958, was thus
all the more significant.

In 1937, on the other hand, the critics had been generally
enthusiastic about *Grand Illusion*, making it almost unique
among Renoir's films, which have often received bad press, or
mixed notices at best.

The film was an immediate success not only in France but
also abroad. It would certainly have won the grand prize at the
Venice Film Festival of 1937 (instead of *Carnet de Bal*) if the
award of the "Mussolini Cup" to a democratic and pacifist film
had not seemed impossible. A prize for the "best artistic ensemble" was created especially for it, to ease the consciences of the
jurors. Despite this official recognition, the film was banned in
Italy and, naturally, in Germany. In America, on the other
hand, it had a triumphant success (fifteen weeks at a major
first-run house in New York and distribution throughout the
country). President Roosevelt said, "Everyone who believes in
democracy should see this film."

In the introductory sound track made for the 1958 reissue
Renoir himself explained how the film was born:

> The story of *Grand Illusion* is strictly true. It was told to me by
> my friends in the war . . . notably by Pinsard. Pinsard flew
> fighter planes; I was in a reconnaissance squadron. One day I
> had to go to take photos of the German lines. He saved my life

on several occasions when the German fighter planes became too persistent. He himself was shot down seven times. His escapes are the basis for *Grand Illusion* . . .

But . . . an escape story, however gripping, is not enough for a film. You must make a scenario of it. For that, Charles Spaak lent me his talents. Our collaboration was smooth and without incident. The ties of our friendship were reinforced by our common faith in the equality and fraternity of men.

In fact, the scenario of *Grand Illusion* went through several transformations after Spaak's initial treatment.* First, because as is the case with all Renoir's films, the director made allowances for improvisation, but also because an unforeseen situation that developed at the beginning of the shooting in Alsace completely altered the film: the producers had succeeded at the last minute in engaging Erich von Stroheim (banished from Hollywood) for the role of Commandant von Rauffenstein. Renoir had always proclaimed his admiration for this controversial director who had considerably influenced his own work, and he could not resign himself to confining von Stroheim's prodigious talents to the modest role which the original script provided. Between von Stroheim and Renoir there developed a productive collaboration from which emerged not only the extraordinary final portrait of von Rauffenstein but also one of the most beautiful aspects of the film: the additional elaboration on the theme of aristocracy made possible through the interplay between the French captain and the German commandant. This relationship allowed Renoir to develop the dialogue and the portrayal of nobility far more subtly than the simple antithesis of Maréchal and de Boïeldieu alone would have permitted.

It would nevertheless be unjust to dismiss Charles Spaak's contribution to *Grand Illusion*. He certainly played a significant role in its success, being responsible above all for the dramatic structure and the delineation of character, qualities which Renoir has not always been able to reconcile in his other films with the aims he regarded as more important.

* An early treatment of *Grand Illusion*, which preceded the casting of Erich von Stroheim and Dita Parlo, appears in Part II. F.T.

How has *Grand Illusion* held up over the years? It is not enough to say that it has retained its power. Not only has the stature of the film remained undiminished by the passage of time (except in a few minor details), but the innovation, the audacity, and, for want of a better word, the modernity of the direction have acquired an even greater impact.

I am not sure that *Grand Illusion* is the most realistic of Renoir's films, but certainly if the film's effectiveness has survived undiluted, it is largely due to its realism. The most obvious of the many instances of Renoir's realistic treatment of his material is the use of languages. In the aftermath of the Liberation, films like *La Dernière Chance* and *Paisan* happily swept aside the old dramatic conventions which allowed protagonists of almost any background to speak in the language of Shakespeare, Dante, or Molière. But only for a while, alas! Now we see films from supposedly realistic British film makers which portray the Resistance in a Paris where the concierges speak English. Long before neorealism, Renoir based his film on the authenticity of spoken language. (Pabst, it is true, had done this in *Kameradschaft* [1931], but in a far less subtle manner.) Here, the touch of genius which produces a delightful human insight is the use of a third language, English, between von Rauffenstein and de Boïeldieu. No longer a national language, it becomes a *class* language, that sets the two aristocrats apart from plebeian society.

Another addition which greatly benefited both the scenario and the *mise en scène* was the invention of Rosenthal, who did not exist in the original script. His character, which adds the dimension of race to the theme of class, deepens the meaning of the film in an important way and at the same time adds nuance to what could have been an overly schematic treatment of the Fresnay-Gabin antithesis.

There is also a realism of human relations, or better still, an authenticity—although less perhaps in the relationships of the principal protagonists, who, though vividly characterized and never reduced to mere symbols, are inevitably determined by the dramatic requirements of the scenario, than in the relationships of the characters that Renoir was able to create between the level of the protagonists and the level of the extras. The German guards, simple soldiers, noncommissioned officers, and officers are drawn with stunning verisimilitude. This realism is not the result of simple copying from life; rather, it is the product of a careful re-creation of character through the use of detail which is not only accurate but meaningful as well, and this is accomplished without recourse to dramatic conventions. The invention of a character like Monsieur Arthur, the guard, and of his subtle complicity with the prisoners is a creation which approaches the sublime. The bit in which Carette, in the midst of his talent-show number, calls over the heads of the superior officers in the crowd, "Get it, Arthur?!" is a brilliant moment of pure cinema. And so are the brief scenes in which we see the English officers; an entire civilization is evoked in a few seconds, and yet the suggestive details are neither "typical" nor the standard traits so often caricatured.

What we are considering here is a faculty for *invention*, not simple documentary reproduction. The accuracy of detail in Renoir's work is as much the result of imagination as of observation. He does not indiscriminately record reality. Rather, he singles out the telling—but not conventional—detail. The sequence which best illustrates Renoir's use of detail is probably the scene of the talent show, when the recapture of Douaumont is announced. Given this brilliant idea, a clever director could not fail to produce an exciting scene. But Renoir adds the little touches to it which make the scene far more than just a standard treatment; for example, the idea of having the "Marseillaise" led, not by a Frenchman, but by an English officer dressed up as a woman.

It is the multiplicity of "realistic inventions" which accounts for the substance of *Grand Illusion* and which explains its undiminished impact years after it was made.

The realism is also enhanced by the photography, or more precisely, by the way scenes have been broken down into shots. Certainly the verisimilitude of *Grand Illusion* owes much to Renoir's decision to shoot all the exteriors (and even some of the interiors) on location. Unable to shoot in Germany, he chose Alsace, as close as possible to the border. Above all—even though Renoir has pushed this technique even further in other films—one notices the constant concern not to allow the photography or the editing to break up the dramatic focus of a scene.

This concern is implemented in several ways. Depth of field is one, of course, but even more important is Renoir's use of camera movement to avoid excessive cutting. By moving the camera to "reframe" the scene instead of cutting, Renoir is able to treat the sequence not as a series of fragments but as a dramatic whole. For example: For certain interior scenes which could have been shot in the studio, Renoir had movable partial sets constructed in the courtyard of the actual barracks used on location. This permitted him to have his actors "inside" and at the same time show the bustle of the camp through the window (e.g., the scene of the young recruits exercising). It is through such techniques that Renoir attempts to portray realistically the relations between men and the world in which they find themselves.

Without attaching undue importance to it, we might inquire into the film's title, *Grand Illusion*. The phrase was explained in the ending of the original version of the scenario. The two fugitives had set a rendezvous at Maxim's for the first Christmas Eve after the end of the war, but on December 24, 1918, their table, reserved so long in advance, remains empty. For this pessimistic comment on the grand illusion of friendship, Renoir substituted a far more optimistic message. Of course, the theme of illusion is also scattered throughout the film (the illusion of sexuality fostered by the soldiers in women's costumes, the illusion of love in Maréchal's improbable and probably ill-fated romance with the farm woman, the illusion of liberty behind every attempt to escape, the illusion of approaching peace). But the illusions are more beneficial than harmful: they help the men to overcome their trials and give them the courage to persevere.

But it is necessary to carry the idea even further and give to the word "illusion" a resolutely positive, even militant, significance. Grand illusions are doubtless the dreams which help men to live, such as a simple obsession with pyrography or translating Pindar, but more than this, the grand illusions are the illusion of hatred, which arbitrarily divides men who in reality are not separated by anything; the illusion of boundaries, with the wars which result from them; the illusion of races, of social classes. The message of the film is thus a demonstration *a contrario* of the fraternity and equality of men. The war, the product of hatred and division, paradoxically reveals the falseness of all the barriers of prejudice separating man from man.

If, however, these boundaries can be attacked, it is because they do indeed exist. Here another theme dear to Renoir emerges, one he has often mentioned in his interviews. It is that men are less separated by the vertical barriers of nationalism than by the horizontal cleavages of culture, race, class, profession, etc.

Grand Illusion does pay homage to one such division, the one between the nobility and the common people. In all his work Renoir constantly expresses his respect for the nobility, but for the true nobility, titled or not; for the aristocracy of the heart, or of sensibility, and above all of art or simply *métier*, which makes equals of de Boïeldieu and Maréchal. Unlike von Rauffenstein, de Boïeldieu recognizes and admits this. He also understands that the outward signs of *his* aristocracy are now anachronistic and doomed. Thus his supreme affirmation of his nobility is to sacrifice himself for Maréchal.

For this episode and others, *Grand Illusion* can be considered a political film (in 1937 Renoir did not hide his sympathies for the Popular Front; he was soon to make *La Marseillaise* for the Confédération Générale de Travail*). But one must admire how little this "political" film appears to be partisan. The genius of Renoir lies in the way he gets his point across without ever seeming biased. Even when defending a particular moral or social truth, he always does justice to the men who oppose this truth and to *their* ideals as well. He gives every chance to ideas, and every chance to individuals. This artistically fruitful

* The principal French labor organization. Trans.

approach is particularly apparent in *La Marseillaise* in the manner in which he presents the émigrés and the court of Versailles.

La Marseillaise (1937)

MANUSCRIPT NOTES

First of all, note the contrast of tone and acting between the court and the people. The common people speak loudly and with spontaneity. On the other hand, at the court, voices are never raised; the most serious and the most trivial statements are offered in measured, almost whispered tones.

The film starts at Marseille, where we see the formation of a battalion of 500 volunteers. They leave on July 2, 1792, and march to Paris, where they arrive on the 30th, the day before the publication of the Brunswick Manifesto. The film ends a little after August 10, just before the battle of Valmy.

The aristocrats are marvelously individualized. Under their aristocratic comportment, Renoir gives each a character, a precise and subtle style, which immediately attracts us to them. The most developed from this point of view is, of course, Louis XVI (Pierre Renoir). The primary goal of the film, the one which determines its entire style, is to go beyond the historical images to uncover the mundane, human reality.

Historical reality first (the profusion of concrete details, the accurate reconstruction of daily life, particularly the culinary aspects), but above all, reality of characterization.

Renoir puts the heroic acts in concrete perspective, in psychological relief. He demythologizes history by restoring it to man. Not to bring history down to the level of trivia, but simply to bring it to the level of individuals. This effort had already been foreshadowed by *Le Tournoi*.

In this light, take note of the long march of the troops to Paris, punctuated by excellent dialogues on the subject of feet, the different ways of protecting and taking care of them. The first time he hears the "Marseillaise," one of the representatives of the common people does not hold back his criticisms: "There is something wild and bombastic about this song which I do not like at all."

An admirable touch: as he reviews the troops in the Tuileries, Louis XVI is hindered by the fact that his wig is askew.

The Human Beast (1938)

MANUSCRIPT NOTES

Zola's novel is not without faults.* For one thing, the writing is grossly uneven. Beside some marvelously crafted scenes—the opening, for example—one finds pages of sloppy or conventional writing. The construction of the plot seems arbitrary, since it is rarely determined by the psychology of the characters (or by anything else). The events seem to be ordered by some *a priori* postulates of the author, or merely by whimsy. We sense that he set out to describe a single situation in a particular milieu. Ironically, it is the novel rather than the film which seems to rely on "stock scenes" as in the American spectaculars. Here the novelistic rhetoric serves the same function as cinematographic effects: for example, the derailing of the train, described hastily and without conviction and with tremendous improbabilities (the survival of Lantier and Pecqueux). The ending (the train speeding out of control) is also a piece of rhetoric.

* The reader may have noticed that several of the manuscript notes concern the adaptation of the film from the original literary sources. They were written after a systematic reading of all the novels on which Renoir drew for his films. F.T.

Simone Simon and Fernand Ledoux in *The Human Beast*

Jean Gabin and Blanchette Brunoy in *The Human Beast*

It is an example of Zola's "cinematic" vision which Renoir did not film.

As for the writing, the best examples of laxity occur in the metaphors and the images relating to the locomotive, *La Lison* and to Flore (the virgin warrior, the Amazon, etc.).

Another improbability of the story: it includes no less than six murderers, potential or actual, nearly everyone in the book. Lantier, Roubaud, Séverine (when she wants to do away with her husband), Misard, Flore, and even, at the end, Pecqueux. This accumulation of criminals would seem improbable even in a detective story.

Again note the weakness or the cursory nature of the psychology, with the possible exception of Séverine. The only consistent characters are social stereotypes (Philomène, the neighbors). Jacques Lantier is certainly not the strongest character. He is rather crudely discussed by the man from the caverns, but besides that, is given almost no psychology at all (notice his indifference after the murder of Séverine).

On the whole, we can say that Renoir has in almost every way improved on the book. The sense of milieu in the film is not inferior to that of the book, and the explanation of the characters is much better. Renoir founds this explanation not on psychology but on a metaphysics of actors. What we see on the screen is not the murderous anger of Lantier, but that of Jean Gabin. Even when the actor does not correspond physically or morally to the character in the book, the "error" of casting offers more advantages than disadvantages, because the presence of the actor, his powers of suggestion, are clearly superior to what is in the book (Roubaud, played by Fernand Ledoux; Pecqueux, played by Carette; and even Flore, played by Blanchette Brunoy).

Note the intelligence of the changes. The scene of the railroad workers' hall, which Renoir added, is a piece of social observation completely in the spirit of Zola and certainly not inferior to what the novelist would have done with it.

On the whole, Renoir judiciously simplified and dramatized the story to suit the demands of the cinema, and the result is better than the novel. You could almost say that the only lapses in the scenario are the remnants of the novel: the role of Flore, the role of Séverine's lover, that of Cabuche, which Renoir plays himself, as if he gave himself the part as a trial run for his role as Octave in *The Rules of the Game*.

Finally, note the use in several scenes of dialogue taken directly from the book. The effect is one of a slightly literary affectation, which is not at all unenjoyable.

The Rules of the Game (1939)*

I am convinced that the importance of Jean Renoir will continue to grow. His films of the prewar years alone are of such importance that when looking at them it is difficult to realize that they are the work of a creator who is still in his prime and who continues to produce films of stupefying beauty, originality, and youth.

From *Nana* to *French CanCan*, from *La Chienne* to *The Golden Coach*, from *The Crime of M. Lange* to *The River*, from

* This text is a transcription of an introduction to a showing of part of *The Rules of the Game*, probably to the members of a film society. We have not been able to discover either the date or the place of this talk, but we publish the text because we are certain that Bazin revised it in 1957 after the release of *Paris Does Strange Things*. Curiously, it is to our knowledge the only text Bazin wrote on *The Rules of the Game*, which was his favorite among Renoir's films. I think that Bazin was waiting to see the definitive version of the film which Jean Gaborit and Jacques Maréchal had started to put together. Here is an extract from a letter Bazin wrote me in July 1958: "What you tell me about the work on *The Rules of the Game* is extraordinary; I am very anxious. Could I see it in August?" Bazin died on November 11, 1958, without having seen the definitive version, which was finished the following year and presented at the 1959 Venice Film Festival. The reader will notice that Bazin rarely speaks of a Renoir film without comparing it to *The Rules of the Game*, which is thus indirectly discussed throughout the book. F.T.

Marcel Dalio and Jean Renoir in *The Rules of the Game*

Grand Illusion to *The Southerner*, from *Diary of a Chamber-maid* to *Paris Does Strange Things*, Jean Renoir has not ceased to struggle and to renew himself.

Some great directors have failed because they did not know how to transcend their own success. They become prisoners of the conventions of their first successful films, not realizing that they owe this success not just to a certain cinematic form but to an elusive affinity of subject, style, and the particular expectations of an era. Once this mysterious harmony disappears, the artist whose inspiration does not renew itself finds himself groping desperately. This misfortune could never befall Jean Renoir, whose sensitivity to human nature has enabled him to adapt to the changing concerns of our history, as well as to the differences of various cultures. Some were willing to write off Renoir in 1940 when he abandoned the gloomy skies of the Ile de France for the bright sun of California, red wine and Camembert for American cuisine. But this was to misunderstand the man and the nature of his talent. In fact, for a man like Renoir, such an emigration could only be an opportunity to broaden his human perspectives, to adapt his sensibility to the upheavals of the contemporary world. On the subject of *The River*, which takes place entirely in India, Renoir has written:

"I felt a growing desire to reach out and touch my fellow creatures throughout the world. Perhaps evil forces dominate the course of events, but I sense in the hearts of men, if not a sense of fraternity, then at least one of inquiry. This curiosity is still on the surface, but it is better than nothing."

He says further: "There are creators who sense things in advance and those who understand things only retrospectively. Those who seem to march at the same pace as the great mass of men are obviously the most successful. But the really great ones think ahead, which is not to say that they are always right commercially."

Renoir is too ingenuous to mean to praise himself by this observation, but he is aware of being one of those who, with skill and felicity, have sought to show their contemporaries what the cinema can teach them about themselves, their era, and their problems.

Comparing his feelings during the war, when he was far from France in a time of violence, to the confidence and inspiration which had informed his work when making *The Rules of the Game* in 1938, Renoir said:

"When I made *The Rules of the Game* I knew where I was going. I knew the evil that gnawed at my contemporaries. My instinct guided me, my awareness of the imminent danger led me to the situations and the dialogue. And my friends were like me. How worried we were! I think the film is a good one. But it is not so difficult to work well when the compass of anxiety points in the true direction."

Alas, we know which direction this was. The Munich Pact had just been signed. Georges Sadoul has said quite rightly that *The Rules of the Game* is for the prewar era what *The Marriage of Figaro* was for the Revolution of 1789: the portrayal of a refined, oblivious, and decadent civilization. Renoir was in fact inspired by Beaumarchais, taking as the epigraph of the film a couplet from Cherubin, as well as by de Musset's *Les Caprices de Marianne*, from which he took the basic dramatic situation of *The Rules of the Game*.

Neither the public nor the majority of the critics in 1939 could recognize in *The Rules of the Game* the fullest, most lucid expression of a moribund age. But this was certainly not the principal cause for the commercial failure of the film. As a conventional love story, the film could have been a success if the scenario had respected the rules of the movie game. But Renoir wanted to make his own style of *drame gai*, and the mixture of genres proved disconcerting to the public. Perhaps audiences were also put off by the stunningly mobile *mise en scène* and the subtle irony of the compositions and the camera movements. The photographic style which prefigured the famous depth of field, now returned from America via *Citizen Kane* and *The Best Years of Our Lives*, appeared at the time a droll but dubious curiosity.

Today *The Rules of the Game* is a classic of the film societies. It is admired not only as the most advanced expression of prewar French realism but also for its prefiguration of the most original elements of the cinematographic evolution of the next fifteen years. This legacy has yet to be exhausted.

CHAPTER FIVE

THE FRENCH RENOIR

•

The most immediately noticeable paradox in Renoir's style, and the one which almost always trips up the public, is his apparent casualness toward the very elements of the cinema which the public takes most seriously: the scenario and the action. Slip-ups in detail and even casting "errors" abound in the films of the renowned "realist."

It will be argued that, on the contrary, Sylvia Bataille and Jeanne Marken in *A Day in the Country*, Pierre Fresnay and Erich von Stroheim in *Grand Illusion*, and Jean Gabin and Simone Simon in *The Human Beast* are perfect examples of actors made for their roles. This is true enough. It is certainly not the case, however, for Jacques Brunius and Renoir himself in *A Day in the Country*. None of the major actors in *The Rules of the Game* is in his element (with the exception of Gaston Modot and Paulette Dubost). And who would claim that the cast of *The Lower Depths* stepped from the Gorki play? Gabin as a hero in a Russian novel is a long shot at best; and it would be difficult to conceive of a more spectacular bit of miscasting than Valentine Tessier in *Madame Bovary*. She is appropriate as the Emma at the end of the film, but her obvious maturity makes it difficult to believe in her virginity earlier and certainly impossible to accept her as the extremely young Emma at the beginning of the story. In the film she is not made to age physically in the slightest.

One could go on forever citing similar examples, for Renoir seems to take pleasure in making unlikely choices in about three-quarters of his casting. Rather than give up an actor who appeals to him in spite of what the script calls for, Renoir seems to be able to modify the scenario in order to justify his choice.

Even more than the casting "errors," Renoir's direction of his actors gives the impression of an almost annoying nonchalance. The casting is tangential to the roles, but more than that, the style of acting seems to be irrelevant to the dialogue and the dramatic situation. Given a certain scene to film, Renoir frequently seems to treat it as nothing more than a pretext for a completely new and original creation. The party in *The Rules of the Game* is a perfect example. In *Tire au Flanc* (a very revealing little sketch), Renoir's indifference toward the scenario is apparent throughout. Each scene uses the Mouézy-Eon story merely as a take-off point, rapidly developing into a sort of *commedia dell'arte*, a phenomenon reminiscent of the way Chaplin passes imperceptibly from the simple repetition of a gesture to its pure choreography.

Renoir showed a similar disregard for the script in shooting Boudu's first suicide attempt from the Pont des Arts. Rather than hire extras he simply filmed the group of curious observers attracted by the moviemakers. To understand why this approach is so appropriate for the scene, one must realize that the overriding purpose of the scene is to make fun of the world. With that aim in mind, there would be no other way to film it. As a final example of Renoir's cavalier approach to filming, remember that *The Lower Depths* was shot along the banks of the Marne, with the false beards and wigs of the Parisian muzhiks not even properly attached, at least figuratively speaking.

In short, Renoir directs his actors as if he liked them more than the scenes they are acting and preferred the scenes which they interpret to the scenario from which they come. This approach accounts for the disparity between his dramatic goals

and the style of acting, which tends to turn our attention from these aims. This style is added to the script like rich paint liberally applied to a line drawing: often the colors obscure and spill over the lines. This approach also explains the effort required to truly enjoy half the scenes Renoir directs. Whereas most directors try to convince the viewer immediately of the objective and psychological reality of the action and subordinate both acting and directing to this end, Renoir seems to lose sight of the audience from time to time. His players do not face the camera but each other, as if acting for their personal pleasure. One senses that they become their own private audience, enjoying little inside jokes among themselves. This impression is strong in *A Day in the Country* (Brunius's dance) as well as in *The Rules of the Game*, and in *The Crime of M. Lange*, where Marcel Duhamel and Paul Grimault act like a couple of conniving friends slipped into the real cast.

A glance at the credits of Renoir's films is sufficient to indicate how little regard he had for union codes or specialized labor. Pierre Lestringuez, a scenarist for *Nana* and *Marquitta*, is an actor in two other films. André Cerf was both assistant and actor in *Le Petit Chaperon Rouge*, along with Pierre Prévert. And Renoir himself was not hesitant about appearing in his own films.

The party at the château in *The Rules of the Game*, an elaborate game organized for the pleasure of the people making the film, is symbolic of all of Renoir's French work. What is more, this aspect of Renoir's films is almost certainly one of the major reasons for their commercial failure. To appreciate a Renoir film, one has to be "in," one has to catch the winks exchanged between actors and the knowing glances tossed over the camera. And the spectator who does not pick up the invitation to play the game necessarily feels a bit left out. It is not surprising to note that Renoir's most commercially successful films are the ones where this sort of internal play is the least marked, the films which direct themselves most openly to the public: *The Human Beast* and *Grand Illusion*. The presence of major stars in these films was a further guarantee against incongruities in

Catherine Hessling and Pierre Lestringuez in *Nana*

the casting, ruling out any possibility of the kind of inside jokes so dear to the less-known actors. At the other end of the scale lies the classic example of a film which demands considerable participation from its viewers: *The Rules of the Game*. The title itself is indicative of the nature of the film.

These remarks could be taken as reservations in my assessment of Renoir. Movies, after all, are not made for the people who produce them. But we should not push this line of reasoning too far, for it might lead us to consider Renoir's work as nothing more than a sort of modern-day *théâtre de salon*, a minor form dedicated to a limited audience. And to accept this judgment is to deny both Renoir's "realism" and the most striking elements in his work: the power, the fullness, the variety, and the creativity, to say nothing of the international influence of his long career. These are qualities hard to reconcile with a desire simply to entertain one's friends.

My point is that Renoir's tendency to hesitate between the scene in the script and the one he ends up making is only a dialectical moment of his realism. The party at the château is a game, but it is nevertheless a game whose absurd rule is to die of love. Roland Toutain, struck full force by a shotgun blast, rolls to the ground much like the rabbit we have just seen writhing in agony in front of the society folk, who like to kill in comfort from their hunting blinds. If Renoir is enjoying himself, if he entertains us by pushing his actors to the limits of parody, if he seems to linger over apparently incidental attractions, it is only the better to impress us with a sudden revelation of truth when we are no longer expecting it.

One of the most beautiful sequences in all of cinema is the moment in *A Day in the Country* when Sylvia Bataille is about to accept the advances of Georges Darnoux. The scene opens in a light, comic vein which one would logically expect to turn bawdy. We are ready to laugh, when suddenly the laugh catches in our throat. With Sylvia Bataille's incredible glance, the world begins to spin and love bursts forth like a long-stifled cry. No sooner is the smile wiped from our faces than tears appear in our eyes. I can think of no other director, except perhaps Chap-

Georges Darnoux and Sylvia Bataille in *A Day in the Country*

lin, who is capable of evoking such a wrenching bit of truth from a face, from an expression. Think of the look on Nadia Sibirskaïa's face when René Lefèvre makes awkward advances to her on the bench in *The Crime of M. Lange* or the ridiculous grin that spreads across Dalio's face when he shows off his calliope to the guests in *The Rules of the Game*.

Renoir's sense and taste for comedy is deeply rooted in his awareness of human tragedy. The temptation to parody, the tendency to enter into a sort of game with his actors, is only a preliminary modesty or hesitation necessary to the dialectic of game and rules, of pleasure and love, and love and death. I mentioned earlier that the acting in Renoir's films is frequently inappropriate for a certain scene, much like a color not quite right for a given drawing. But this apparent incongruity only serves to set off the dazzling moment which will reveal how right Renoir has been all along. We say to ourselves that the actor is definitely not the character up until the instant when all falls into place and he becomes the perfect incarnation of that character. In this way Renoir moves from an original discordance to an incomparable human harmony. The need which brings the actor and the character together lies deeper than superficial appearances. The truth which illuminates the faces of Renoir's actors, is testament to a veritable revelation.

The cinema as a whole still suffers from the mentality of the kind of people who like slick color prints. It confuses the beauty of the model with that of the painting, whereas the painter's aim is not to depict a particular woman but to reveal a universal beauty. Renoir does not choose his actors, as in the theater, because they fit into a predetermined role, but like the painter, because of what he can force us to see in them. That is why the most spectacular bits of acting in his films are almost indecently beautiful. They leave us with only the memory of their brilliance, of a flash of revelation so dazzling that it almost forces us to turn our eyes away. At moments like these the actor is pushed beyond himself, caught totally open and naked in a situation which no longer has anything to do with dramatic expression, in that most revealing light which the cinema can cast on the human figure more brilliantly than any other art except painting.

Parenthetically, one can see by what I have just said how much Renoir owes to the crucial influence of von Stroheim. But if Stroheim came eventually to a sort of obscenity in acting, it was by a different route. While Renoir pretends to play with his actors so as to catch them unawares, Stroheim proceeds with an unrelenting insistence and obsessive patience which pushes acting to its limits.* Stroheim's influence is nonetheless curiously

---

* Bazin wrote elsewhere that "It is certainly von Stroheim who is the most firmly opposed to both pictorial expressionism and the artifices of montage. In his work reality yields its meaning like a suspect under the

apparent in Renoir's last silent films and as late as *La Chienne* (1931). It is perhaps most striking, because unexpected, in *Tire au Flanc* (1929), which includes a fabulous bit of pure Stroheim: the scene of the lieutenant picking a rose for the prisoner's wife, while the prisoner tries to observe the painful scene through his small barred window.

It is of course only a critical ploy which allows us to distinguish the direction of the actor from the interpretation of the scenario. The elements of *commedia dell'arte* which creep into the acting or the discrepancy between a given role and the way it is acted are examples of the liberties Renoir takes with a story. They are probably also reasons for the misunderstanding between Renoir and his public. The spectator wants to believe in the story that the actor brings to life. Psychological or physical verisimilitude is less important for him than respect for a certain dramatic logic, for a formal verisimilitude based on the conventions of storytelling. But it is precisely this sort of formal logic of which Renoir is incapable. What counts for him is not verisimilitude but accuracy of detail, and to achieve this he frequently takes dramatic shortcuts. Thus at the beginning of *The Human Beast* the pretext of the fat industrialist's little dog is rather unbelievable, all the more so since it is presented in a comic interlude. What Renoir needed was a justification for Ledoux's approach to his wife's godfather, and he seized upon the first excuse that came along. Even at that he could have made an effort to make us believe in the incident, but the little track-side episode amused him and he did not care that it revealed in his hero a courage and sympathy that would be belied by the following sequence.

Furthermore, we know how Renoir works, how important improvisation is to his technique. We know how he rewrites and

relentless grilling of a police inspector. The principle of his *mise en scène* is simple: Look at the world close enough and insistently enough until it eventually reveals its cruelty and ugliness. Theoretically one could imagine a von Stroheim film composed of a single shot as long and as close as you like." André Bazin, *Qu'est-ce que le cinéma?*, Vol. I, p. 135. Trans.

polishes scenarios in advance only to modify them a final time on the set. These are hardly methods conducive to the development of dramatic logic and verisimilitude. But they are fertile indeed in the hands of a Renoir, who can infuse them with pure cinematic inspiration.

Renoir brings to the screen not a story but themes, for which the scenario is ultimately nothing more than a physical support, like props for a set. His themes are visual and plastic: the theme of water, for example, which we find throughout his work, from *La Fille de l'Eau* to *The River*, the Marne of *Boudu* and *A Day in the Country*, the swamp of Sologne in *The Rules of the Game*, the Louisiana bayous of *Swamp Water*, the flood in *The Southerner*. Or they are dramatic and moral themes, such as the theme of the hunt in *The Rules of the Game*, or the metaphor of man and machine, which is the organizing principle in *The Human Beast*. This latter is by no means an abstract metaphor. It is earthy and physical, as in the scene where Jean Gabin, attentive and friendly but sensual as well, caresses his locomotive, *La Lison*. If we interpret the film as nothing more than a love story played against the realistic backdrop of the railroad, and poorly played and put together at that, we have not understood it at all.

By the same token, to grasp the subtle organization of *The Rules of the Game* we have to go from the general to the specific, from the action to the plot and from the plot to the scene. To grasp the scheme of the film, we must see the music boxes, the bearskin which gives Octave so much trouble, the agony of the little rabbit, and the game of hide-and-seek in the corridors of the château as the essential realities of the film from which unroll the dramatic spirals of each particular scene. This accounts for the integrity and independence of each scene relative to the scenario as a whole. But it also explains the unique quality and orientation of these scenes, which develop cinematically in concentric layers, much like the grain of sand within an oyster gradually growing into a pearl.

It is precisely this treatment that makes *The Rules of the Game* Renoir's masterpiece, for in it he has succeeded in dispensing entirely with dramatic structures. The film is nothing more than a tangle of reminders, allusions, and correspondences, a carrousel of themes where reality and the moral plane reflect one another without disrupting the movie's meaning and rhythm, its tonality and melody. At the same time, it is a brilliantly constructed film in which no scene is unnecessary, no shot out of place. *The Rules of the Game* is a work which should be seen again and again. As it is necessary to hear a symphony more than once to understand it or to meditate before a great painting in order to appreciate its inner harmonies, so it is with Renoir's great film.

The fact that *The Rules of the Game* was so long misunderstood is not simply the result of its originality and the public's psychological inertia, but also because it is a work that reveals itself only gradually to the spectator, even if he is attentive. *Citizen Kane* is a similar film in this regard. In retrospect it is surprising how obscure the Orson Welles film seemed when it first appeared, and hard to believe that nine out of ten critics found it impossible to recount the plot correctly. If there is any film which seems to us today to be simple (though ambiguous, it is certainly not obscure) and perfectly constructed, it is *Citizen Kane*.

From a dramatic point of view, the death of Toutain, running toward the greenhouse in *The Rules of the Game*, is a coincidence difficult to accept. The mistaken identity is too easy. If we accept this kind of turn of events anything could happen to anyone. But Renoir makes the whole sequence indispensable to his movie, and marvelously apt, through the metaphor of the hunt, which implicitly alludes to the case of mistaken identity in *The Marriage of Figaro* and reminds one of the tragic ending of Alfred de Musset's *Les Caprices de Marianne*. It is the glimpse of a rabbit rolling over dead and the memory of Beaumarchais and de Musset which elevate the hero's death and make an apparent coincidence into an aesthetic necessity.

In other words, Renoir does not construct his films around situations and dramatic developments, but around beings, things, and fact. This assertion, which explains his method of handling actors and adapting the scenario, also gives us the key to understanding his method of filming. Just as the actor does not "play" a scene which itself will be just another episode in the scenario as a whole, so the camera does not simply record the dramatic relationships and underline the main lines of the plot; on the contrary, it focuses on whatever is original and irreplaceable in the scene.

In this way Renoir reminds us that he is his father's son. It would be a mistake to look for the heritage of Auguste Renoir in the formal, plastic elements of his son's movies. For it is precisely here that painting had its worst influence on the cinematic image. And the stunning pictorial quality of Jean Renoir's work is by no means the result of his photographic composition, but of the originality of his vision and the ideas behind his images. What is more, if *A Day in the Country* plays at evoking the subject matter and the lighting of the Impressionists, it is out of an exceptional coquetry which only proves the rule. Renoir is playing at being his father, just as he plays at being Beaumarchais and de Musset in *The Rules of the Game*. It is a discreet and playful homage, which is significant not simply as a conscious imitation but as witness to the sensitivity and love which the films of Jean and the paintings of Auguste have in common. Jean made the ideal movies which Auguste himself would have made if he had abandoned his brushes for the camera.

Jean Renoir's pictorial sense is expressed above all in the attention he pays to the importance of individual things in relation to one another. He does not sacrifice the tree to the forest. Herein lies his true cinematic realism, rather than in his penchant for naturalistic subjects.

To define a film style, it is always necessary to come back to the dialectic between reality and abstraction, between the concrete and the ideal. In the final analysis, the principle of a director's style lies in his way of giving reality meaning. It should be kept in mind that the art of the film, so often considered the most concrete of all, is also the most easily abstracted. Look carefully at bad films and you will see that they are composed of nothing but symbolism and signs, of conventions, of dramatic, moral, and emotional hieroglyphs. It is this fact which lends a certain validity to the common sense critical standard which considers "realism" as a criterion of quality. The word "realism" as it is commonly used does not have an absolute and clear meaning, so much as it indicates a certain tendency toward the faithful rendering of reality on film. Given the fact that this movement toward the real can take a thousand different routes, the apologia for "realism" *per se*, strictly speaking, means nothing at all. The movement is valuable only insofar as it brings increased meaning (itself an abstraction) to what is created. Good cinema is necessarily, in one way or another, more realistic than bad cinema. But simply being realistic is not enough to make a film good. There is no point in rendering something realistically unless it is to make it more meaningful in an abstract sense. In this paradox lies the progress of the movies. In this paradox too lies the genius of Renoir, without doubt the greatest of all French directors.

Renoir the moralist is also the most "realistic" of film makers, sacrificing reality as little as possible to the thrust of his message. The last scenes from *Boudu* could serve as the epigraph to all of Renoir's French work. Boudu, newly wed, throws himself into the water. Dramatic or psychological logic would demand that such an act have a precise meaning. Is it despair, suicide? Probably not, but it is at least an attempt at escape. Boudu is fleeing the chains of a bourgeois marriage. This interpretation, although more ambiguous, would still lend a certain meaning to the shot. Boudu's fall would remain an *act*. But Renoir, like his character, quickly forgets the *act* in favor of the *fact*, and the true object of the scene ceases gradually to be Boudu's intentions and becomes rather the spectacle of his pleasure and, by extension, the enjoyment that Renoir derives from the antics of his hero. The water is no longer "water" but more specifically the water of the Marne in August, yellow and glaucous. Michel Simon floats on it, turns over, sprays like a seal; and as he plays we begin to perceive the depth, the quality, even the tepid warmth of that water. When he comes up on the bank, an extraordinary slow 360-degree pan shows us the countryside he sees before him. But this effect, by nature banally descriptive, which could indicate space and liberty regained, is of unequaled poetry precisely because what moves us is *not* the fact that this countryside is once again Boudu's domain, but that the banks of the Marne, in all the richness of their detail, are intrinsically beautiful. At the end of the pan, the camera picks up a bit of grass where, in close-up, one can see distinctly the white dust that the heat and the wind have lifted from the path. One can almost feel it between one's fingers. Boudu is going to stir it up with his foot. If I were deprived of the pleasure of seeing *Boudu* again for the rest of my days, I would never forget that grass, that dust, and their relationship to the liberty of a tramp.

This has been a rather long and lyrical treatment of a scene in which nothing happens. I could choose many others, each of which would bring out Renoir's feeling for the appearances of things, or at least the important role that these appearances play in his art.

A particular predilection for water is easily discernible in his work. I have just cited one example. Water evokes a theme of *mise en scène* which has become a screen classic: the boat scene which poses all sorts of complicated technical problems, such as the changing of camera angle, the dolly out and the other movements of the camera, and the sound recording. Often directors content themselves with a series of general exterior shots intercut with close-ups shot in the studio against backgrounds simulated by the transparencies. This technique would be unthinkable for Renoir, for it necessarily dissociates the actors from their surroundings and implies that their acting and their dialogue are more important than the reflection of the water on their faces, the wind in their hair, or the movement of a distant branch. All of Renoir's boating scenes are shot entirely on location, even if he has to sacrifice the shooting script to do so, and their quality is a direct result of this technique. A thousand examples could illustrate this marvelous sensitivity to the physical, tactile reality of an object and its milieu; Renoir's films are made from the surfaces of the objects photographed, and his direction is frequently but a caress, a loving glance at

these surfaces. His editing does not proceed from the usual dis-
section of the space and duration of the scene according to a
preestablished dramatic formula. Rather, it follows the dictates
of his roving eye, discerning, even if occasionally distracted or
willfully lazy.

Throughout the entire last part of *The Rules of the Game*
the camera acts like an invisible guest wandering about the
salon and the corridors with a certain curiosity, but without any
more advantage than its invisibility. The camera is not notice-
ably any more mobile than a man would be (if one grants that
people run about quite a bit in this château). And the camera
even gets trapped in a corner, where it is forced to watch the
action from a fixed position, unable to move without revealing
its presence and inhibiting the protagonists. This sort of personi-
fication of the camera accounts for the extraordinary quality of
this long sequence. It is not striking because of the script or the
acting, but as a result of Renoir's half amused, half anxious way
of observing the action.

No one has grasped the true nature of the screen better than
Renoir; no one has more successfully rid it of the equivocal
analogies with painting and the theater. Plastically the screen
is most often made to conform to the limits of a canvas, and dramatically it is modeled after the stage. With these two traditional references in mind, directors tend to conceive their images
as boxed within a rectangle as do the painter and the stage
director. Renoir, on the other hand, understands that the screen
is not a simple rectangle but rather the homothetic surface of
the viewfinder of his camera. It is the very opposite of a frame.
The screen is a mask whose function is no less to hide reality
than it is to reveal it. The significance of what the camera dis-
closes is relative to what it leaves hidden. But this invisible witness is inevitably made to wear blinders; its ideal ubiquity is
restrained by framing, just as tyranny is often restrained by
assassination.

Another scene which I would like to use as an epigraph is
the shot from *The Rules of the Game* after the chase by the pond,
where Nora Grégor, fooling about with a little spyglass, happens

to spot her husband kissing his mistress. Just as it was chance that brought the husband into her field of vision, so it is chance that determines to a certain degree what part of a scene the lens will uncover. And, paradoxically, it is this chance which makes the perspicacity and the vigilance of the eye so important. The point of view of the camera is not that of the novelist's omniscient third-person narrator; nor is it a stupid, unthinking subjectivity. Rather it is a way of seeing which, while free of all contingency, is at the same time limited by the concrete qualities of vision: its continuity in time and its vanishing point in space. It is like the eye of God, in the proper sense of the word, if God could be satisfied with a single eye. Thus when M. Lange decides to kill, the camera stays in the courtyard with Jules Berry, watching through the windows of the stairway as René Lefèvre descends from one floor to the next, faster and faster, as if pulled along by his resolution. He emerges suddenly onto the stoop. At this point the camera is between the two protagonists, with its back to Berry. Instead of panning to the right to follow Lange, it swings deliberately 180 degrees to the left, sweeping the empty set to center once again on Berry, placing us at the side of the victim just as Lefèvre comes back into our field of vision from the left.* The intelligence of this bit of camera work is all the more admirable for the fact that it is doubly audacious, doubly effective. On the one hand, the whole scene rests on a continuity of point of view expressed by a camera precisely located in the center of the action. On the other hand, the personified camera takes it upon itself to turn its back on the action in order to take a little shortcut. Only in the work of F. W. Murnau can one find similar examples of a camera movement

---

* A look at what would have been the traditional handling of this scene will make clear exactly what I mean. Two approaches seem likely: (1) A continuous shot, a pan or dolly shot following René Lefèvre across the courtyard to the right, from the stoop to the fountain where Berry is standing. (2) Better, a discontinuous, edited sequence. René Lefèvre emerges from the stairway and heads toward the camera. Cut to Jules Berry behind the camera. Lefèvre re-enters the camera's field of vision.

In both cases the approach would be purely descriptive, directly determined by the action and the position of the actors.

so liberated from the characters and from traditional dramatic geometry.

Technically this conception of the screen assumes what I shall call lateral depth of field and the almost total disappearance of montage. Since what we are shown is only significant in terms of what is hidden from us and since therefore the value of what we see is continually threatened, the *mise en scène* cannot limit itself to what is presented on the screen. The rest of the scene, while effectively hidden, should not cease to exist. The action is not bounded by the screen, but merely passes through it. And a person who enters the camera's field of vision is coming from other areas of the action, and not from some limbo, some imaginary "backstage." Likewise, the camera should be able to spin suddenly without picking up any holes or dead spots in the action.

What all of this means is that the scene should be played independent of the camera in all its real dramatic expanse and that it is up to the cameraman to let his viewfinder play over the action. Reframing, then, is substituted as much as possible for a switching of points of view, which not only introduces spatial discontinuity, a phenomenon foreign to the nature of the human eye, but also sanctions the concept of the reality of a shot on a single plane, the idea of each shot as nothing more than a unit of place and action, an atom which joins with other atoms to make the scene and then the sequence. When a film is made in this way, with each shot lit and played separately, the screen hides nothing, because there is nothing to hide outside the action being filmed. And as cleverly as these separate bits are stitched together, they cannot fool the attentive spectator. The little moment of hesitation at the beginning of a first line, the little something in the fixed nature of the camera and above all in the framing, where nothing is left to chance—everything betrays the existence of a preconceived "shot."

Never do we have this feeling in *The Rules of the Game*, where the action plays hide-and-seek with the camera and the set, passing from the pantry to the second floor, from the great salon to the smoking room, from the pantry to the corridors. In all this ceaseless action the slightest detail in this great complex of reality never ceases to be a living part of the rhythm, whether it is before our eyes or far away.

I should mention here how and why this deliberate use of realism which goes beyond the image itself to include the very structures of the *mise en scène* brought Renoir to the use of depth of field ten years before Orson Welles. Renoir himself explained it in the famous *Le Point* article:

"The farther I advance in my profession, the more I am inclined to shoot in deep focus. The more I work, the more I abandon confrontations between two actors neatly set up before the camera, as in a photographer's studio. I prefer to place my characters more freely, at different distances from the camera, and to make them move. For that I need great depth of field . . ."

This modestly technical explanation is obviously only the immediate and practical consequence of the search for style which we have struggled to define. Simple depth of field is only the other dimension of the "lateral" liberty which Renoir requires. It is just that our commentary proceeds from the screen, whereas Renoir's explanation starts at the other end of his creation, with the actors.

But the function of depth of field is not only to allow more liberty to the director and the actors. It confirms the unity of actor and decor, the total interdependence of everything real, from the human to the mineral. In the representation of space, it is a necessary modality of this realism which postulates a constant sensitivity to the world but which opens to a universe of analogies, of metaphors, or, to use Baudelaire's word in another, no less poetic sense, of correspondences.

The most visual and most sensual of film makers is also the one who introduces us to the most intimate of his characters because he is faithfully enamored of their appearance, and through their appearance, of their soul. In Renoir's films acquaintances are made through love, and love passes through the epidermis of the world. The suppleness, the mobility, the vital richness of form in his direction, result from the care and the joy he takes in draping his films in the simple cloak of reality.

CHAPTER SIX

RENOIR IN HOLLYWOOD

●

The Southerner (1945)*

MANUSCRIPT NOTES

After the death of his uncle, Sam Tucker (Zachary Scott), a cotton farmer, decides to try to work a patch of land which has been abandoned for several years. With his wife, Nona (Betty Field), their two children, and an aging grandmother (Beulah Bondi), Sam takes to the road in a battered car and heads for the new tract.

The abandoned farm, the untilled earth, winter, and the sickness which one of the children develops from malnutrition pose seemingly insurmountable problems. A torrential rain causes a flood, which wipes out several months of work. Only the courage of the women keeps Sam from giving up and looking for a job in town. He will stay on the inhospitable land and start again to try to cultivate it.

I was quite bothered by certain things which prevented me from getting into the story.

---

* For Renoir's first two Hollywood films, *Swamp Water* (1941) and *This Land Is Mine* (1943), see the notes by Jean-Luc Godard and François Truffaut in the Filmography. F.T.

I found the conditions of life of the characters hard to accept without further explanation (for example: Where does the little girl go to school? Are they really unable to buy even half a quart of milk a day? Where are the other buildings on the farm? the stable? the barn?). But perhaps this impression is a consequence of ignorance. If we were Americans, we would see no more problems in *The Southerner* than in *Toni*, where the improbabilities do not bother us French at all.

The same goes for the actors: Zachary Scott is good, but Betty Field is hardly credible. One cannot lead a life like hers and still maintain such grace. On the other hand, the grandmother seems to be overdone in the opposite direction.

Note that casting in the French films is often no more convincing, but since the actors are French the line between realism and fantasy is easily perceptible to us. Here we have a mixture in which the two are difficult to distinguish. Add to this the theatricality of the actors, which clashes with the realistic set. (The sound track—in both music and sounds—is much more professional than that of *Swamp Water.*) *The Southerner* suggests a pastoral drama transplanted to the universe of Erskine Caldwell.

But probably this reaction is very unjust. First, because the Americanism excludes us from the participation possible in the French films; and with Renoir, when you are not a participant . . . (We regain this participation with *The Diary of a Chambermaid.*) We must break through the crust of realism which blinds us and reach beyond to the tender, cruel, ironic, playful, almost dreamlike universe of Renoir. The fact is that the images which *The Southerner* leaves with us are more surreal than dramatic.

Diary of a Chambermaid (1946)

I have written that Renoir's American films are admirable. Nonetheless, in my heart of hearts I have always suspected that they were inferior to the French films, and if I did not take more advantage of opportunities to see them again, it was more for fear that my disappointment would be confirmed than that I might find cause to revise my original unfavorable opinions. At least that way I could still tell myself that I might have been too severe. I did have the slightly morbid curiosity to look back at what I had written on *Diary of a Chambermaid* in *L'Ecran français* of June 15, 1948. Here are some extracts:

> What mental aberration, what failure of self-analysis, or what dangerous taste for irony led Renoir to make a film in America on the subject closest to him, on the very subject which he would least be able to treat outside of France? . . . This drama of ambition and domestic service strikes no chord in America, where the problem of domestics does not exist (except as an aspect of the racial problem). . . . Renoir has gone to ridiculous lengths to re-create around his heroes the French milieu in which they live and die. But we sense the glare of the studio lights on Burgess Meredith's rosebushes. The entire film is bathed in this aquarium light so typical of Hollywood. Everything, even the actors, seem like Japanese flowers under glass. Still there is a melancholy pleasure in re-encountering Renoir, even in such an unsuccessful effort. We sense him constantly squirming under the limitations of his situation, hampered by the scenario, unable to give the right tone to his actors. His American works are still "Renoir films," as characteristic as his French films, but this time characteristic in their failures.

Today I can see clearly what critical preconception blinded me; it was that of Renoir's "realism." I projected this notion on *Diary of a Chambermaid*, whose naturalistic aspects seemed to doubly justify the application of such a standard. Does not Renoir seem to be preoccupied with the design of the costumes (copied from Berthe Morisot), the sets, and the furniture (by Lourié)?

Of course, this realism of detail was obliterated by the effects not only of shooting the exteriors in the studio but above all of having the characters played by Americans. However slightly less inaccurate than the usual American film portraying France, *Diary of a Chambermaid* leaves us with the same impression of falseness. Hence my original judgment.

The Crime of M. Lange, which I saw again recently just before *Diary*, and which seemed more admirable the tenth time than it did the first, could only confirm my prejudice, and after being overwhelmed with admiration for *Lange* I expected only the "melancholy pleasure" of finding again the same Renoir in *Diary*, but this time wrestling with the wrong subject and the wrong style.

Then the film started, and this was indeed the unfortunate feeling I had during the first few minutes. But that was all the time it took me to realize my error, to see how absurd it was to persist in seeing failed realism in the most surreal and deliberately imaginary of all Renoir's films. The point of the meticulous design was not to reconstruct an impossible, synthetic France, but rather to give the images the precision of a nightmare. As for the "aquarium light" which had so upset me, it was still there all right, but this time it appeared like the illumination of some interior hell, a sort of telluric phosphorescence such as Jules Verne imagined to illuminate the journey of his voyagers to the center of the earth. Everything, including the meticulous details of the costumes, is organized into a vision of cruel fantasy completely removed from the real world. Here perhaps was the source of the obsession with the theater that was more and more to characterize Renoir's development. Before *Diary* the theater had offered little more to the director of *Boudu* than a few pretexts for scenarios. But here for the first time we see in Renoir's work not theater, but the purest theatricality.

Once I had abandoned the futile criterion of realism and allowed myself to dream the film with Renoir, I could see the precision of the film, in its construction as well as in its style, and above all in the direction of the actors, which is accomplished with a freedom and an audacity equaled only by *Paris Does Strange Things*. Certainly Renoir has never gone further than in *Diary* toward the marriage of the dramatic and the comic. It is not realism which puts *Diary* on a level with *The Rules of the Game*, but the fact that the French film was a "comic tragedy," the American film a "tragic farce." Renoir succeeds in harmonizing the two most extreme colors of his palette, that of *La Chienne* and that of *Boudu* or *Tire au Flanc* (although in *Tire au Flanc* the grotesque has already begun to mingle with the burlesque). In *Diary* the marriage of the two extremes is the basis for the film. The "happy ending" flows from both cruelty and joy, despair and happiness.

The old image of the director exiled to Hollywood, of the colossus bound up by the Lilliputians, is at least in this case absurd. None of Renoir's films reflects more freedom of invention and style.

MANUSCRIPT NOTES

(on the adaptation of *Diary of a Chambermaid*)

Renoir's work in adapting the novel consisted in shifting around the chronology of some of the episodes in the diary. For example, the story of the tubercular boy with whom Célestine falls in love is a combination of two independent stories which take place in two of the different places where Célestine is employed.

In the book the priory is more the place where Célestine records her adventures than the place where they happen. In Célestine's biography the priory has hardly any importance except for the conclusion, the marriage with the valet, Joseph. From the dramatic point of view the adaptation is judicious and astute, because the diffuse, episodic quality of the novel is not appropriate to the unified construction of a film. This is particularly so considering that a major strong point of the film is the successful effort to achieve a unity of action and atmosphere, to create a consistent universe around the characters.

Diary is cruel and grotesque, but not evil. In every instance, evil is punished in the end. The film is dominated by a fantasy and a humor completely foreign to Mirbeau's novel.

The captain and "Monsieur" are without grace in Mirbeau; the one is a heartless maniac, and the other is a cowardly old bastard. On the other hand, the valet, Joseph, ambiguous in Mirbeau, is a monster in Renoir's film. Or, more precisely, we see that Célestine spurns him because of his monstrousness, while in Mirbeau it is this monstrousness which attracts her.

This brings us to Célestine. Either from taste or from necessity (this point should be checked), Renoir has sweetened Célestine's character. She does not really contradict the Célestine of the book, and many of her characteristics are the same, but they are almost all favorable characteristics. We do not find in the film the vulgarity and the unrestrained sexuality of Mirbeau's Célestine. In the book Célestine is sympathetic not because her own feelings and actions are better than those she attributes to the others, but simply because the others are hypocrites while she is sincere. This quality would not be enough to make her sympathetic on the screen if the scenario attributed to her a tenth of what she does in the book, and particularly if she fell in love with Joseph.

Note, in addition, the influence of the book on all of Renoir's work. First, of course, the theme, so important with him, of subordination (the innumerable servant scenes in *Diary*). But also the way details from the past reveal character. *Orvet* is full of memories of *Diary*, and so probably are *Marquitta* and *Nana*.

Always you realize to what extent naturalism is only a point of departure for Renoir; how he uses it with freedom and intelligence, on the one hand, to create a moral universe (*Diary*), and, on the other hand, to portray contemporary subjects realistically (*The Human Beast*, *The Rules of the Game*).

The Woman on the Beach (1946)

MANUSCRIPT NOTES

A Coast Guard officer, Burnett (Robert Ryan), is engaged to Eve Geddes (Nan Leslie), the daughter of a shipbuilder in the area in which he is stationed. He is awaiting his discharge so they can marry. Meanwhile, on the beach he meets Peggy Butler (Joan Bennett), the wife of the painter Tod Butler (Charles Bickford). Butler is blind and lives in an isolated house with only his wife for company.

Burnett is charmed by Peggy's beauty and thinks she is unhappy. She leads him to think that her husband confines her and beats her. Burnett suspects Butler of feigning his handicap to ensure the devotion of his wife. To see if Butler is really blind, Burnett leads him on a walk on a cliff and abandons him at the edge of the abyss. Butler falls and escapes death only by miraculous good fortune.

Burnett is now convinced that Butler is really blind, but he is not cured of his passion for Peggy, and he neglects his fiancée. A confrontation finally comes about between the two men, and Burnett realizes that despite their constant quarrels Peggy and her husband are strongly attached to each other. He decides to break with her and go back to his fiancée.

But that night, a hysterical telephone call from Peggy summons him back. During a violent scene with his wife, Butler has decided to destroy his remaining paintings, worth a considerable fortune, and to burn down his house. Burnett arrives as Peggy is struggling to keep Butler from throwing the paintings into the flames. The paintings will burn with the house, but Peggy saves her husband and, finally, leaves with him to help him start a new life.

It is a strange film, stubborn, sincere, elusive, obscure. Renoir says that he wanted to portray pure sexual attraction, but between which characters? The sensuality is there certainly, but it goes from one character to another like a mysterious ball of fire. We don't know exactly where it is.

The nightmare is curiously done. It is difficult to tell how much of it is just a typical Hollywood nightmare and how much consists of images really conceived by Renoir. The question is important because the nightmare sets the tone for the film. The hero lives the adventure like a real nightmare. The ending is curious for its rapid brutality.

It seems to me that the final editing, after Renoir's troubles with the studio, must have massacred and obscured the film, but even so, it remains at once one of the most sincere and one of the most hampered of Renoir's works.

Was not *The Woman on the Beach* conceived and executed in the manner of the mystery film, pressed in its mold but with another material, not at all conventional, rather very personal? The strangeness of this film results, at least in part, from the contrast between the material and the mold.

CHAPTER SEVEN

RENOIR RETURNS

●

As he was passing through Paris in 1951 following the opening of
The River, *Jean Renoir granted a rare interview to André Bazin.
What follows is the text of an article which Bazin wrote about this
conversation, as it appeared in the June 3, 1951, edition of* Radio-
Cinéma-Télévision. *More significant than a simple interview, the
article recounts the first meeting of Renoir and Bazin at the Invalides
Aérogare and later at the Hotel Royal Monceau. It is an account of
the beginnings of a friendship.* F.T.

Anyone who ever doubted, not being acquainted with his work,
that Jean Renoir was a great man, would have only to spend a
little time with him to be convinced that he is.

"Great" first of all physically. Tall and fat, all smiles, with
his slight limp, he reminds you of a cross between a playful bear
and an elephant with a sprained ankle. We have already seen
him as the great bear and the prankster in *The Rules of the
Game.* Perhaps he developed an affinity for elephants while
shooting *The River* in India. But let us leave aside the bestiary,
to which we would be obliged to add the little rabbits shot from
blinds in Sologne and the ones who beat the drums on calliopes.
Renoir's resemblance to these animals only makes him more
charming to us humans.

Renoir's charm is part strength, part kindness. And I have

not found a kindness like his in any other director in the world, with the possible exception of Orson Welles (and I think his is superficial), certainly not in any of the run-of-the-mill directors. A single example: During our conversation at the hotel the telephone rang constantly. After the third or fourth call my wife, who was sitting next to the phone, offered to ask who was calling before passing the phone to Renoir. Surprised, Renoir said, "What for? I always answer."

"In France," Renoir told me, "after shaving, one carefully wipes the blade with a little gadget. But in America razor blades are so cheap that men throw them out after each shave. I could never get used to that. Throwing out a blade which is still sharp? Why, it's inhuman."

Let those who have known and loved Renoir be reassured. America has not devoured him. At the very most, and this is hardly a misfortune, it has distilled his French virtues, eliminating the impurities and leaving only the essentials.

A kind of Franciscan serenity and tenderness tempers his Rabelaisian paganism now. A sense of the universal, of the relativity of history and geography, situates and confirms his Frenchness: "I think we are entering a new Middle Ages," he says. "We should not complain. The Middle Ages was a great era."

Renoir is now hoping that he will be able to work in France. Aside from the private difficulties, which have now been resolved, and the fact that his son is living in America, Renoir did not want to return to film in France before he was assured of success in the States.

"I had ups and downs in Hollywood," he says, "but to leave after a partial commercial failure* would have been a bit low. So I am pleased by the good reception that the New York distributors have given *The River*. Now I am morally more free to consider the offers I receive to work in France. Nothing specific yet. These things cannot be handled at a distance. I'll think about them a little more seriously after *Le Carrosse du Saint-Sacrement*, which I am about to start in Rome."

* *The Woman on the Beach*. Trans.

Another phone call: "Oh! Hello, Pierre, so happy to hear from you . . ." "It's amazing how many friends I run into who remember me as if it were yesterday . . ." "*The River*, which I shot on location in Technicolor with my nephew, Claude, as cameraman, is basically the story of *Toni*, a *Toni* moved to India. I consider it as a follow-up to my efforts in *The Rules of the Game*." Clearly, Renoir has not renounced his French work. How will he take it up again?

The man who made *La Chienne, Nana, The Crime of M. Lange, Madame Bovary, Grand Illusion, The Human Beast, A Day in the Country, The Lower Depths*, and *The Rules of the Game* is without question the greatest French director, or at the very least, the greatest sound director. The son of the painter Auguste Renoir, he has in his blood what he has called "a certain feel for French gesture," the gesture of Degas's ironing woman or of the locomotive engineer touching the overheated axle. More generally, he has inherited from the literary and pictorial sensibility of his father's era a profound, sensual, and loving sense of reality. His genius is not just to translate, but to reinterpret in the cinema all that made the writers and the painters of his childhood great. He is certainly one of the two or three directors who have made films worthy of the literary masterpieces which inspired them. And maybe history will consider Renoir's *A Day in the Country* superior to de Maupassant's original.

With *The Rules of the Game*, his last French film, Renoir freed himself from the literary and pictorial sources which dominated a great part of his work up to that time. True, *Grand Illusion* and *The Crime of M. Lange* were made from original screenplays, but *The Rules of the Game* brings together and surpasses, transcends all of Renoir's earlier works. One can and should consider this film the most highly developed and the most instructive in terms of scenario and direction of all French sound films.

The films Renoir made in Hollywood probably disappointed his French admirers. Still people will probably reconsider their first opinions of *Swamp Water* and *The Woman on the Beach*. But Renoir only flourishes when he is free, when he does not have to conform to anyone's rules, when he can let himself be inspired on the spur of the moment by people and things. It is for this reason that *The Southerner*, based on the importance of the earth, the water, the countryside, is the most human and most beautiful of Renoir's American films.

If Renoir returns to making films in France, I don't think we should expect him to be just as he left us. His art will be perhaps more spare, more serene and tragic. A renewed classicism could well be the result of the American experience and of the past ten years of world history. One thing we can be sure of: his style will not have become academic.

CHAPTER EIGHT

A PURE MASTERPIECE: *THE RIVER*

●

Jean Renoir is the greatest living French director. This judgment implies a choice of Renoir over René Clair, the only other
French director of comparable stature. I choose without hesitation, not from personal preference, but on the basis of a criterion
I think is objective. Clair is a man of the silent film. That he
adapted himself to sound to produce his masterpiece, *Le Million*,
is proof enough of the intelligence and suppleness of his talent,
but in the final analysis, he did no more than *adapt* himself to
it. His use of sound implies an a priori commitment to the pre-
eminence of silence. With Renoir, on the other hand, sounds and
words are an expressive addition which is assimilated naturally
and immediately. Now *The River* has shown that color did not
present him with any more problems than had sound. For Renoir, the cinema means the maximum in the realism of the
image, both plastic and aural.

Except for Malraux's *Man's Hope*, *The Rules of the Game*
was the only film which did not seem to age in the immediate
postwar period; on the contrary, it seemed to incarnate the future. Marcel Carné's *Le Jour se Lève* (also made in 1939) was
the culmination of poetic realism, but the very perfection of the
achievement left him no place to go. Carné has yet to go beyond
this impasse. *The Rules of the Game* too was the culmination of
all its director's previous efforts, but at the same time it opened

up a new path. One could almost say that with it the silent film finally died completely. The revolution of realism, begun by von Stroheim five years before the appearance of sound, was now finally fulfilled with the appearance of a cinematography which clung firmly to reality while repudiating all plastic symbolism and the artifices of montage. "Cinema" no longer imposed itself between the spectator and the object, like a set of prisms and filters designed to stamp their own meaning on reality. With Renoir, expressionism had had its day. By expressionism I mean not just the German school and its influence, but everything which manifests an explicit imposition of technique on the meaning of the film. I know that this seems obscure; I shall attempt to elucidate it.

Imagine a love scene on the screen. The impression which the director communicates to us has two essentially different elements:

1. The object of the scene itself, which is to say the characters, their behavior, and their dialogue; in other words, reality in its objective time and space;

2. The sum of the artifices which the film maker uses to emphasize the meaning of the event, to color it, to describe its nuances, and to make it harmonize with what precedes and follows it in the story.

We can easily see that if it is to be a romantic scene, the set, the lighting, and the framing would not be the same as for a scene of violent sensuality. Then comes montage. The shots will be more numerous and closer for the depiction of sensuality. The romantic scene will demand two-shots at first, and the close-ups at the end will be long ones. We can also see all the imaginable variations.

I call expressionist any aesthetic which in this situation places more confidence in the artifices of cinematography—which is to say, in what is generally meant by "cinema"—than in the reality to which they are applied.

When I speak of a cinema without "cinema" (where, then, would be the difference between art and reality?), I mean another conception of cinematographic style which does not permit the distinction I have just made between subject and expression. I would rather crudely call this tendency "realistic." But this realism does not at all mean a renunciation of style. It only postulates that cinematic expression must be dialectically fused with reality and not with artifice. This is the case with the most abstract, the most intellectual, of our directors: Robert Bresson, whose *Diary of a Country Priest* is in this sense an eminently realistic work.

Renoir is one of those directors who create their own scenarios almost singlehandedly. While the subjects and the adaptation are only rarely Renoir's, he reshapes them so much before and even during the shooting that it is impossible to think of the result as someone else's. The nature of this reshaping is almost always the same: to make the story more closely dependent on several visual themes. A dramatist constructs his play on a theatrical structure. The action is a sort of pure movement toward certain events, which are the heart of the plot. Contrary to this approach, Renoir begins with two or more tangible realities and creates relationships among them. The action proceeds from them like the concentric circles which radiate from a stone thrown into the water. Thus in *The Human Beast* the moral credibility of Gabin's character resides not in his hereditary alcoholism—this is just Zola's pretext, which Renoir has kept— but rather in the thematic relationship created by the *mise en scène* between the man and the machine. Renoir's film is a tragedy, but the metaphor for the fate which destroys the hero is not the rotten blood of the Rougon-Macquart family as it was in Zola's novel; it is the locomotive. This and this alone makes his death credible and necessary. Not that Renoir makes the machine a "symbol" of a blind and omnipotent force which traps and crushes. Nothing is more foreign than symbolism to Renoir's familiar, loving, sensual style, to his intimacy with things. On the contrary, Renoir identifies the object with the man to characterize the *object*.

The Rules of the Game is basically constructed on two sets of themes which crisscross each other like two sets of ripples on the surface of the water: the hunting party and the party at the château. The hunting party is really nothing more than a dress rehearsal for the party at the château. In spite of the ironic and the comic elements in them, the race through the hallways, the exchanges of identity between the masters and the valets, the shots from Schumacher's revolver, constitute the real hunt, which is ended by an "accident": the death of André, shot by the gamekeeper after a double misunderstanding.

The characters do not act according to psychological probability in terms of their "personalities." They move according to a mechanism of the heart, like Dalio's musical dolls, in the concentric circles of analogies. André (Roland Toutain) receives a blast of buckshot in the stomach and rolls dead like the little rabbit we have just seen in its delicate and terrifying spasm of agony. I am simplifying some out of necessity. This analogy is not the only one, although it is probably the most significant. The entire film is an extraordinary web of allusions, references, parodies, of scenes which refer to one another like motifs recurring in different tones and styles. But have I made myself understood? The freedom of this construction, the contempt for dramatic and psychological verisimilitude, are the height of realism in the sense that Renoir—instead of taking the usual path from the idea to a simulated reality—imposes the idea by departing from reality. It is through Renoir's love, his sensibility, his intimacy with objects, animals, and people, that his moral vision confronts us so strikingly. With Renoir a swallow is enough to suggest spring.

The *mise en scène* flows directly from Renoir's reversed approach to the scenario. He understands the true nature of the screen, which is not so much that it frames the image but that it masks out what lies outside it. From this principle flows an entirely new idea of composition (*"une révolution du découpage"*). This is precisely the revolution brought about by *The Rules of the Game*. For the structure of images in the anecdotal or theatrical film inherited both from painting and the theater, for the plastic and dramatic unity of the "shot," Renoir substitutes the stare of his camera, which is at once idealized and concretized. Henceforth the screen will not try to offer us a sense of reality, but will deliver it to us in the manner of a cipher grid moving across a coded document.

This revolution is not without analogies to Impressionist painting. Until Impressionism the "composition" of a painting was also theatrical or decorative: it depended on the structure of the frame (cf. Raphael's "Madonna of the Chair"). After Manet, and above all Dégas and Renoir, the frame was no longer a stage. If it still sometimes played a role in the composition, it was negatively, through its discordance with reality. By interrupting the continuum of reality, the frame suggested what lay beyond it (cf. Bonnard). We can see how this transition served the Impressionists' desire for realism.

Throughout his French films Renoir has put this principle of *mise en scène* in the service of a set of themes which I would also characterize as generally realistic. The influences which determine his choice of subjects and his treatment of them clearly belong to the era of naturalism. We have already noted the ones which originate in painting. Even more apparent and more explicit is Renoir's predilection for the literature of the time (Zola, *Nana* and *The Human Beast*; Maupassant, *A Day in the Country*) and for "realism" in the general literary sense of the word (*La Chienne*, by La Fouchardière; *The Crime of M. Lange*; and *Toni*, which was inspired by a newspaper story).

But this undeniable affinity is only the point of departure for a rather profound transformation. The themes and the moral and philosophical context of naturalism are only the soil which nourishes the roots of a temperament, a sensibility, a personal vision. Is it really necessary to define it? A Renoir film identifies itself instantly: the sensuality, the sense of happiness with its sharp counterpoint of skepticism and irony—but a smiling skepticism and an irony without bitterness. Cruel sometimes, but only out of tenderness. Its cruelty is objective; it is nothing more than the acknowledgment of destinies at odds with happiness, the measure of a love without constraint and without illusion. Its sympathy always goes out to the victim. Renoir has a sense of the tragic, but he does not dwell on it; not because he does not respect it, but because the only way to overcome destiny is to believe in happiness in spite of it. His most characteristic film from this point of view is *The Lower Depths*, a tragic story with a scenario as grim as could be, which Renoir leads into the comic. It is the subtle play of this constant moral counterpoint against the themes of his scenarios which gives Renoir's French work this verve at once tender and satiric, this air of goodwill and maliciousness, this slightly cynical ingenuity, this casual way of believing in both joy and despair, this tone worthy of the great tradition of French moralistic novels.

The Rules of the Game is a wild imbroglio, a farandole danced to a frenetic rhythm in the corridors of a château and ending with an absurd cadaver. *The River*, on the other hand, is a more refined work, devoid of this sort of frantic comic-macabre activity and strictly limited within the confines of time. What happens to its hero in the course of the film is an almost imperceptible modulation of a pervasive eternity. The swamps of Sologne reflected the picaresque silhouettes of the weekend guests; the waters of the sacred river reflect nothing. Serene and majestic, they flow without change, cleansing man of his blemishes, mixing his ashes with their silt.

But a closer look reveals the affinity of the two films. Beneath the contrasts in subject matter and tone, we see the same indifference to dramatic scaffolding, the same delicate sculpting of characters barely sketched out in the scenario. No theatrical convention interferes with the pure interest which we take in their existence. The film is merely an intimate and indiscreet way for us to live with them. As in *The Rules of the Game*, nothing happens to the heroes but the fortuitous. On the one hand there are the ironic absurdities of the amorous mistaken identities—the vain and pleasant activities of a decaying society which at least knows how to die; on the other, there are the slight events, accidental in the profoundest sense, accidents controlled by a stable force, the perceptible signs of a fundamental cycle of the world and its souls. André's accidental death at the hands of a stupid gamekeeper, is balanced by the cry of a newborn baby. Renoir is faithful to Renoir, but the pagan has become a mystic. His sensual pantheism has become religious.

Why, then, instead of blaming the unevenness of Renoir's American period on the fluctuations of economic and social conditions, do we not see it as part of a profound moral evolution of the artist? Why not suppose that for Renoir it was less a question of adapting himself to Hollywood than of developing himself, of at once mastering a new way of thinking and feeling and creating an adequate means of expressing it. In our belief that *The Rules of the Game* incarnates the avant-garde of the cinema of 1939, that its legacy is far from being exhausted, that this master stroke on which Renoir left France perfects and condenses the meaning of all his French work, and in our implicit hope that he would limit himself to repeating this success, we have made Renoir a prisoner of our admiration. In so doing, we condemned ourselves to a negative criticism—through misguided loyalty to the past of a man who was always in the avant-garde—and let him pass us by without our noticing it. Thus were we unprepared for *The River*, which startled us with a perfection this time too obvious to be mistaken and compelled us to recognize how far its author had advanced. *The River* is the *Rules of the Game* of Renoir's second period.

Renoir recently wrote: "I spent ten years outside of France. The first time I came back to Paris, I sat down with some old friends and we took up our conversation not where it had stopped when I left, but where it would have been if we had continued to see each other all those years." I suspect that this statement is more of a wish than an objective fact. But whatever it is, consider the idea of evolution which it implies. And again:

> To make a path in the jungle it is a good idea to strike out in front of you with a stick to push aside the invisible dangers. Sometimes the stick hits a solid branch and breaks in your hand; sometimes it holds firm, but your arm is stunned. It is a little like what I did during those ten years. I didn't want to stay still, but the needle of the compass I consulted was spinning, and I had difficulty finding my way. Yet I am quite proud of it; it proves that I have not lost contact with our unstable world. . . .
> I recovered a similar certainty with *The River*. I felt growing

within me a desire to reach out and touch my fellow creatures throughout the world.

These notes (with their tone of exemplary honesty and modesty which in no way hides the assurance and authority of the true artist) impress me particularly with their indication of Renoir's profound concern for his era and, inevitably, its expression in the cinema. This is the language of a man reaching out toward the future, intent on placing himself at the front of the attack, at the cutting edge of his art, on that extreme point where the artist carves out a new trail, where the artist's understanding of his time leads to the invention of a new form.

Now perhaps we can see why and in what ways *The River* is dynamically faithful to *The Rules of the Game*. We shall not, however, forget to make important distinctions. What has become of the tender, mocking skepticism, the social satire of *The Rules of the Game?* *The River* describes the life of two English families someplace in Bengal. They are wealthy and without material worries. Renoir never subjects this colonial bourgeoisie to antipathy, to the slightest critical irony. Of course, the characters of *The Rules of the Game* had his sympathy too, but the tenderness they inspired in him did not in any way mitigate his mercilessly lucid appraisal of them. After all, his heroes were equally conscious of their fate. Their destiny had been ordained. The love and attention which Renoir gave them was a tribute to a world which knew how to die with a slightly ridiculous grace, which achieved a sort of grandeur in its amused consciousness of its own anachronism and vanity.

There is nothing anti-aristocratic in the novel by Rumer Godden on which *The River* is based. Furthermore, in the film Renoir explicitly takes the point of view of Harriet. The events are thus filtered through the memories and sensibilities of an English adolescent with a lively but still naïve mind, scarcely aware of social problems. She sees India, like her garden, her friends, and her parents, from the viewpoint of a stable family life which takes for granted the social and economic stabilities

The River

on which it is based. Thus Renoir's point of view as it is expressed by her is exclusively moral. To reproach him for not using this fleeting love story as a vehicle to describe the misery of India or to attack colonialism is to reproach him for not treating an entirely different subject. I have it from Renoir himself that before he found a producer with resources in India he had considered for some time making the film in Hollywood. If this had happened we would have lost much, but nothing of the essential theme of the film, which is the discovery of love by three adolescents.

However, I am not being altogether sincere in pleading Renoir's case this way. I think that his fidelity to his central theme made for a vision of English society in India which, though not at all false, may be a little superficial, overly optimistic, and implicitly imperial.

But then Renoir never hesitated to take liberties with historical facts in his French films either. As a matter of fact, the choice of point of view would seem to argue for a certain partisanship, not (as only an absurdly narrow-minded critic of *The River* would contend) on behalf of colonialism, but rather on behalf of morals over sociology. The latter were not separable in *The Rules of the Game*. They are in *The River*. Made in Hollywood with a simulated Indian decor, the film would have had a completely different tonality. What the geographic and human realism adds, however, is not a social dimension, but a religious and mystical meaning. The problem of the confrontation of the Occident and the Orient is not posed in terms of economics or politics, or even history, but exclusively in terms of religious spirituality. India figures only as a setting, but more as a moral than as a geographical setting. Its silent presence, to which the protagonists pay only half-conscious attention, acts on their minds as a magnetic field influences the needle of a compass.

With this in mind, just as it was ridiculous to complain that Renoir did not make a documentary on famine in India, so it is equally absurd to reproach him for not having made an exhaustive study of religious problems there. During the shooting of *The River* Renoir witnessed bloody battles between the Moslems and the Hindus. There is nothing of this in the film, however, because what interests Renoir is not the Indian religious mentality in itself, but rather its insidious attraction for Westerners.*

There was no more reason for Renoir to understand India after three months than for his heroes after ten years, but some-

---

* Since writing this we have seen an Indian (or more precisely, Bengali) film, *Pather Panchali*, the young director of which (Satyajit Rey) had worked with Renoir on *The River*. This work, typically Indian, made in India by Indians, based on a famous Bengal novel, has the same spiritual tone as *The River*. Appearing in 1955, it confirmed that Renoir's vision of India was neither naïve nor superficial, but rather that it went straight to the essential.

how, even while standing so close to the false perspective of the Protestant, imperialist bourgeoisie, he was able to render the mute, diffuse, and inexhaustible light of *The River*.

There is at least one character who incarnates the mystical temptation of the Orient, and this is Bogey. Remember his games with his little native friend, as mysterious and taciturn as a bronze statue? He is the only witness to Bogey's death, and he is the only one at the burial who does not grieve, because he alone understands the vanity of the tears and the ignorance which the Westerners' love conceals: ignorance of the profound secret to which "the Unknown" has initiated Bogey for eternity.

Renoir took great liberties with Rumer Godden's novel, as he always does with the sources which inspire him. But significantly, the changes he made were of an entirely different sort from those he made with his material in the 1930s. They suggest a conversion to spiritual values, to something like, if not a faith in God, then at least a faith in man and in the transcendence of man.

I feel sure that Pierre Laroche and others will be quick to attack this turn in Renoir's work, sneering at what will seem to them a "reactionary" development and even insinuating that it suggests senility. And certainly this type of spiritual adventure will not appeal to Henri Jeanson.* *The River* can flow over them without even getting them wet. I will not do the film the indignity of defending it against this type of critic. We love the irony of Renoir; we delight in his humor. But there are other criteria of beauty, and it is to them that *The River*—with its majestic dimensions, its sense of grandeur, its universal spirituality—pays brilliant homage.

Rather than undertake a pointless and vain defense of *The River* against *The Rules of the Game*, it might be interesting to discuss the significance of Renoir's transition from one to

---

* Laroche and Jeanson are highly caustic and witty film critics with considerable experience as screenwriters. Laroche wrote *Lumière d'Eté* (1943), *Les Visiteurs du Soir* (with Jacques Prévert, 1942), *Gigi* (1949), and *Huis Clos* (1954), among others. Jeanson's writing credits include *La Dame de Chez Maxim's* (1933), *Carnet de Bal* (1937), *Carmen* (1942), *Nana* (1955), *L'Affaire d'une Nuit* (1960). Trans.

the other. Almost everything of any importance in the cinema of the past five years* reveals in some way a spiritualistic inspiration, an optimistic humanism, a re-embracing of the ethical as opposed to social criticism or moral pessimism. It is worth noting that this movement does not at all coincide with developments in literature. The great era of the *film noir* (1935–1939), such as it was, had been over for several years before the current success of the *série noire* began.† Delannoy failed with *Les Jeux Sont Faits*, but he was successful with *Dieu A Besoin des Hommes*.

The greatest development in the recent history of the cinema is the appearance of good treatments of religious subjects. *Diary of a Country Priest* is the most significant product of this paradoxical avant-garde. *Miracle in Milan*, done in a much different style with a much different story, is also part of it. In addition, it is only from this perspective that we can find any unity in inspiration between the recent Soviet cinema and the best work of the West.

No doubt about it; the future, at least for the next few years, will belong to films favoring virtuous and elevated sentiments. The convergence of works of such diverse origins and styles cannot be attributed to fashion. The films must spring from deeper sources. Perhaps they are the groping response to an appeal from the people of this era. Those whom Renoir calls "the truly great" have no need to conspire with each other to bring to their contemporaries the message of love and confidence which the world awaits so anxiously and which surely only the cinema can deliver.

Some are surprised by the slightness of the content of *The River*. Others make fun of the sappy adolescent loves and accuse them of bearing traces of Hollywood psychologizing and rosewater moralism. I think they are blinded by their literary frame of reference. They judge the film on the basis of the novel it could be turned into. I am quite willing to admit that this novel would be inferior even to Rumer Godden's, which itself

* Bazin wrote this in the early 1950s. Trans.
† *Série noire, film noir:* violent mystery novels and films. Trans.

is difficult to see as anything but an interesting but minor work. But I marvel that a story so "slight," with such conventional elements, and which I would have no desire to read, has yielded one of the purest, richest, most touching works in the history of the cinema, one which moved me to tears. Many of the admirers of *The River* detest rosewater literature, conventional moralism, and facile optimism as much as the film's detractors. Is it possible that they would love here what they detest elsewhere? It seems much more likely that some reflex of literary culture has prevented the detractors from appreciating the film's cinematic pleasures. Such people are happy to acknowledge the transmutation of content by style in literature, but they are blind to Renoir's promotion of themes through style, which is to say, to art itself. It takes a man of letters like André Saurès to speak of the "ignoble heart" of Chaplin. It's because when he looks at a film he imagines himself reading it.

Everyone recognizes that writers have different styles, but not so with directors. Thus we have Kléber Haedens describing *The River* (in *France Dimanche*) as a "long, slow, and rather dull documentary" and proclaiming that there are no traces of Renoir's personality in the film and that it is most interesting as evidence of the difficult progress of Technicolor. The truth is that there is probably no other film which is so completely and precisely controlled by its author. Most of the best films depend to some degree on God, on a lucky or unlucky chance which belongs not to the film maker but to the film, an uncertain and involuntary poetry of the machine. Not a frame of *The River* gives us this feeling: its images always suggest exactly and only what their creator intended. From this point of view, the two high points are the burial and the amorous hide-and-seek of the girls chasing the young man. This latter scene beautifully conveys the feeling of excitement checked by sexual modesty. It is no exaggeration to compare such moments to the great achievements of the older, more refined arts. I cannot imagine what a brilliant painter, novelist, or poet could have added to the kiss Valerie gives to Captain John.

Renoir's mastery of his material in this film, his power to

mold it in the shape of his vision, may surpass even that of *The Rules of the Game*. Certainly it is not inferior to it. Yet this time Renoir's achievement rests on techniques considerably different from those he used until 1939. For the fluid camera, the lateral reframings of the deep-focus shots, Renoir here substitutes a pictorial stability in which the scenes are framed only once. There is not a single pan or dolly shot in the entire film. Renoir used his lens like a telescope, moving in and out on reality, revealing and concealing things according to the instincts of his shrewd, mischievous sensibility. Here he seems interested only in showing things precisely as they are. Even when he falls back on traditional montage, using many shots, as in the scene of the siesta, there is no hint of expressionist symbolism. He uses it only as a narrative convention, and it does not for a second destroy the concrete reality of the moment.

Furthermore, the classicism of the editing in *The River* is perhaps more apparent than real. It is in no way a return to the traditional forms which *The Rules of the Game* destroyed and supplanted, but rather an extension of the same revolution begun in the earlier film. For the decorative or expressionist *frame* of the traditional shot, for the artificiality of discontinuous montage, Renoir has substituted the *mask* and the living continuity of reframing. By this he brought to the cinema at once more realism and more expression. He allowed it to mean more by showing more.

But in this negation of cinematographic canons, in this destruction of the *shot* as the basic unit of screen narrative and of the screen itself as the unit of space, there remained an implicit acknowledgment of the "cinema" as a means of expression. Even as a mask, the screen remained a screen. Even in reversing its function Renoir had not destroyed it. This final step remained to be taken. In *The River* the screen no longer exists; there is nothing but reality. Not pictorial, not theatrical, not anti-expressionist, the screen simply disappears in favor of what it reveals.

This classicism goes beyond *The Rules of the Game*; it is the culmination of its realism. *The River* sits at the avant-garde of the cinema, along with *The Bicycle Thief*, *Diary of a Country Priest*, and everything which really counts in the contemporary cinema; that is, with those works which contribute to the transparency of the medium. Whether it veers toward the theater or the novel, or whether it relies on original scenarios, the cinema must restrain itself from using its techniques to amplify objects which express themselves through it. The cinema will be fulfilled when, no longer claiming to be an art of reality, it becomes merely reality made art.

CHAPTER NINE

RENOIR AND THE THEATER

●

Julius Caesar (1954)

It was love for the cinema as much as for the theater which drew me to the arena at Arles to see Renoir's theatrical debut in 1954.* My presence at the opening is little to brag about, since I was in southern France at the time anyway. Many of my young friends from the cinémathèque had come from much farther than I. One in particular had hitchhiked from his military post in Baden-Baden. Since most of them could not afford even the cheapest reserved seat and since the dozen places set aside for the critics had already been taken by the local bullfight fans, the young followers of Renoir managed as a last resort to get jobs as extras in his production. In the South of France, anything is possible!

I recall these unimportant details because they shed some light on the rather peculiar circumstances of Renoir's first theatrical production. And what a production it was, a real test in radically different conditions for the author of *The Rules of the Game* and *The River*. Of Renoir the film maker it has always been said that he is a director and an improviser capable

* Bazin left nothing that he liked very much on *The Golden Coach*. For this film see François Truffaut's and Eric Rohmer's notes in the Filmography. F.T.

of getting not only the best but the most unexpected responses from his actors. The Arles adventure was going to show whether at sixty years of age this great pink man with the white hair was going to be able to do the same thing in the theater. We awaited this turn in his great career affectionately, hopefully, a little anxiously.

For the 10,000 bullfight and light-opera fans packed into the stone seats still warm from the afternoon sun, Shakespeare's *Julius Caesar* represented something entirely different from their usual fare. Between the two different expectations, theirs and ours, a horrible misunderstanding could have arisen. In a sense, of course, *Julius Caesar* is the business of the people of Arles. After all, his name is everyplace in the town. But the people are nonetheless still a bit vague about his historical and theatrical significance. This fact was brought home to me by a woman I overheard explaining to her husband before the opening curtain: "Caesar is in this play, but not Borgia." Another lady, satisfied with the performance, commented on the way out: "They would have done better, though, to choose Pagnol's version." Between that first marvelous comment and the comments of the lady impatient with English literature or ancient history, the miracle of the theater had been revived in this arena. The miracle was doubly impressive for those who knew the conditions under which it was produced.

When Renoir and his troupe arrived in Arles only ten days before the performance, they had only rehearsed in Paris. For various reasons (among others a bullfight) the set was not entirely ready until the day before the performance. Renoir had been able to work with the local extras for only a couple of hours on the last two days. There was no complete rehearsal of the play. Everything had to be straightened out as it became technically possible, and there was never any continuity. Up until the very last minute Renoir was experimenting with various scenic effects. In fact, the first and only performance of *Julius Caesar* before the 10,000 citizens of Arles, who were drawn by the prestige of the title and their fondness for the arena, was scarcely even a dress rehearsal. Renoir saw his light-

Jean Renoir at the Arles arena during a rehearsal of *Julius Caesar*

ing and various special effects for the first time along with the
members of the audience.

The first minute was awful. Various odd noises were heard
as the first spotlight cut through the darkness to frame Flavius
and Messala. And when Caesar made his entrance the stands
broke into laughter and amused applause as the spectators recognized their friends in the emperor's cortege.

Then came Casca's speech! In a second the theater's magic
finally took hold of the vast arena and the audience listened,
awed and enraptured. Parédès, resolutely comic, had won over
the audience by the fourth time he dropped his cape. The tone
of the laughter changed to reflect the collective joy of 10,000

individuals. Ruse, ambition, and courage were going to develop their tragic spiral around the memory of Caesar as if around the axis of destiny itself.

But perhaps a couple of dozen spectators were impressed by more than what was happening on stage. The tragedy of Caesar's ghost was the triumph of Jean Renoir. We had imagined him dying in the shadows of some ancient vomitorium, but he was, in fact, very much present in that arena.

We had seen once again the miracle of the theater, not only the miracle which made Elizabethans out of 10,000 southern Frenchmen, but also the miracle of the concrete existence of a spectacle which would have been inconceivable without the improvisational genius and the human presence of Jean Renoir.

We were no less delighted to see Renoir respond to the crowd's ovation by appearing and bowing with the same ursine demeanor as Octave in his bearskin at the party in *The Rules of the Game*. And in the tearful voice in which he thanked the public I recognized the emotions of La Chesnaye showing off his calliope. The distance between that ironic, cutting masquerade and this *Julius Caesar* played in the open air before an entire town is an indication both of the artistic integrity and of the spiritual odyssey of our greatest film artist.

Orvet (1955)*

Since his first return from America, I have had the honor and pleasure to talk with Jean Renoir about his work on several occasions and at considerable length. I followed the last three days of rehearsals for *Julius Caesar* at Arles, I have seen him work at the studio, but I don't think I have ever heard him formulate a systematic statement on his art or attempt to de-

* *Orvet* is a three-act play which Renoir wrote and produced in Paris. It opened at the Theater of the Renaissance on March 12, 1955. Gallimard has published the text. F.T.

fine his conception of directing. Not that he is put off by general concepts, quite the contrary; but as a rule his general statements of principle can be practically interpreted in numerous ways. They delimit a morality rather than an aesthetic. The following statement, written in 1952 after he had finished *The River*, is illustrative:

> Few people today can pretend to know where they are going. Whether it is individuals, groups or nations, chance is their guide. Those who advance toward a specific goal owe it to their instinct more than to their intelligence . . . Men are tired of wars, of sacrifices, of fear and of doubt. We have not arrived at the age of great inspiration, but we are entering into an age of goodwill. My comrades and I sensed this when we were in India, even during the awful days when the Hindus and the Moslems were killing one another. The smoke from the burning houses did not stifle our confidence. We thought simply that these men were behind the times.
>
> All this is a bit vague. They are feelings which are difficult to formulate. It is dangerous to write down that I think I sensed these benevolent tendencies. If I am wrong, I will be laughed at; but it is a risk I take confidently.

The text is indicative of what is both general and specific in Renoir's creation. The work of art, be it a painting, a film, or a play, should bring to man the spiritual nourishment which he needs, albeit unconsciously. Awareness of this need and the fertile anxiousness which results from it are Renoir's only interior directives. The specific aesthetic solutions are born unforeseeably from the tension which exists between the fundamental moral aims of the artist and the technical and human resources which he has at his disposal. (Renoir likes to say that in making a Bayeux tapestry Queen Matilda had no better reason for placing a knight in a given spot than the chance presence of a certain clump of blue or green wool.)

One thing that Renoir reaffirms clearly every time he is questioned about his work, and one thing that is obvious through all his work from *La Chienne* to *Orvet*, is the prime importance of his actors. Not the actor *per se*, the super-marionette animated from the exterior to move with the precise rhythm of the action, but the individual performer whose physical and psychological qualities color the direction and can go so far as to modify the meaning of the work itself.

Renoir wrote *Orvet* for Leslie Caron, whom he had met at Charles Boyer's house in Hollywood. It was at a time when Renoir probably more or less consciously wanted to try the theater. The play is without question the product of this desire, coupled with a childhood memory (an eleven-year-old girl he had met in the Fontainebleau Forest) and the encounter with Leslie. It is also a result of Renoir's desire to consider certain moral verities with his audience. But in the final analysis, it is Leslie Caron who made *Orvet* what it is. Renoir was perfectly straightforward in telling me that for another actress the play would have been considerably different. Specifically, what he found so seductive in her was her voice and her way of pronouncing *les bois* with her mouth full of big round *o*'s. He went on to explain:

> The little actresses from the dramatic art courses these days have an impossible pronunciation. Perhaps it is the way they are taught to pose their voices. Or maybe it is the result of the lycée, but girls today almost all have the same sharp, affected voice. And, strangely enough, it is above all the girls of common background. It is frequently in the solid bourgeoisie that you find from time to time a pleasant, natural voice. When I was starting in Hollywood and had to make *Swamp Water*, the production director insisted that I hire Linda Darnell, on the pretext that she came from peasant stock and was used to the country. She is a good actress but her voice has nothing peasant about it. I held out for Anne Baxter. She was unknown at the time, and came from a perfectly bourgeois and urban background, but she could talk like a farm girl.

So it is scarcely exaggerating to say that Renoir wrote *Orvet* because of the way a young French dancer he met in Hollywood had said *les bwooah*. She seemed to me indeed perfect and sometimes sublime, without ever giving that composed effect which the Conservatory seems to teach. Renoir knew just how to direct her expressive body and her delicious voice. This direction, along with her own dancing technique and sense of spectacle, assured the perfect interpretation of a stylized, choreographed, half-real character. Only a dancer could pass as naturally as Leslie Caron from acting to the little ballet of the first slippers.

The critics seemed to be expecting one of the greatest film directors in the world to enter the theater and turn it upside down in the name of the cinema. But Renoir certainly did not come to the theater to make more movies. If he came with any intention at all, it was to create a spectacle and to carry on a dialogue with his public which would be perhaps a bit more personal than was possible in the cinema.

In response to my insistent questions about why he turned to the theater, Renoir offered only answers which would seem laughable if their offhandedness did not hide a magnificent humility which is more instructive than most manifestoes. Beyond his desire to renew the dialogue with his audience, Renoir perceived in his interest in the theater the need to face new technical challenges. From the time when he abandoned ceramics and turned to the cinema, up to perhaps the 1940s, the language of the film was being created, its technique was evolving. Inventing a style, the director ran into technical difficulties. Surmounting them, he created his art. It now seems to Renoir that the cinema offers no more obstacles to expression. Even changing screens will not pose much of a problem. The cinema has become a perfected medium in which only the subject matter will count from now on.

In turning to the theater, which he scorned before the war, Renoir has the impression that he is returning to an art where material difficulties, the precariousness and uncertainty of the medium itself, can still be sources of inspiration.

As for his way of conceiving a play, it can be deduced from his cinematic past:

I realized [he wrote] that theater professionals expect that a play be first of all a well-constructed dramatic machine, and they are probably right to the extent that great works illustrate this principle, but personally I conceive my plays as I conceive my films, not as the result of a plan, but the result of situations which charm me and the creation of the actors who find themselves in these situations. From another point of view, the theater is for me a dialogue with the public, a way of telling the public things which I hold dear and things which could move them, without at the same time boring them. It seems to me that this was the aim of Giraudoux as well, a man whom I knew and admired.

But Giraudoux worried little about theatrical production as he wrote his plays. With Renoir, one always has the impression that his creation is aimed at scenic rather than dramatic effectiveness. Another thing that Renoir learned in the rehearsals for *Orvet* was that traditional theatrical direction is much more worried about the placement and the movements of the actors than it is about their expressions. Renoir believes, on the contrary, that the actors' movements should be subordinated to their expressions and flow directly from them. He did not direct *Orvet* from the orchestra as is usually done, but from the stage itself, as he would have done in a film studio.

If the theater is first of all a dialogue between the author and the spectator with the actor as go-between, and if directing is the art of making this dialogue effective—and I mean emotionally effective, the art of transforming the dialogue into an act of friendship, of intimate persuasion—then Renoir seems to me to have succeeded perfectly.

Orvet received a generally lukewarm reception. I saw the play the night before the premiere with a full, paying house and there was no mistaking its enthusiasm. The applause stopped the action on several occasions, and there were six curtain calls. That particular public in any case responded to the dialogue. They did not seem to think it necessary at all to ask whether a dancer had the right to act without having studied dramatic arts for three years. Leslie Caron seemed to them perfect in the role and touching to the point of making them want to cry. Nor did they wonder whether *Orvet* would have made a good film, whether the play was written according to the rules of the avant-garde, or whether a film maker had the right to be familiar with Giraudoux and Pirandello. They did not reproach him for having failed to choose between the real and dream worlds but listened, charmed, to his music of words and beings and marveled at the interweaving of themes and the harmony of breaks in tone within the carefully preserved unity of style. In short, they seemed to think that it was theater and good theater at that.

CHAPTER TEN

RENOIR'S THIRD PERIOD

●

French CanCan (1954)

Because of its subject matter and because Renoir seems to have tried to make it a light and pleasant film without any pretensions, *French CanCan* came to us with the reputation of a tasteful *divertissement*. It was an entertainment which could have been a failure, and at best promised only the rewards of a minor and rather superficial subject. The film is based on several episodes from the life of Zidler (Danglard), the man who created the Moulin Rouge on the site of the old Cabaret de la Reine Blanche. From such a script we expect recreation of the atmosphere on Montmartre during the *belle époque* by a man whose background is a double guarantee of good taste. And *French CanCan* may indeed be considered as exactly that. But by the same token, can it be said that Auguste Renoir's "Bal du Moulin de la Galette" is nothing more than a diverting painting inspired by a social pastime? If I invoke Renoir's father it is not because the obvious plastic similarities between the film and the painting demand a comparison, but because Renoir's is the only film I have ever seen which is as successful as the painting which inspired it in evoking the internal density of the visual universe and the necessity of appearances that are the foundation of any pictorial masterpiece.

Let there be no mistake. I mean that if Jean Renoir managed to create on the screen a visually satisfactory rendition of a certain style of painting, it was never simply by a superficial copying of its formal elements but rather by placing himself in an inspirational situation in which his course would spontaneously conform to the Impressionist style. We have already seen examples of this phenomenon in films such as *A Day in the Country* and in certain sequences in *The Crime of M. Lange*. But those earlier films, made in black and white, had a built-in guarantee of originality. Color, on the other hand, carries the awful risk of a literal copying from paintings. John Huston's *Moulin Rouge* is a good example of a film which fell into this trap. It is little more than a decorative and dramatic rehash of the paintings which provided its sources.

It is no surprise that Renoir did not succumb to these temptations. We expect nothing less of him. Only technical considerations could have betrayed him—and in a way they did. I saw an early copy of *French CanCan* which had not been perfectly graded and several of the reels had a greenish hue to them. But the internal balance of the shots was such that this imperfection did not at all destroy their harmony. The same phenomenon holds true for certain Impressionist paintings which retain their beauty in spite of the fact that their colors have turned with time. The pink tones of "Bal du Moulin de la Galette," for example, have turned bluish with age, but the painting's grace and harmony remain intact. The reason is that any great painting is first of all a creation of the spirit which is sustained by the spirit. It has an existence beyond its material elements, which are only mediators. The disappearance or alteration of a single one of these elements simply engenders a spontaneous compensation, much as the human body tends to compensate for loss or injury of an organ in an attempt to maintain its vital equilibrium.

French CanCan seems to me to be more, however, than just the successful integration of a static pictorial style with film, for in film there is a new dimension: the dimension of time. And I daresay that this movie is not only as successful as Renoir's painting; it is like a painting which exists in time and has an interior development. This proposition suggests some contradictions which should be taken care of immediately. If true painting is not anecdotal (and Auguste Renoir's, above all, certainly is not), then any temporal development of that painting cannot be dramatic. The inestimable importance of *French CanCan* lies in its implicit understanding of this logic and in its original treatment of pictorial inspiration which at once fulfills and casts new light on the evolution begun in *Coach*. In the past we have probably praised films which freed themselves of dramatic categories, but that was by way of affirming their literary inspiration. In this case it is a question of an entirely different aesthetic approach. The painting is only temporally static in an objective sense. In fact, for the person who looks at it, it represents a universe to discover and explore. This sort of study takes time; so, practically speaking, the dimension of time is indeed inherent in the painting. But if this painting came to life, began to *last*, and to undergo changes affecting its plastic equilibrium as well as its subject, it is clear that this sort of objective time would not take the place of the subjective time experienced by the viewer, but would on the contrary reinforce it. And this is precisely the impression one has after seeing *French CanCan:* that the movie exists in two modes of duration at once, the objective mode of events and the subjective mode of contemplating these events.

Gianni Esposito and Françoise Arnoul in *French CanCan*

A couple of examples will clarify what I mean. The first is elementary. A certain shot in the film, taken from the outside through a gable window, shows a young woman going about her housework. The decor, the colors, the subject, the actress, everything suggests a rather free evocation of Auguste Renoir, or perhaps even more of Degas. The woman bustles about in the half shadow of the room, then turning around, leans out of the window to shake out her dustcloth. The cloth is bright yellow. It flutters an instant and disappears. Clearly this shot, which is essentially pictorial, was conceived and composed around the brief appearance of this splash of yellow. It is equally clear that the event is of neither dramatic nor anecdotal significance. The flash of yellow remains purely pictorial, like Corot's spot of red, but in eclipse.

It should be pointed out that to endow a painting with a temporal dimension means more than creating an animated picture. The animated films of MacLaren, Fishinger, and Len Lye have given us an idea of what that can be. It is probable that animated painting can only be abstract or very close to it: essentially a system of forms in motion. Nor is Renoir trying to achieve what Monet did with his grindstones or his series of cathedrals. Impressionism led Monet almost to abstraction by dissolving the subject in light.

Renoir's work is something quite different. It re-creates a specific social universe, but the re-creation is mediated by the greatest of the earlier historical portrayals of that universe, those of Renoir, Lautrec, Degas. Renoir began with the vision they had created of reality and then restored the dimension of change and time. In other words, the painters took certain aspects of their era and gave them pictorial immortality. Renoir took this second, artistic reality and gave it life. Not the objective, realistic life of the historian, but the potential, artistic life, held prisoner in the painter's static medium.

This sort of aesthetic re-creation demands much more than a simple faithfulness to forms. The film maker must follow not the techniques of the painter, but his vision. The shooting script from *French CanCan* is full of examples of how Renoir

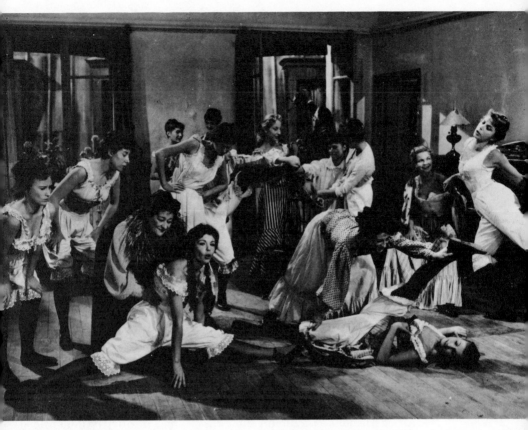

French CanCan

succeeded in doing this. The second example I have chosen is considerably more complex than the episode of the yellow dust-cloth. What follows are the definitive stage directions describing Mother Guibole's dance studio, where Danglard has just presented his latest discovery, Nini, whom he hopes to make into the star of the French cancan.

General Shot: What was once the living room of a bourgeois home. Two windows overlooking the courtyard. One of them is open. The piano. Two folding beds on which are seated two students looking over the lesson of the Conception. The lighting comes from a lamp on the piano. A bedroom and a bathroom are visible through an open door. A girl, perfectly indifferent to what is going on, is taking a bath.

One of the girls on the folding bed, who is making hair curlers, turns as Danglard and Nini come in. The other keeps reading her novel. As she finishes each page, she tears it out and hands it to her companion, who rolls it up as a curl paper.

Nini, a bit suspicious, like an Indian visiting a hostile tribe, stands apart from the others. Danglard: "Good evening, Guibole . . . In the middle of a bullfight?"

Are not these stage directions, the lighting notes, and movements of the characters the description of a great composition which could be titled "The Dancing Class" or perhaps "Mother Guibole's Studio"? The composition includes a detail which deserves comment: the girl in the tub. She appears in the background through a half-open door, which she finally closes with a rather nonchalant modesty. This could well have been a subject dear to Auguste Renoir or to Degas. But the real affinity with the painters does not lie in this specific reference. It is in a much more startling phenomenon: the fact that for the first time in the cinema the nude is not erotic but aesthetic. I mean that the nude is presented to us here precisely as all the other objects in the scene. As in painting, it is just another genre alongside the still life and the portrait. The splendid objectivity of Manet's "Picnic on the Grass"* had implicitly denounced the senile salaciousness of the academic painters who camouflaged their concupiscence with mythological trappings, and Renoir carried this revolution to the screen. Nudity did not regain the innocence of paradise, where temptation was not yet sinful, but was now touched by the serenity of art before which all subjects are equal.

I saw *French CanCan* only once and frankly cannot recall if the scene of the dancing school is handled in a single shot. It is hardly important. Such scenes are often cut up into little fragments which destroy, or rather ignore, the plastic balance of the whole. Here, however, is further evidence that Renoir's pictorial style is never formal and reconstituted from the exterior, but is a completely natural and integral element of his

* When Bazin wrote this, in 1955, he did not know that Renoir himself would make a film entitled *Picnic on the Grass* four years later. F.T.

direction. The camera does not film a re-created painting for us (as in *Moulin Rouge*); it operates easily and naturally from inside the painter's conception. Even if the scene were broken down into a series of separate shots, none of them would necessarily recall the painting which inspired it, and yet the sequence would derive no less directly from its pictorial source. The sum of its parts would be the cinematic equivalent of the painted original.

I have written that what forces us to admire the Japanese cinema, even in its worst productions, is that it is always faithful to a refined and powerful culture. Western films, produced in a culture where art and society have been divorced since the nineteenth century, do not benefit from this resource of cultural unity. Renoir, however, is an exception to this rule. He represents a brilliant marriage of culture and art. He brings together both individual cinematic genius and the infallibility of a culture, or at least of one of the highest aspects of Western culture, its painting. Renoir is Impressionism multiplied by the cinema.

Jacques Rivette pointed out to me that, unlike those who think that to be inspired by painting means to compose a shot imitating a painting and then bring it to life, Renoir starts from a nonpictorial arrangement and cuts when the framing of a scene has evoked a painting. Take, for example, the admirable shot where Françoise Arnoul crosses the entire set to sit at the foot of the column right in front of the camera. Suddenly it is a Degas, but the scene shifts immediately. Renoir never starts from a painting, he ends there.

French CanCan is based on the birth of the Moulin Rouge under the guiding hand of an energetic cabaret director. By studying the romantic intrigues of the diverse people who gravitated to the new night spot, Renoir manages to evoke the various aspects of Parisian society, or at least that part of Parisian society immortalized in the Impressionist paintings of the turn of the century. It is clear what this art has in common with Renoir's ethic: it affirms precisely that extremes come together and that vulgarity exists only in form and is not a question of subject matter. The Count de Toulouse-Lautrec was the perfect incarnation of an aristocracy whose extreme self-consciousness had thrown it into the lower depths, not to deny itself or to flee from itself, but on the contrary to find at the bottom of the scale the essential dignity which the nobility at the top was lacking. Painting became the symbol and the guarantee of that nobility: La Goulue was worthy of the Mona Lisa or the Venus de Milo. In the same way Renoir professes that there is no hierarchy in the performing arts and that only love of one's art and professional skill make the difference between a street singer and an opera tenor. The only hierarchy is determined by talent and heart.

We have seen that Impressionist painting—even more than its contemporary, the naturalistic novel—was the best expression of this popular dignity in the eyes of the artist. It is important once again to recall that Jean Renoir is the son of Auguste Renoir, whose favorite model was his maid. The moral and social lesson joins the artistic education. *French CanCan* is the film of a man who knows Impressionist painting better than anyone. He is not simply an admirer of the works, he knew the movement from the inside and was an intimate friend of its creators. Even as a child he must have been influenced by the artistic climate of the time. And now Jean Renoir has reached the age when a mature sensibility likes to return to its sources. *French CanCan* represents such a return. I cannot imagine a more perfect homage to Auguste Renoir.

Paris Does Strange Things (1956)

Jean Renoir is rare among the world's great directors in that each new film he makes is startling in its originality and yet also profoundly faithful to the same inspiration which animated its predecessors. Only Chaplin intrigues and surprises us as much in this way. Renoir's mastery, confirmed once again in

Paris Does Strange Things, in no way hampers his youthful audacity and willingness to take risks.

While the normal instinct of a successful film maker is, if not to imitate himself, then to try to perfect and deepen the themes and forms which made his original success, Renoir seems concerned only with questioning his most secure accomplishments. Not from any primordial instinct for formal renewal, nor from any desire simply to astonish people. And certainly not from any obstinate singlemindedness. On the contrary, all the reports on his work indicate that his weakness (if it is one) is rather to be more open than most to suggestions—even from producers. If necessary Renoir has adapted and will adapt to the most varied working conditions. The fact is that Renoir sees novelty as an essential part of artistic creation, that his passion for novelty is at the very source of his inspiration, and that this passion is strong enough to accommodate a wide range of practical contingencies. However, the result can be disconcerting for his audience, especially when it thinks it recognizes familiar landmarks in a completely unknown terrain. Also like any great artist Renoir is obsessed by a thematic strain, which is expressed in both form and content. Thus we find in *Paris* the theme of the "party at the château," obviously revived from *The Rules of the Game* but transposed into a new climate with a different significance. The result is that this recognition perplexes more than it comforts.

And it is undoubtedly for this reason that *Paris Does Strange Things* has excited as much controversy as admiration. Few films could provoke the critics to a greater variety of positions. Worse, or perhaps even better, no two admirers of the film like it for the same reasons, and I am not even sure that I myself will not like and dislike different things in it the third time I see it than I did the first two times.

This indicates, among other things, that Renoir is more of an artist than any other film maker. I mean that with him the forms are less determined by intellectual principles or aesthetic systems. Not that Renoir hesitates to formulate ideas on art and morality, and not that one cannot in a sense consider his works as the expression of a continuing ethical meditation pursued throughout his life—but clearly his ideas are the consequence of a strictly artistic inspiration. At the level of creation where this film belongs, invention could only proceed, in the last analysis, from an implicit morality; but this morality can only be embodied in aesthetic forms. The ideas which the film formulates are little more than precarious and provisional buttresses, intended merely to prop up the artistic construction.

Renoir has never been known to shrink from contradicting himself, and there is more than one inconsistency in *Paris Does Strange Things*. But it does not take a great deal of familiarity with Renoir's work to see beyond the relatively opportunistic use of ideas to the distant point of convergence where order is established and incongruity vanishes. This is why Renoir should be credited only with the profound and revealing ideas and the others should be dismissed. For example, there is a speech in *Paris Does Strange Things* which I continue to find extremely weak even after a second viewing: the one in which Henri tells the princess that in a country where love is so important (France) the dangers of politics, and particularly of personal power, could never be very serious. As if the Italians, for instance, had no interest in love! It would have been much better to eliminate these clumsy lines and let the admirable *mise en scène* of this sequence speak for itself. Happily, the true significance of Renoir's sensual lyricism goes well beyond this sort of naïvely demagogic pronouncement.

In *Paris Does Strange Things* Renoir took the risk of treating a serious subject lightly. The irony of this approach was compounded by the internal contradictions of the subject itself. *Boulangisme** could have turned into a tragedy rather than an operetta, but the decisive fact was that in the end the saber-rattling general was more interested in his mistress than he was in power. Nevertheless, if *Paris Does Strange Things* had been a historical, political, or social film, Renoir's position would be

* *Boulangisme:* a right-wing political movement of the 1880s led rather ambivalently by General Georges Boulanger, the prototype of the protagonist in Renoir's film. Trans.

Pierre Bertin and Ingrid Bergman in *Paris Does Strange Things*

untenable, even distasteful, in the same way as the unfortunate
bit of dialogue mentioned above. But the film is an advance in
the same tradition as *The Rules of the Game*. It is concerned
only with morality; that is, morality in the broadest sense: the
concern with illustrating through a story, with its rhythms
and characters, a certain attitude toward the problems of life.

Renoir has said that the subject of *Paris* is Venus, and in
this light the film can be seen as an illustration of both the
sovereignty and the fallibility of the goddess. Throughout his
life General Rollan is torn between glory and love. His friends
who know him well understand that the only solution is to
bring the two forces together, and so they persuade a beautiful

Polish princess to become his political adviser. Eléna, who really loves a charming friend of Rollan's whom she has met at a military parade, is so excited by her mission that she compromises her true love. The dénouement—which takes place, not coincidentally, in a bordello—restores everyone to his proper partner. Rollan allows his mistress to take him away, and Henri recovers Venus after she loses her prey.

It is not that Renoir has shrunk from political commentary, but his satire of manners inevitably focuses exclusively on the moral element in the historical tableau. The human fauna surrounding General Rollan illustrate in dazzling color the entire gamut of political *arrivisme*, and the Caran d'Ache–style* caricature is pushed to an even greater extreme here than in *French CanCan*. But far more than the political regime, it is the idiosyncrasies of character which interest Renoir. The secondary characters are all puppets carefully manipulated within the limits of their stereotypes. Renoir is no more interested in psychological realism than he is in historical accuracy, and it would be a great mistake to look for verisimilitude or psychological consistency in his protagonists. Each one acts, not according to a specific character endowed him by Renoir, but rather within the framework of the artistic conventions he invokes, and it is these conventions which once again suggest a particular approach to life.

Certainly this is completely traditional, at least in the perspective of literature and particularly dramatic literature. Neither Molière nor Racine was a psychologist in the nineteenth-century sense. Yet these days the cinema feels compelled to bedeck itself with the trappings of psychology. From this point of view Renoir's freedom of action in regard to his characters might well seem incongruous. Nevertheless, Renoir finds his own references and meanings. Like René Clair, although with a completely different temperament, he is fascinated by the audacious style of the early slapstick comedies. Rejecting

* Caran d'Ache was the pseudonym of the artist Emmanuel Poiré, whose caricatures of major political figures appeared in the French press in the late nineteenth century. Trans.

the varied and subtle perspectives of psychology, he is not afraid to push his players to an extravagant acting style which is at once tragic and comic. It is in this single, flat dimension that the truth asserts itself so forcefully. It was because I didn't understand this that I originally thought *Diary of a Chambermaid* a failure. Its sociological and psychological improbabilities, emphasized by the Hollywood technical realism, seemed inexcusable. I recently took another look at this admirable film, and found it one of Renoir's most beautiful, one of those which most precisely incarnate his aesthetic aims. Everything which had originally shocked me now appeared to be the very essence of a film whose extraordinary audacity is to venture so far at the same time into the tragic burlesque and the comic burlesque: *Tire au Flanc* and *La Chienne* simultaneously.

Paris Does Strange Things is probably, along with *Diary*, Renoir's most daring film in terms of the direction of the actors. The entire tone of the work, its intimate rhythms, depend on it. Here the paradox lies in the synthesis of the quasi-burlesque style, which is much closer to farce than to music-hall comedy, with a highly refined, delicate, and subtle observation of detail. There is no film with a more complex structure than this "musical fantasy" in which each shot is an extraordinary lesson in *mise en scène*. The abundance of group shots and the rarity of close-ups are only the most superficial characteristics of this amazing style. I would call attention, in particular, to the remarkable ingenuity of the sound track.

Finally, however, I must admit that *Paris Does Strange Things* leaves me with, if not disappointment, a certain regret in the fact that Renoir seems here for the first time to have abandoned that dialectic between the comic and the bitter, the gay and the serious, which is one of the surest signs of his genius. This becomes apparent when it is compared to almost any scene from *The Crime of M. Lange*, such as the dialogue on the bench between René Lefèvre and Nadia Sibirskaïa, from *The Lower Depths*, or from the violently contrasted *Diary of a Chambermaid*. In this respect *French CanCan*, though less perfect in other ways, seems to me more faithful to the body of Re-

noir's work in its passages of tenderness that turns suddenly ex-
cruciating. But then perhaps I am wrong and the director of
Paris did well to maintain the tone of optimism and fantasy
throughout the film, precisely because the subject offered him
innumerable opportunities to turn toward bitterness.

It can be argued that *Paris* is less than perfect. One might
find that the third part drags a little and that it lacks the com-
pelling verve of the first two, although after a second viewing
I no longer think so. There are two or three mistakes in casting.
The sad Gréco could never make a gay gypsy. Mel Ferrer,
badly dubbed, is not very convincing in the major supporting
role. But the rest of the large, varied, and talented cast more
than makes up for these relative weaknesses. The leads are admirable. Jean Marais marvelously incarnates his character, and
Ingrid Bergman, by no means an obvious choice for Eléna,
never permits us, once the film begins, to imagine her otherwise.

The Wisdom of Jean Renoir

Jean Renoir is still the greatest living French film director. His superiority cannot be disputed. It is confirmed not only
by the quality of his work but by its variety, from *La Chienne*
to *The Golden Coach*, from *The Crime of M. Lange* to *The
River*, from *Grand Illusion* to *The Southerner*, from *Diary of
a Chambermaid* to *Paris Does Strange Things*, to say nothing of
The Lower Depths, *A Day in the Country*, or *The Woman on
the Beach*. Jean Renoir has never ceased, in the course of a long
but completely uncompromising career, to search and to renew
himself.

Renoir is one of the few talented directors who have not
been trapped by their own success and been doomed to spend
their later lives trying merely to repeat their initial triumphs.
He has known how to adjust to the evolution of the cinema and
the tastes of his contemporaries because the impulse for self-
renewal is an integral part of his genius. At the time of a recent

Anna Magnani and Jean Renoir during the filming of *The Golden Coach*

revival in Paris of *Toni*, Renoir wrote: "Today I am going through a period in my life in which I am trying to get away from surface realism and to find a more controlled style, closer to what we call 'classic.' This is not to say that I repudiate *Toni*, but rather that I am the victim of my spirit of contradiction."

Renoir's entire career has been marked by this sort of self-contradiction. In 1938, for example, he wrote:

"Man, even more than by his race, is shaped by the soil that nourishes him, by the living conditions that fashion his body and his mind, and by the countryside that parades before his eyes day in and day out. . . . A Frenchman, living in

France, drinking red wine and eating Brie cheese against gray Parisian vistas, can only create a work of merit if he draws on the traditions of people who have lived as he has.''

But in 1940 Renoir left the Ile de France for sunny California, where he made five films which owe nothing to the gray Parisian vistas. One of his most incontestable masterpieces, *The River*, was made in India with a sympathy for a civilization which was not even Occidental. After returning to Europe, he made *The Golden Coach* in Rome. And while *French CanCan* and *Paris Does Strange Things* were made in Paris, these films, inspired by Impressionist painting and made in studios, have only an indirect relation to the grayness of the French skies which lit the images of *A Day in the Country*. This sort of anomaly gives some idea of how difficult it is to analyze his talent. Yet for all its apparent contradictions, few bodies of cinematic work demonstrate such unity. Let us try then, despite the obstacles, to propose a few guidelines.

First of all, unlike a René Clair, whose methodical intelligence always dominates his working conditions, Renoir is the most easily influenced of directors. His inspiration, though essentially faithful to a central core of feeling, needs to nourish itself on the human milieu which surrounds it before it can take form. The climate of friendliness in which his French films were made is well known, and has left unforgettable memories with those who worked with him. It was not uncommon, for example, for writer or technician friends to take small roles here and there in the films of this period. For Renoir, making a film was always a pleasant occasion, a game in which everyone was supposed to have a good time. The climate of fraternity which reigned within his company eventually established itself between the film and the spectators, for it was always Renoir's desire to elicit from the public not admiration but a sense of complicity, a friendly connivance quite foreign to the mechanical impersonality of the medium. In this way Renoir's films have something in common with the theater: they demand that we enter into the game.

In addition, the creator of *The Rules of the Game* is by nature an improviser incapable of following a work plan (although he carefully prepares one). The final appearance of the set, and particularly the actors as they assume their roles, always spurs his imagination at the last minute. Like his father the painter, Renoir the director works more or less on impulse, and this is what accounts for the communicative fervor, the direct and personal character of all his films.

Renoir's sensitivity to his surroundings extends beyond his immediate environment to include the entire society in which he lives. His French films, particularly the ones of the immediate prewar period, provide a profound and lively commentary on the France of the day. *The Crime of M. Lange*, for example, came out of the atmosphere of the Popular Front, whose hopes, and perhaps also its naïveté, it brilliantly portrays. But certainly Renoir made his first social commentary in 1938 with *The Rules of the Game*. In this film, so extraordinarily audacious in subject, story, and technique, Renoir gave to French art on the threshold of the war something comparable to what *The Marriage of Figaro* had been to the French Revolution. Not that this story of love in a château at Sologne, inspired by Beaumarchais, Musset, and perhaps Marivaux, has anything to say about politics; rather, it implicitly translates the entire crisis of consciousness of a civilization on the verge of destruction.

The great success of *The Rules of the Game* has tended to compound a critical misunderstanding, however. It has often been said that the essence of Renoir's French work lies in its social realism. Renoir himself, in the examples cited above, seemed to confirm this notion. It is this idea which accounts for the unfavorable prejudice with which Renoir's American work has been received in France. Indeed, we are unable to find intimate social truth in the work of the exiled, transplanted Renoir. But this is because Renoir has passed beyond this contingent reality to pursue another goal, or perhaps the same goal but now stripped of the dimension of social circumstance. Renoir has become a moralist.

Renoir's emigration did not cause him, as some critics have too hastily concluded, to lose his taste for social realism. It simply enlarged his human perspectives and deepened his moral preoccupations. Transcending the varied categories of race and nation, Renoir has come a little closer to mankind.

Similarly, Renoir's later French films, despite their superficial differences in style and subject (many owing to the exigencies of color and costume drama), are permeated by the great themes which characterize all his work.

If the social and historical commentary of *The Rules of the Game* retains its force today, it is because it embodies a moral message, a vision of man, love, and happiness. Essentially *The Rules of the Game* is a dazzling variation on the theme of true and false nobility, which is not a matter of blood but of the heart. I find the same message, which was already apparent in *Grand Illusion*, refined and polished with age in *French Can-Can*, where we learn also that all vulgarity comes from the soul. A ragpicker who knows what she is talking about assures us that Danglard, the proprietor of the "Caf'-Conc' " (cabaret) is "a prince." Furthermore, is not the French cancan itself a denial of the hierarchy of genres, an example of vulgarity transfigured by art? The lesson of Impressionism which Renoir so beautifully paraphrased here is not only plastic. Toulouse-Lautrec in immortalizing La Goulue or Auguste Renoir offering the figure of his maid for the admiration of posterity proved that there is as much nobility and grace in such humble models as in the Venus de Milo.

The other great lesson which Jean Renoir may owe to his father is an infallible appreciation of the quality of the image, the worship of vision and all else which comes to us through the senses. The entire work of Jean Renoir is an ethic of sensuality; not the affirmation of an anarchic rule of the senses or of an unrestrained hedonism, but the assurance that all beauty, all wisdom, and even all intelligence live only through the testimony of the senses. To understand the world is above all to know how to look at it and to make it abandon itself to your love under the caress of your eye.

•

PART TWO

•

"*Memories*" by Jean Renoir

[reprinted from *Le Point*, XVIII, December 1938]

●

I have loved the cinema since the year 1902. I was eight years old and boarding in a sort of elegant prison which passed for a school. One Sunday morning an individual who looked like a photographer came into the parlor dragging behind him a lot of queer-looking equipment. It was the cinematographer. He was wearing a floppy bow tie and artist's pants, and had a pointed goatee. For more than an hour we watched him set up his projector, try out his acetylene lamp, and place his screen, all with the help of two assistants. Then the show began. The cameraman showed us a few shots which he had taken around Paris. I remember that these pictures seemed confused to me at first, probably not because of the quality of the photography but because of the fact that I was not used to them. But children, like savages, accustom themselves to films quite rapidly, and after a few minutes I understood what was happening. My schoolmates understood also, and we started naming out loud the areas of the city which we recognized.

Next we were shown a comic film, *Les Aventures d'Auto-Maboul* ("The Adventures of Auto-Nut"). Auto-Maboul was dressed in a goatskin driving cape, the hair of which had been starched in such a way that they poked out cantankerously in every direction. An enormous cap and gigantic pair of goggles rounded out the accouterments of this grotesque hedgehog. He was trying to get his car started in front of a garage. His efforts were fruitless, producing nothing but great clouds of smoke, explositions, and backfirings. Suddenly the car started up in reverse all by itself. It stopped just in front of a terrified passer-by, then took off again at top speed in forward. As the car passed by, Auto-Maboul managed to scramble behind the wheel, getting all tangled up in his goatskin in the process. The film faded out as the car and its driver were disappearing into a pool of water.

I would give almost anything to see that program again. That was real cinema, much more than the adaptation of a novel by Georges Ohnet or a play by Victorien Sardou can ever be.

My second step on the way to the movies was a showing of *Mysteries of New York* during the war. I think it was at the American Cinema, Place Pigalle. I was a flyer, and when I returned to my squadron I excitedly recounted the entire story to my comrades. My enthusiasm earned me the nickname "Elaine Dodge."

My friends were soon bitten by the bug themselves, and they too became avid fans of the film's heroine. Later I met the actress herself, a solid American woman who could not have been nicer, not at all up in the clouds.

My third story is more important. It too dates from the war. Let's call it "the revelation of Charlie." I owe it to the farsightedness of one of my friends in the squadron. He had been greatly affected by Chaplin's first films and was convinced that the cinema was going to play an important role in the future development of nations. He went so far as to predict that movies would one day be judged by high-class critics, just like theater, poetry, novels, and music. My friend's father shared these views. This prophetic father was none other than Professor Richer.

The years after the war were a sort of golden age for film lovers. It was the great age of the American film. The big theaters looked down on the American movies and preferred to show pretentious nonsense awkwardly acted by worn-out old actors or else the totally ridiculous Italian films. The Americans found their audiences in the little theaters, which were very cheap. We got to see two or three films per show and the program changed twice a week. Sometimes for months at a time I would go to the movies three times a day. That meant that by the time I went to bed I had absorbed seven or eight films, fifty by the end of the week, and about two hundred after a month.

The idea of working in the cinema did not occur to me. It seemed to me impossible to do anything worthwhile in France. Weren't the American films I loved so much, and the actors who transported me, scorned and even totally ignored by most of our critics? How could I, who dreamed timidly of following in their footsteps, but never hoped to equal them, how could I have conceived of having the slightest chance of success in this pedestrian country of mine? As for actually going to America, I never would have had the gall to even consider such a utopian scheme.

One day at the Coliseum I saw *Le Brasier Ardent*, directed and acted by Mosjoukine and produced by the courageous Alexander Kamenka of Albatros Films. The audience howled and whistled, shocked by a film so different from their usual pap. I was ecstatic. Finally, I had before me a good French film. Of course it had been made by Russians, but in Montreuil, in a French atmosphere, a French climate. The film was released in a reputable theater, not successfully, but at least it had been released.

I decided to abandon my job, ceramics, and to try to make movies.

My first efforts are, in my opinion, without interest. They are only worthwhile at all because of Catherine Hessling's acting. She was a fantastic actress, much too fantastic for timid French merchants. That is why she disappeared. Naïvely and laboriously, I struggled to imitate my American masters. I had not yet learned that, even more than by his race, man is shaped by the soil that nourishes him, by the living conditions that fashion his body and his mind, and by the countryside that parades before his eyes day in and day out. I did not yet know that a Frenchman, living in France, drinking red wine and eating

Brie cheese against gray Parisian vistas, can only create a work of merit if he draws on the traditions of people who have lived as he has.

The only benefit I derived from these first naïve works was a fairly good knowledge of the use of the camera, of lighting, of set design, and above all of special effects. I became skilled at making models: constructing a landscape to scale or a miniature street was a real pleasure for me.

I went to the movies less then, because I no longer had the time. And my taste was no longer exclusively for American films. Perhaps it was just to be contrary, because by that time the snobs had discovered and claimed them. It was also because having become a film maker myself, I was becoming aware of the flaws in the American products.

It was a great stroke of luck that in 1924 brought me into a theater which was showing Erich von Stroheim's *Foolish Wives*. This film astounded me. I must have seen it at least ten times. Destroying my most cherished notions, it made me realize how wrong I had been. Instead of idly criticizing the public's supposed lack of sophistication, I sensed that I should try to reach the audience through the projection of authentic images in the tradition of French realism. I began to look around me and was amazed to find quantities of subjects both intrinsically French and perfectly adaptable to the screen. I began to realize that the movement of a scrubwoman, of a vegetable vendor, of a girl combing her hair before a mirror, frequently had superb plastic value. I decided to make a study of French gesture as reflected in the paintings of my father and the other artists of his generation. Then, inspired by my new discoveries, I made my first film worth talking about, *Nana*, from Emile Zola's novel.

I saw *Nana* again a couple of years ago. There is a great sincerity in its awkwardness. When one is young, and constantly attacked and scorned as I was, it is natural to take refuge in a certain pretentiousness. That is apparent in *Nana*. But, however that may be, I still like the film. And one of the greatest moments in my life occurred three or four years ago in Moscow when a Russian friend of mine introduced me at a convention.

The members of the audience, who scarcely knew my name, started cheering for my old *Nana*!

Nana was one of the first films to have a run of several weeks in one of the boulevard theaters; it commanded a very good price for the time, and the sale of the foreign rights brought a price that we would be happy to get now. In spite of all that, the film was a commercial disaster. I lost everything I had, down to the very last cent. What I earned was a healthy respect for the power of the big producers. I was convinced that as long as they held sway, an independent movie maker could do nothing on his own.

I learned something else too: that the cinema, like any other profession, is a special milieu and that for an outsider to make his way in is not simply a question of ideas or attitudes; it is a question of language, dress, habits. History teaches us that great transformations in peoples and organisms come from within. My mistake was not starting out as one of the insiders in the film world.

I found work and made a series of insignificant films on commission. They were not successful, but the producers were happy. They said my work was "commercial." In cinema jargon, a commercial film is not one which necessarily makes money, but one which is conceived and executed according to the businessmen's standards.

I should like nevertheless to point out two exceptions in my work of the period. The first is *La Petite Marchande d'Allumettes*, which was an excellent opportunity to perfect my technical knowledge. The other is *Tire au Flanc*, a silent version played by the dancer Pomiès and the actor Michel Simon, and which has nothing to do with Bach's *Tire au Flanc*. I made *La Petite Marchande d'Allumettes* with Jean Tedesco in a tiny studio we had fixed up in the attic of the Vieux-Colombier Theater. The reason we were forced to set up our own studio was that we were convinced of the need to switch from orthochromatic to panchromatic negative film, and the industry was not ready to change over.

I *had* been able to convince the studios I was working for

to use very fast lenses, which yielded pictures on orthochromatic film similar to what we get now. Now everyone uses these lenses, the Cook 2 for example; but at the time it was a real struggle to get the people to buy them and even more difficult to convince them to use them.

Ironically, I have now turned against these lenses. For one thing, highly sensitive modern emulsions and advanced laboratories have done away with the need for such wide lens apertures. Another consideration draws me away from these lenses: the farther I advance in my profession, the more I am inclined to shoot in deep focus. The more I work, the more I abandon confrontations between two actors neatly set up before the camera, as in a photographer's studio. I prefer to place my characters more freely, at different distances from the camera, and to make them move. For that I need great depth of field, and it is my feeling that this sharpness is more pleasing when it is achieved with a lens made for deep focus, rather than with a shallower lens which has been stopped down.

The style of photography popular in France in 1925 was unnaturally harsh, and I was deeply opposed to the number of shadows on people's faces. If I chose to use fast lenses at that time, it was because they offered the obvious advantage of allowing me to use fewer lights and thereby to simplify the problem of unnatural shadows.

But let us get back to the Vieux-Colombier. Tedesco and I, along with some other friends, had constructed a lighting system which is the ancestor of all such systems used today. The system was characterized by slightly stepped-up light bulbs. We placed these bulbs either in metal reflectors, or in front of painted surfaces, which yielded a softer light, or in front of spotlight mirrors, by themselves or in groups, exactly as is done today. We kept a few arc lights so that we would still be able to throw great shadows on the actors or the sets if we wanted to. Of course the studio technicians did not give a hoot about what we were doing, but we were confident because other technicians like my old master Ralleigh and the engineer Richard approved of our experiments. The current for all these bulbs came from a power plant which we had arranged ourselves. It ran on a motor from a wrecked car, which was cooled with water from the tap.

We conceived and executed our own sets, our own costumes, and our own models as well. In addition, we developed and printed our own film. So it was that in the course of a year we practiced on a very small scale all the specialized skills of our profession. The result was a film no worse than the next, which boasted some fantasy scenes that interested the public and photography by Jean Bachelet that was truly dazzling. Unfortunately, a rather silly lawsuit* cut short our career and doomed our workshop to failure.

As for *Tire au Flanc*, it was a commercial-type film, made rapidly and with limited funds. I had the good fortune in this film to introduce Michel Simon, who was already the great actor that he is today. And I remember the collaboration with the dancer Pomiès, who was to die soon thereafter, as a pleasant episode in my career. Making this partly tragic, partly whimsical burlesque, with no clear relation to the play it was taken from, gave me great satisfaction.

We arrive at last at the event which more than any other marked the lives of all those trying to make a living in films: the release of *The Jazz Singer*. The success of this film upset all established standards. The French, hesitantly at first and then enthusiastically, started making sound pictures. I would have liked to do as everyone else was doing, but I was classified once and for all as a director of silent dramas and as an enemy of the theater. As a result I was not welcome in the new profession, which set about filming successful stage productions word for word.

I had to wait almost two years before I got my chance. During this time the entire commercial edifice on which the industry had been built came crashing down. The cause was simple. Before the talkies there had been a surplus of films. Practically all foreign films had been adapted for the French public simply by the addition of subtitles. As a result the theater owners had had great power. Sound changed all that because the

* See page 215. Trans.

language itself became a barrier which kept out the foreign products and protected ours. The producers replaced the theater owners as the captains of the industry.

The foreign film-makers opened the battle. It did not take them long to find an effective weapon in dubbing. As for the producers, they overinvested after they saw the first miraculous receipts from the talkies and soon fell back into the hands of the middlemen, that is to say, the distributors. That is approximately the situation today. It is safe to say that, with perhaps a few rare exceptions, the French film industry belongs to those who managed to step in between the men making the films and the people willing to pay to see them. They risk little or nothing and are sure to profit at every turn.

My first talking film was a sort of test. People didn't trust me. So I had to prove myself. I managed to get *On Purge Bébé*, based on Georges Feydeau's play. The film is not much. I shot it in only four days. Even so, it is more than 2,000 meters long. It cost the producer less than 200,000 francs and earned more than a million.

I probably did well to start out with a modest film. It is likely that I would have regretted it if I had made my debut in sound with a more ambitious project. It was the age of bad sound. The props and the sets were arranged around the mikes with an unbelievable naïveté. These practices annoyed me, and to show how dissatisfied I was, I decided to record the flushing of a toilet. It was a kind of revolutionary act which did more for my reputation than a dozen brilliantly filmed scenes ever could have. The most respected scientific and artistic figures from the great sound companies declared that it was an "audacious innovation." After such a stroke I could no longer be refused the job that I had been after for a year: the chance to make *La Chienne*, based on La Fouchardière's novel.

In *La Chienne* I must admit that I was ruthless and unbearable. I made the film as I wanted, as I understood it, without the slightest regard for the wishes of the producer. I never showed him a single page of my shooting script or a word of the dialogue, and I arranged it so the rushes would remain unavailable until the film was completed. That was when the scandal broke. The producer, who had been expecting a vaudeville, found himself with a serious drama on his hands, a pessimistic story revolving around a murder.

I was kicked out of the studio and barred from my editing room. Every time I tried to get in, they called the police. Finally, after the producer had tried to have the film re-edited the way he wanted it and had realized that his ideas would not work, he decided that perhaps it would be best to let me go ahead after all. I was allowed back into my editing room and managed to repair most of the damage. The film was released first in Nancy, where it met with unprecedented disaster. Apparently the audiences had been led to expect an uproarious comedy. I insisted that all future publicity faithfully reflect the mood of the film. A courageous distributor in Biarritz did just that and presented the film with good success. It was then decided to release the picture in Paris, at the Colisée. It ran for several weeks, giving me ample opportunity to enjoy the pleasant atmosphere of a critical battle similar to that which had accompanied the release of *Nana*.

Unfortunately for me, this fight gave me the reputation of being difficult to get along with, and I had a hard time finding work afterward. I was supposed to be impossible to work with, capable of perpetrating the worst outrages upon the persons of directors hapless enough to disagree with me. I got along as best I could, making occasional poor films, until Marcel Pagnol gave me the opportunity to make *Toni*.

I saw *Toni* as the chance to really direct and to get free of the stupid conformism which afflicts so many of the people who run our industry. In short, *Toni* represented for me that liberty of *esprit de corps* without which no one in the world is capable of doing good work.

I learned a lot from *Toni*. This film gave me the courage necessary to try new things, to move in new directions.

Next I made *The Crime of M. Lange*, *La Vie Est à Nous*, *The Lower Depths*, *Grand Illusion*, *La Marseillaise*, and I have just finished *The Human Beast*. I do not know whether these films are good or bad. In my humble opinion, it is without importance. What I know is that I am beginning to understand how one should work. I know that I am French and that I must work in an absolutely national vein. I know also that in doing this, and only in doing this, can I reach people from other nations and act for international understanding.

I know that the American cinema will collapse because it is no longer American. I know too that we must not spurn the foreigners who come to us with their knowledge and talent; we must absorb them. It is a practice which has served us rather well from Leonardo da Vinci all the way to Picasso. I believe that the cinema is not so much an industry as people would have us believe and that the fat men with their money, their graphs, and green felt tables are going to fall on their faces. Film making is a skilled trade and it is craftsmen grouped together for their own protection that will perhaps make French cinema the best in the world. Knowing that, I feel that I still have everything to do in a profession which, if it were free, could add so much to our understanding of men and things.

The First Version of The Crime of M. Lange

●

This first version of The Crime of M. Lange *was written before Jacques Prévert arrived to collaborate on the scenario.*

The two main characters, Lange and Batala (here called Cathala), are already well established, as are the essential elements of the social commentary and of the detective-story plot. The tentative title, "The Rise of M. Lange," foreshadows Brecht's The Irresistible Rise of Arturo Ui *of six years later. It is obvious that this first draft overlooks the possibility of unifying the film by grouping all the characters around the same courtyard: the concierges, the washerwomen, the employees at the press. Mlle. Marion will become the washerwoman, Florelle (Nadia Sibirskaïa). Messrs. Buisson and Meunier (the son) will become less important, and Pietrini will disappear altogether as the female characters and the amorous intrigues take on added significance in the final version. Renoir's film is almost here. It awaits the contributions of two other geniuses: Jacques Prévert and Jules Berry.*

François Truffaut

Jean Renoir and Jean Castanier
THE RISE OF M. LANGE *(tentative title)*
Scenario filed at the Société des Auteurs de Films, 9 rue Ballu
Oberon, 22, place de la Madeleine, Paris Opéra 04-30

Preamble

This film is based on the idea that any man who has carved out a place for himself in society and is worthy of his position has the right to keep his place and to defend it against one who would take it from him, even if this thief bases his action on legal principles.

Specifically it is the story of an employee in a publishing office who takes over the direction of the business when the owner leaves. In the absence of his boss, he proves to be a remarkable businessman and a talented promoter. The business, which had been failing, becomes profitable again. The backers are pleased, and the employees are able to live comfortably.

The owner returns and wants to resume his rightful place. Our man will kill him in order to defend his position, and with it his own happiness and that of his colleagues.

Is such a crime justified? The people who hear the story, simple mountain folk living on the border between Spain and France, think that it is. Before fleeing his country, our hero has taken refuge at an inn in this region. The people recognize him, but instead of handing him over to the authorities they will help him escape across the border.

This subject will be treated in a perfectly realistic way, which is to say that many of the situations will lend themselves to laughter because the milieu where the characters will evolve can be rich in comic situations. Nonetheless, the players will not act according to the traditions of vaudeville. They will avoid trying to provoke laughter by facial expressions or by excessively exploiting situations. If there is laughter, it shall have to come from the situations themselves and the personalities of the characters. We hope that these characters will be sufficiently varied so that the merciless exposition of their oddities can produce some amusing contrasts.

The central character, M. Lange, appears to be a puny little functionary. But under his unimpressive exterior seethes an intense imagination. The minute he has the opportunity to daydream, his thoughts turn to his favorite heroes: the cowboys and Indians of the Far West. In his dreams he gallops alongside them over the prairies.

It seemed to us that a crime of passion that is also a social protest, like M. Lange's, does not necessarily have to be situated in a sinister milieu. Rather, a study such as ours gains in dramatic intensity and in true humanity if it is surrounded by real everyday elements likely to amuse the public.

The Action: Prologue

The police in a little border outpost in the Pyrenees receive a photograph of an individual who, having committed a crime, has evaded the police and will no doubt be trying to cross onto foreign soil. The man is named Lange, a rather well-known former writer accused of having murdered his boss, M. Cathala. A policeman complains to a peasant about the extra work necessitated by the search for the accused man.

We switch to Lange himself, who is walking calmly along a little mountain path, accompanied by Mlle. Marion. They do not look like fugitives, but rather like a couple of casual strollers, pleased to be enjoying the superb view. Some girls offer them wild flowers, adding to the idyllic atmosphere of the scene.

The prologue could be characterized by the same calm beauty as that of mountain landscapes where it takes place.

Tired after a long day's walk, M. Lange and Mlle. Marion decide to spend the night at an inn near the border. Unfortunately, the peasant we have seen talking with the policeman is at the inn, and he recognizes Lange from the police photograph.

He tells his friends of the discovery. Will they turn the fugitive in?

Lange, very tired, has stretched out on his bed and fallen asleep. Mlle. Marion has overheard the men's conversation. Just as one of them is about to go tell the police, she enters the room and asks the strangers to listen to her. She thinks that by explaining the circumstances to these simple people she can convince them to change their minds and close their eyes to Lange's escape.

They decide to listen, and it is her story which provides the substance of our film.

Part One

Lange and Mlle. Marion work together at the offices of Popular Publications. Specifically these publications are three weeklies: *The Boy Scout,* whose adventurous contents are Lange's creation; *The Petite Lisette,* a collection of bright little stories edited by Mlle. Marion, an ageless, lackluster woman; and *The Illustrated Weekly,* the largest of the three publications, written by the entire staff under the direction of the company's owner, M. Cathala.

In back of the editorial offices, on the dark and stifling courtyard side of the building, is the printing press itself, which also does job printing, but for a progressively smaller clientele.

M. Cathala has an office overlooking the street, where he smokes huge cigars in the company of Pietrini, his editor-in-chief. These two live fairly well and always manage to find enough money in the cash register to pay for their sumptuous lunches. The blond Edith, although she does not know how to type, serves as a decorative secretary.

In addition to his responsibilities with *The Boy Scout,* Lange corrects proofs, composes dummies, and does a little of everything. He helps the cashier put off the most insistent of the company's creditors.

The business is going poorly; the employees wait in vain for their salaries, always a question mark. Cathala senses that he is going to have to give up his elegant life style. He would very much like to sell the business to some big publishing house. But Lafayette Publishers, sensing that something is wrong, let Cathala know in no uncertain terms that his offer does not interest them.

As a final stroke of bad luck, M. Meunier, the man holding Cathala's mortgage, sends his representative, M. Buisson to look at the books; and Cathala receives word that he has been officially charged with fraud.

Cathala and Pietrini decide to resort to exceptional measures: to wit, they will invite M. Buisson to a lavish lunch in a posh restaurant, where they will try to buy him off.

The scene in the restaurant revolves around Lange's awkwardness and his several blunders. He has been brought along to present some papers relative to the affair if they are needed. Cathala thinks it looks impressive to be accompanied by a secretary. Cathala is apparently a habitué of the restaurant. He refers to "my port" and "my oysters." He is hoping to overwhelm M. Buisson.

Lange, hardly worthy of notice, is allowed to sit down at the table, but not to eat. Very ill at ease, he blushes as the waiters push him out of the way to serve the others. He wishes he could disappear. He provokes a catastrophe, causing the gravy to be spilled on M. Buisson.

Cathala is very unhappy, and worried too. He is afraid that M. Buisson will be ill disposed toward him as a result of the accident and more difficult to corrupt. Also, he seems afraid to make his move in the presence of Lange. Suddenly solicitous, he notices that Lange has not had a chance to eat and sends him off. Lange returns to the office, where Mlle. Marion is waiting for him. She is surprised that he has had nothing to eat. Always imaginative, he has her believe that he did not accept Cathala's invitation to eat at the restaurant because the cuisine was not up to his standards.

Mlle. Marion has not forgotten that it is Lange's birthday. She has brought him a present: a gas lamp for camping. She hopes that this lamp will be only the beginning of a complete set of camping equipment which will enable them to go camping together the next summer beside a beautiful river somewhere. For Mlle. Marion loves Lange and sets hopelessly naïve traps in an effort to win him. But Lange turns the conversation toward Cathala, whom he admires. Mlle. Marion does not like Cathala at all and says that he is a thief. Lange claims that he is a gangster, something quite different and worthy of admiration.

At this point the beautiful Edith appears, returning from her lunch at the restaurant. Forgetting everything, Lange dashes after her in an effort to strike up a conversation. He loves her, or at least desires her passionately. In his confusion he forgets even his own lunch, which Mlle. Marion has finally succeeded in warming up over the camping lamp. It is a mistake, for it is clear that the coquettish secretary is not about to waste her time on a mere employee.

Cathala and Pietrini return crestfallen from their great luncheon. They lock themselves in their office and set to arguing violently. M. Buisson, a man of integrity, has rejected their offer indignantly. The coffers empty and the prospect of jail looming before him, Cathala decides to flee abroad and abandon his company. Pietrini, envisioning the worst, asks his accomplice for a little money to tide him over. They quarrel again, and Cathala leaves on the sly, having bought Pietrini's silence.

Cathala is seated in a first-class compartment on the express train to Brussels. He is counting his money and writing figures with a pencil. He has not lost his arrogance—or his fat cigar. A sudden accident: the train goes off the tracks.

Having passed out briefly, Cathala comes to on the track bed. In the distance men are helping the injured. Cathala has an idea. He takes the wallet from a dead man, which supplies him with new papers and a bit of extra money, and places his own wallet in the dead man's pocket. Armed with new identity papers and well supplied with money, Cathala disappears into the night, rather satisfied with the unforeseen turn of events.

Part Two

Following the presumed death of Cathala, M. Buisson, in the name of M. Meunier, the magazines' major creditor, has come to an understanding with the heirs: they will gladly renounce any claim to the enterprise in exchange for payment of the money owed them.

M. Buisson is perfectly willing to let Popular Publications continue to operate, his only desire being to make more money for his boss. The sale of the old equipment would not have produced much profit in any case. He calls a meeting of the staff, explains the situation to them, and informs them that he has decided not to invest another cent in the enterprise. The employees are already behind in their salaries and do not want to work unless they are paid up.

The cashier comes up with a solution that is acceptable to both sides: the workers will share in any future profits if they stay on.

Assuming that Pietrini will be the new boss, Lange is thinking only of how to convince him to give *The Boy Scout* a page in color. Economic questions leave him cold. What he is interested in is the technical side of the operation, and he is pushing for a new policy which would allow the readers to participate in the editing of the magazine. But no one listens to Lange. Everyone is thinking of his own immediate concerns rather than the long-term good of the magazine.

The agreement between M. Buisson and the staff has to be approved by M. Meunier, so M. Buisson suggests that the three main representatives of the company go down to see the industrialist. He means Pietrini, the cashier, and Lange.

At the hotel they are told that M. Meunier has stepped out. They decide to wait for him. Lange goes out to buy some cigarettes. At the tobacco stand he makes the acquaintance of a pleasant drunkard and starts playing little games with him. They meet thanks to the difficulty the drunk is having with an electric lighter. Lange forgets about his meeting and becomes quite friendly with the drunk, then suddenly remembers that he has an appointment at the Hotel Ritz. "Say, so do I," says the drunk, who is none other than M. Meunier himself.

The others are quite surprised to see Lange and M. Meunier return arm in arm. M. Meunier is even more surprised to learn that his new comrade is a member of the magazine of which he finds himself the owner. M. Meunier is quite thrilled to find that Lange is a proofreader. In his drunken condition he reasons that a proofreader must be correct and therefore be superior to everyone else. He states that he will not accept the agreement unless

Lange assumes the management of the company. He even signs a contract by which he promises to take no action without the signature of his new manager.

Pietrini is mortified, but he has no choice but to go along. Lange is frightened and considers the prospect of taking over from Cathala, whom he admired so much, with apprehension.

It is now three months later. A creditor, whom we have already seen at the beginning of the film, reappears. Much to his surprise the ramshackle old offices are full of life, well organized and . . . he is paid.

M. Lange is talking with the envoy from Lafayette Publishers who earlier turned down Cathala's offers to sell. Now he has gone out of his way to try to buy out Lange, but the new manager refuses, in agreement with his fellow workers, who now feel that they have a stake in the business.

Everyone is now happy except Pietrini and Edith, who has been kept on to brighten up the office a bit. They are bored and miss the privileges they enjoyed under the Cathala regime.

Suddenly a loud noise brings all work to a halt. It is M. Meunier, returning from Lille, drunk as usual. He falls all over Lange with expressions of friendship, says he is delighted with the company's success, and proposes to drink to it. He takes Lange for an apéritif at the café. Lange, not used to drinking, feels quite gay. Then he wants to leave, but Meunier will not hear of it and takes him to dinner.

Lange has asked Meunier to take him to the restaurant where he was shamed during the famous luncheon which Cathala gave for M. Buisson. Timid at first, Lange gradually gains confidence and ends up asking for "my port" and "my oysters" as Cathala did. He is carried away by his drunkenness, unlike Meunier, who although inebriated maintains his propriety and is much amused by Lange's eccentricities. In his drunken state, Lange sees Edith everywhere. He thinks he recognizes her at the next table and among the restaurant employees.

The soirée concludes at a night club, the Prince Igor, amid

hundreds of Ediths whom Lange chases madly, causing great damage to persons and property. The waiters learn that he is an editor and call him "Big Shot" and "Mr. Manager." Convinced of his own importance, Lange finally leaves the night spot.

Full of new-found dignity, Lange decides he wants to go to the office, in spite of the late hour. Alone, he enters the building and wanders through the deserted premises. This marvelous evening has left him exalted, and for the first time he enters the director's office without knocking. He takes possession, opening drawers, going through files. Ideas crowd into his head, he takes notes. As each new idea supersedes the previous one, he crumples up his notes and tosses them into the wastebasket.

Suddenly a sound makes him shudder. There is someone in the next room. Worried, he takes a revolver out of the drawer and prepares to confront the intruder. It is Cathala, the supposed dead man, come back to pay a visit on Lange. He has observed the whole scene and laughs at Lange. Lange loses some of his self-assurance. But Cathala does not intend to reclaim his company, at least for the moment. The police have not yet forgotten his earlier peccadilloes, and now he is carrying false identification papers as well. He has just returned to draw a little money. Cathala leaves when he has gotten what he wanted, and has made Lange promise not to say a word.

Completely sobered, Lange feels depressed and small. As his boss leaves, delighted with himself, Lange humbly picks up the papers that have fallen on the floor and places them in the wastebasket.

Part Three

The offices of Popular Publications are now completely modernized, and one has the feeling that the company has enjoyed several months of prosperity. We see the improvements as the staff is preparing a great celebration out in the country, to which the readership of all three magazines will be invited.

The party is aimed at the younger readers, and of course Lange has given it a Wild West motif. At last he can give life to the heroes of his stories—cowboys, and Indians attacking stage-coaches, shooting at one another, etc.

During the preparations Pietrini receives a mysterious telephone call. It is obvious that Cathala has chosen this moment to reveal himself to his old accomplice. The phone call clearly has something to do with the current situation vis-à-vis M. Buisson, who has received a new offer for the company from Lafayette, and this time the price is so high that he would be crazy to turn it down.

Lange is scarcely listening. A cowboy hat on his head, he is testing his aim with a bow and arrow. In any case, the other employees have told him that they do not want to sell.

Noon. Everyone goes out to lunch.

Only Pietrini stays at the office. It is not long before Cathala sneaks in. Cathala knows about the offers from Lafayette and he too, for reasons far removed from Buisson's, would like the offer to be accepted. What does he have to lose? A few months in prison for his past and present mistakes? That little vacation would be well worth the several hundred thousand francs he would stand to gain from the sale. He knows a way to force Lange into signing the bill of sale: a year earlier he managed to delay payment on a major debt for twelve months. The cashier thinks that Cathala has since paid the debt, but actually he took the money from the company coffers and kept it for himself. So, if Lafayette bought Cathala's note from the original creditor and ruthlessly demanded payment from the company, Lange, caught without the money on hand, would have no choice but to accept Lafayette's terms.

Pietrini is delighted by the ploy. He foresees the possibility of picking up a few crumbs himself (from Cathala, from Buisson, and perhaps even from Lafayette) and plots to reinforce the effectiveness of the scheme by playing on Lange's naïve passion for Edith.

A lucky or unlucky stroke of fate has it that the IOU will be presented to Lange at the very moment of his Far West festival.

The festival is in full swing. Scores of little boys and girls are enjoying themselves immensely in the midst of a large field, which has been transformed into a Sioux Indian camp for the occasion. There are little donkeys harnassed like wild mustangs, lassos, and even a goat cart serving as a stagecoach. In a tent Mlle. Marion, dressed up as an Indian, warns Lange against Edith. She has noticed that her rival has changed her attitude toward Lange, a turn of events which she finds suspicious. Lange replies that she is incapable of understanding great passion.

In another tent Pietrini is giving his final instructions to Edith. She is to pretend to give in to Lange's advances and ask him to take her away to a foreign country. With Lange out of the way, the company can be sold without his approval.

Meanwhile Lafayette himself has appeared at the office, the overdue draft in hand. Buisson has brought Meunier along to precipitate the matter. He has kept his boss practically prisoner for the past forty-eight hours, absolutely forbidding him to take a drink, under some vague medical pretext. Meunier signs anything they like without question. He is counting on the good judgment of Lange, whose signature is needed for final approval.

The agreement being reached, everyone heads for the festival, to have Lange sign the bill of sale and to let the new owner participate in the promotional celebration.

Edith has found a moment to put on her act of love for Lange. She has changed into a magnificent cowgirl's outfit, which greatly excites the naïve Lange. He is all set up to commit the irreparable blunder.

Mlle. Marion, still dressed as an Indian, intervenes in time to thwart Edith's schemes. With Edith at her mercy, she forces her to confess that it is Pietrini who tells her what to do. Lange is very upset.

M. Meunier has observed this last scene, and he realizes that there is some scheming going on. He has regained a little of his self-assurance, thanks to a couple of drinks at the festival bar. Outraged, he writes a check to cover the draft which M. Lafayette is holding and declares that he wants to hear no more about the sale. The company will continue to operate as it has been.

In a burst of enthusiasm, everyone returns to Paris, singing.

Only Lange returns to the office, to straighten out the draft bought by Meunier. There he finds Cathala, furious at the failure of his scheme. Cathala pours invective on Lange, reminding him that he is really nothing but an employee; that he, Cathala, is the real owner of the company; and that Lange's efforts to cross his schemes were to all intents and purposes a form of theft. At first Lange hangs his head, cringing; but then he gets hold of himself and stands up to Cathala. He reproaches him for being selfish and not caring about the company and its staff: Cathala does not know what real work is. Lange, on the other hand, has worked wholeheartedly for the company for twenty years, and now he considers himself to be more the owner than Cathala himself, who only got hold of it in some shady deal.

The quarrel between the two men takes on the aspects of a fight over a woman, Lange playing the role of the faithful lover and Cathala that of the cynical exploiter.

Cathala decides to resolve the matter by telling the police that he is alive and has returned. He will be arrested as a result, but he will also regain ownership of the company. He takes the telephone off the hook, but as he is dialing, Lange shoots him with a revolver.

Terrified by what he has done, Lange wanders about the premises until he comes across Mlle. Marion, who has followed him to the office and overheard everything that happened with Cathala. He collapses at her feet, crying and clinging to her legs.

Mlle. Marion consoles Lange as one would console a child; because Lange, in spite of his age, is like a kid. He used his revolver as he would have a prop in a story of the Far West. Mlle. Marion, who has remained perfectly calm, convinces him to run away. She will accompany him on his flight.

Epilogue

A long dissolve brings us back to Mlle. Marion, who is finishing her story at the mountain inn.

It is dawn, a child sleeps against his mother's knees. Lange appears at the door, surprised by the silent gathering. He asks what is happening. The oldest man present answers simply that his companion has asked for a guide for a mountain excursion and that he will ask his son to accompany them and lend them a mule.

The decision of this improvised jury having been stated, the scene jumps to the little caravan preparing to climb the majestic peaks beyond the border.

An Early Treatment of Grand Illusion

•

This first treatment of Grand Illusion *is not dated, but it is apparent that it was done before the roles were cast. Jean Renoir had probably already thought of Jean Gabin for Maréchal and perhaps even of Pierre Fresnay for Boïeldieu, but not yet of Dalio (Dolette, who later became Rosenthal), and certainly not of Erich von Stroheim or Dita Parlo. Some will regret that Renoir dropped the epilogue at Maxim's, but most of the essentials of the final film are here (developed with or without the collaboration of Charles Spaak—the manuscript is not signed): the escape attempts, the taking of Douaumont, the transfer, the fortress, the prison, the death of de Boïeldieu, the Swiss border, and above all the idea that social conditions are more important than nationality and that people, as Renoir often said, "are more divided horizontally than vertically."*

François Truffaut

1916. Behind the French lines. In an air corps canteen we find the career officer Stanislas de Boïeldieu, a cavalry captain. Monocle in place, riding crop in hand, with a touch of arrogance and impertinence. He asks a pilot to take him on a reconnaissance flight. It is Captain Maréchal, a rugged character, without polish, a mechanic by trade. The fortunes of war and his own merits have brought him his commission very quickly. Boïeldieu and Maréchal are of the same rank, but not of the same world . . .

They are on the runway. The engine starts; the plane moves . . . In the air. Boïeldieu cannot see anything because of the clouds. "Horses," he says, "we'll go back to them eventually. Nothing like them for reconnaissance."

No gunshots, no enemy planes. And then all of a sudden the engine starts to fail. Boïeldieu is disturbed: "Just get me back behind the lines . . ." Boïeldieu's tone and his remarks are grating. On the German side some soldiers, bearded, aged, and sickly, are guarding a bridge. A French plane appears in the sky. Excited, the old Germans send off several perfunctory rounds toward the enemy. And the plane comes down . . . down . . . The Germans think they have shot it down. The motor dead, Maréchal has been forced to land. Boïeldieu finds this "annoying."

The Germans run toward the Frenchmen as fast as their old legs will carry them. The first thing to do is to destroy the plane quickly so that it will be useless to the Germans. To Maréchal's surprise, Boïeldieu is unshaken by the danger and shows remarkable self-control. The Germans reach the two officers; a few blows from their clubs and the Frenchmen are stretched out on the grass.

A German officer, his face thin and scarred, gets out of a Mercedes. He has witnessed the scene. He reproaches his embarrassed men for their pointless brutality. And in impeccable French he excuses himself personally to Boïeldieu, who is just coming to. He assures the French officers that General van der Winter will be happy to receive them at his table.

The dining room of a very luxurious château. The German general is surrounded by his staff. The two Frenchmen are there. The table is sumptuously laid out, and the service is attended to by waiters in formal serving garb. The general apologizes for the modesty of his menu: some requisitioned chicken. But the wines are good. The departed owners of the château knew their vintages.

Boïeldieu is quite at ease in this elegant company, Maréchal less so. He is not at all adroit with his knife and fork, and this is a little disturbing to Boïeldieu. Nonetheless, the conversation sparkles. These men of the world have no trouble making themselves understood to each other. They all speak excellent English. The general, quite Parisian, asks about actors and about Maxim's, where he used to spend his New Year's Eves.

Maréchal notes that the man next to him is no more accustomed to this style of life than he. This brings them together. Surprise: like him, his neighbor is a mechanic-turned-pilot. He speaks good French; before the war he worked in Lyon at Gnôme-et-Rhone. All at once they are talking like old friends about their common interests: have you had trouble with your fuel?

Cannon fire. No one is concerned. The windows are opened. Enemy planes are fighting in the sky. The meal continues. Boïeldieu and his colleagues chat about the last Grand Prix; Maréchal and his pal talk mechanics. The general stands and raises his glass. "Impossible to drink to the success of either army . . . May the better man win . . . And to the coming peace . . ." They touch glasses amid the louder and louder noise of the approaching bombardment.

The next day a foul-mouthed German soldier rather brutally packs a group of prisoners into a wagon; among them are Boïeldieu and Maréchal.

En route to Germany . . .

The prisoners are put in a temporary barracks without utilities. Their quarters occupy one wing of the building, while the other is occupied by German women preparing food. Of course the two wings are completely separated; no conversation or contact is possible. Only through a vent can they catch glimpses of the feet of the women as they go to and from their work.

In the room which Maréchal and Boïeldieu choose, four officers have been preparing an escape for months. They are slowly digging a tunnel which will take them under the road to the air field across from the camp. They are disturbed by the new arrivals. There are so many informers! Still, they have no choice but to tell the newcomers their secret. That night Maréchal and Boïeldieu join the enterprise, which is directed by a curious special officer who was in prison when the war began. He was the leader of a gang which specialized in bank robberies. Their method had been to dig tunnels under the banks. In wartime this type of man and his specialty become invaluable.

Naturally the work on the tunnel, which is interrupted periodically by the guards on their rounds, is a complicated and unpleasant task. In the daytime the rats hide there, and each night before digging, the conspirators have to rout them out. The next day, during their outing, the prisoners dispose surreptitiously of the earth and the dead rats.

The newcomers are informed of a pleasant diversion: twice a day, at the opening and closing of one of the nearby workshops, a woman whom no one has seen rests her foot on one of the bars in front of the vent to adjust her garter, provocatively revealing two beautiful legs. The prisoners joke about it a lot.

The morale of the conspirators is excellent. Whatever the discomfort, no matter how bad the food, the officers respond with the refrain "The war to end all wars; that's a good one!" All except Boïeldieu, who in the midst of these simple men retains his natural stiffness and the manner of expression which amuses and annoys them.

This is how the days pass: at night, work on the tunnel; during the day, play rehearsals. For in this camp, as in others, the prisoners have built a stage in a wooden shack. Musicians, designers, male and female performers, have been recruited from the camp. The great Parisian fashion designers send costumes. The rehearsals of this curious production are nothing if not picturesque.

One night, after the customary appearance of the woman with the beautiful legs, our heroes are waiting for the hour to begin their ditch digging. But they hear a great commotion among the German guards. The news spreads quickly: Douaumont has just fallen to the Germans. The guards are celebrating with beer and songs, which they sing so well.

The prisoners are disconcerted. They are upset by the news and affected by the force of the music, which rises up to them in waves. They wonder if, under the circumstances, they should not put off their production for a few days. They decide to go ahead with the show as a reply to the Germans' obnoxious celebrating. Meanwhile they return to the tunnel with vigor. The following night the soldiers assume the incongruous role of dancers—and they acquit themselves quite well. In a box, surrounded by his subordinates, the commandant of the camp laughs uproariously at the verve and spirit of the Frenchmen.

In the show Maréchal acts as Master of ceremonies. He is in the wings, gluing on a false beard, when he suddenly learns the news. He leaps onto the stage, stops the scene, goes to the edge of the platform, and in a thundering voice announces: "Men, we have just retaken Douaumont!"

A second of silence, and then in a corner of the room some-one starts singing the "Marseillaise." All the men are standing. All sing. The commandant rises, infuriated. On the stage the thrilled soldiers are dancing as if it were Bastille Day. No way to stop them from taking revenge for the day before. The German guards, armed, rush into the room. The men refuse to leave, refuse to be quiet.

And the Germans advance, clubs raised, among the dancing, howling madmen, carried by a wave which nothing can stem.

For Maréchal, guilty of instigating the outburst, it is forty-five days in solitary; forty-five days of complete darkness and silence. "The war to end all wars; that's a good one," he thinks the first day . . . But the silence and the darkness, these are hostile forces to which even the strongest succumb.

Each day for five minutes the guard comes to watch him and light the cell while he eats. An old guard with sympathetic eyes who doesn't speak a word of French. In the five minutes Maréchal speaks to him without stopping. He must hear a human voice; he must hear someone reply to him. But the guard doesn't understand; he nods his head and says nothing. And Maréchal becomes desperate, dangerously so. He can't take it any more. He howls in his cave. He thinks of killing himself.

The old guard intervenes, calms him with his friendly smile and eyes. Only the mute compassion of this old German saves Maréchal from insanity and death.

Maréchal rejoins his friends. The tunnel, which they have continued to dig, is almost finished. However, they take no pleasure in this fact. They are dejected and querulous for a reason which Maréchal does not understand at first.

It is because of the woman, because of her beautiful legs. What started as a joke has become an obsession, and the men have begun to take out their frustration on each other. They must do something to get back at the bitch, to teach her not to tantalize love-starved men. One of them, hidden by the vent, will grab the foot which she rests on the bar and make her their prisoner.

They wait. She comes. Her usual merciless display. She is seized. Everyone dashes to grab hold of the leg sticking through the vent. Hearing her cries, the woman's friends grab her shoulders and pull her back. The men take off her shoes, tear off her stocking. Everyone wants to touch the fresh, gleaming skin. And Maréchal, cruelly, bites her. The woman screams. The men retreat, and her friends pull her out. "Now she'll leave us alone!" cry the men.

The same night, the soldier who has been working on the tunnel comes rushing out like a madman. Tomorrow night they can leave!

But everything cannot be foreseen . . . At roll call the next morning the sergeant tells them they have one hour to get ready to move. They are being transferred to another camp. They are being separated. Their tremendous efforts, their dogged persistence, was all for nothing.

Then they are in the courtyard. If their tunnel could at least be used by others . . . The sergeant shows them six British officers who have just arrived at the camp. "These are the ones who are going to occupy your quarters . . ."

By all means, they must tell them. Maréchal leaves his group and manages to accost one of the British soldiers. He explains: on the left, in the corner; all you have to do is remove the bricks to find the tunnel . . . The Englishman doesn't understand a word of French. He smiles. Maréchal persists; he gestures. The Englishman laughs heartily and slaps him on the back. Maréchal, unable to communicate the secret, has to go back to his group. With Boïeldieu, he is sent to the heart of Germany.

The British move into the room which the French have just left. They calculate the disposition of the room, and right away one of them comes up with a plan of escape: exactly the same as that of the French. But the hole, where to make it? To the left? To the right? They argue and then agree on the right. Five meters from the completed tunnel left by the French prisoners, the British, with the same faith and the same obstinacy, begin to dig theirs!

The second camp is located in a gloomy region far from neutral borders. The men are imprisoned in a medieval château, complete with towers, ramparts, and stone walls. A frightful discipline reigns. And everyone feels weary. This war, the war to end all wars, just doesn't end . . . No theater here, no more glimpses of female legs, no more Count of Monte Cristo–type tunnels; nothing but boredom and despair.

Maréchal and Boïeldieu find themselves with a new group of companions. A former locksmith turned infantry officer, who will not listen to talk of escape; just mind your own business and wait for the time when we can go back to our old trades. A professor of Greek working on a translation of a minor poet; he is not suffering particularly from his confinement, since it allows him to dedicate himself completely to his monastic labors. Another cavalry officer: Guy de Saint-Privat, from the same world and class as Boïeldieu. In the barracks the two men form their own clique. As soon as the opportunity arises, even in this hell-hole, the social classes align themselves in the old manner. A talkative, sardonic Parisian, whose unquenchable wit no longer amuses anyone. A Negro just out of engineering school, cold, polite, and reserved. Finally, Dolette, a thin boy with handsome features, a broad intelligent forehead, and striking eyes. Apparently there is something in common between this intellectual and the mechanic Maréchal. They are both solid types, both stalwarts. They recognized each other right away. They will become inseparable.

An empty bed . . . The occupant is in solitary. An inoffensive pharmacist's assistant from Brittany. He has an incredible hatred for the Germans. He cannot control his feelings. At roll call, on two occasions, he has stepped forward, saluted respectfully, and coldly declared to the German sergeant: "You are all scum, and you can go to hell!"

The first time it was thirty days in solitary; then sixty. He is serving the latest sentence.

Escape . . . Maréchal is constantly haunted by the idea. But how? The most important requirement is a map of Germany, and little by little he puts one together from scraps the size of postage stamps, smuggled to him in chocolate bars. But many of the bars are lost en route, and there are holes in the map.

One morning the little Breton returns. To those who knew him, he is unrecognizable. He can hardly stand on his feet. He looks so miserable, so pathetic that the Parisian bursts into tears. The others gather around this refugee from hell. Dazed, he doesn't have the strength to reply to them. And then it's roll call.

The men, lined up, respond to the calling of their names: the Breton responds in his turn. But then he advances, salutes formally, and declares in an unshaking voice: "You are all scum, and you can go to hell!"

On the dilapidated stove in the barracks, with the pathetic resources available, the prisoners have made a small forge; they want to make keys. The locksmith, who wants to be left alone, refuses to help. He will give in, however, if only because of his passion for his craft.

With the keys, Maréchal and Dolette are able to get out of their room and roam the corridors. They come across the room where the ammunition is stored. They are going to blow up the camp. But killing a few old Germans would not be worth the death of all their friends. They return from their expedition with two revolvers.

They have to try something. Two men will escape while their companions simulate a revolt at the other end of the camp. The traditional practice will be observed: the two best-qualified officers, Maréchal and Dolette, will attempt to escape, while the two least-valued men, the Parisian and Boïeldieu, will sacrifice themselves. The latter know that they will not get out of it alive. "The war to end all wars; it's worth the price . . ."

One revolver goes to the group which is going to pretend to revolt, the other to the fugitives. The night of the escape arrives. The Parisian refuses to obey an order. Boïeldieu steps in and hits a guard. Wild disorder breaks out immediately, everyone running and shouting. Boïeldieu and the Parisian climb onto a roof. They fire their revolvers. German reinforcements arrive on the run. More gunfire. The Parisian falls. Boïeldieu holds out. Finally, he too is hit. "The war to end all wars . . ."

And this man whom we have found odious in all the small details and magnificent in all the crucial situations dies to assure the escape of his two friends; Maréchal and Dolette have gotten over the walls. With a revolver, a map, some biscuits and sugar, they are going to make it on foot to the Swiss border.

The alarm has been sounded. They will spend the first night in a pine forest. They are hunted with flashlights. After almost getting themselves caught, they escape . . . The road is open, but their destination is far . . .

The sugar and the biscuits are soon gone. Hiding by day in the most improbable places, Maréchal and Dolette walk each night, avoiding towns and even villages.

They are already exhausted. To add to their problems, Dolette twists his foot while crossing a ditch during one of their nocturnal marches. Whether sprained, broken, torn, or what, Dolette doesn't know, but he suffers horribly, and he cannot go any farther. Desperate, the two friends hide in the ditch and take stock. They hear the tramp of boots on the road next to the ditch. Voices sing an old marching song. It is a company of reservists crossing the forest. It passes and continues on.

Dolette insists that Maréchal abandon him and continue on his own. Impossible. They are not far from a village. Maréchal drags his friend and hides him in a stable which seems to be abandoned; the cows were eaten long ago.

Stretched out on the hay, Dolette feels better. He soon goes to sleep. Maréchal cocks his ear at the creaking of a door, the sound of steps. There is light under the door; the door opens. A lamp in her hand, a woman stands in the doorway. She is one of those German blondes made to bring beautiful children into the world.

She is in her nightshirt, with only a shawl over her shoulders. And with her clear, calm blue eyes, she gazes at the two French prisoners whose fate she holds in her hands. Will she call for help?

She is calm; she moves slowly. She looks at Maréchal, and he thinks her beautiful. She removes her shawl, blows out the lamp, and lies down in the warm hay beside Maréchal. And Maréchal listens to her passionate, foreign tongue as she whispers, "It has been over a year since all the men left . . ."

Dawn. Maréchal comes out of the barn and looks for eggs in the yard. Meanwhile, soft and beautiful, her long hair in lovely disarray, the German woman lies in the arms of the sleeping Dolette.

They have to be on their way. The two lovers bid goodbye to the woman they shared. She has the same smile for both of them. And for a long time, she watches them recede in the distance and disappear, going where?

They have reached the Swiss border. Now they must get past the guards to reach the other side. Avoiding the patrols, they reach their goal by a narrow trail, but a lone guard stands in their way.

This guard is no formidable adversary. He is bearded, and his beard appears to be white. It was a strange fate which pulled him from his large family and brought him to this remote corner of the world to play sentry . . .

But they must get past. Maréchal has his revolver in hand. The German has put down his revolver to warm his hands. He takes a long drink from his canteen. Maréchal cannot bring himself to shoot him. He tries to give the gun to Dolette. Dolette refuses: "The old guy looks like my uncle, a mechanic . . ."

A branch snaps, the German seizes his gun and turns toward our heroes. Maréchal aims; two shots and the German falls. The way is clear.

By dawn Maréchal and Dolette are in Switzerland. In bad shape. They are dying of hunger. On the road, where they can now walk during the day, a little girl comes along. She is carrying a beautiful loaf of bread. They steal it from her. And the girl, astounded, looks on through her tears as these two bearded, filthy, unsightly men bite ravenously into the golden crust.

Now free, at ease, the two men chat seated on the edge of the road. Surely the war will be over by the end of the year? They will have to celebrate the adventure they have just survived and the new peace. They will celebrate Christmas at Maxim's! The Maxim's, where neither of them has been, about which Boïeldieu used to talk incessantly. They swear to meet there on December 25, 1918. They will reserve a table eight months in advance.

December 25, 1918. The first Christmas since the peace. Maxim's in the euphoria of the early days of the victory. The room is bursting with officers from all the Allied armies. Splendid, dazzling women . . . With all the commotion and joy, a Christmas like no other . . . But in the center of the room, which is jammed, why this empty table? "Reserved," the sign says.

Where is Maréchal? Where is Dolette?

Before The Rules of the Game:

An Interview with Jean Renoir

●

In the January 25, 1939, issue of Pour Vous, *Jean Renoir explained to Marguerite Russot his plans for the scenario of* The Rules of the Game.

François Truffaut

A TALK WITH JEAN RENOIR

The director of *Grand Illusion* and *The Human Beast* will write the story and the screenplay, direct, and act in his new film: *The Rules of the Game.*

"I'm leaving Tuesday," Jean Renoir said to me the other evening. "So if you want to talk a little, come see me before then."

He greets me with a smile:

"Tomorrow we leave," he says. "I have to finish the screenplay for *The Rules of the Game,* and the work will go much better outside of Paris."

"Where are you going?"

"I don't know. Perhaps to Burgundy, or perhaps to the forest at Fontainebleu. After I start off in the car, I'll flip a coin."

A joke? Certainly not. Anyone who has the pleasure of

knowing Jean Renoir understands that this is exactly how it
will happen.

Why Jean Renoir is becoming a producer.
"So you're a producer now?"
"Oh, yes. If you're interested, I'll tell you why. First of all,
I prefer, when I have a good subject, to shoot right away, instead of going to explain it to the producers, which wastes time,
not to mention the fact that it can be dull. In addition, I will
not have to worry about the kind of thing that happened to *The
Human Beast:* having my film—good or bad, it doesn't make
any difference—mutilated on the grounds that the censor in
some country will not accept certain scenes.* Those who buy
or rent my film will know what they're getting. And I hasten
to add that I received a gracious welcome and a good deal of
encouragement from the distributors to whom I talked—not as
an antagonist, but as a friend naturally. The N.E.F. (La Nou-
velle Edition Française)—that's what I call my production
company—is directed by old friends. One will take care of sales.
Another will be in charge of casting. Another will be executive
producer, and the fourth, André Zwoboda, will help me with
the direction. The five of us get along like the five fingers of a
hand. I will make two films a year, and I'll be able to keep my
crew: de Bretagne, the sound engineer; Bachelet, the cameraman; Lourié, the designer; and the others . . .
"In *The Rules of the Game,* for which I have conceived
the scenario, I will do the dialogue and the shooting script. I'll
also play a major role."
"Just what will *The Rules of the Game* be like?"
"A precise description of the bourgeois of our age. I want to
show that for every game, there are rules. If you don't play according to them, you lose."

His great love for women.
"But what I want to convey in this film is my great love
for women," Renoir continues. "To do this, I have to show
* *The Human Beast* was produced by Robert and Raymond Hakim. F.T.

men, men who talk about women, who say everything that can be said about them.

"My heroine will be Christine, a woman of the world who is bored. The job of the women of the world is a dreary one. Christine is the daughter of a great orchestra conductor from Salzburg. This Stiller was a kind of Toscanini. A young baron (he doesn't have a name yet, so let's call him just 'baron') brings Stiller to Paris, then marries his daughter. Later, old Stiller dies, but Christine has long ago changed her life: she, who was once her father's collaborator, has become just another Madame X, the rich wife who gives receptions . . . and who looks desperately for something to overcome her unhappiness . . ."

"Christine has children?"

"No, because then her life would be different . . ."

A woman must work or be a mother.

"In our age, there are two possibilities for a woman: work, have a career which occupies her, or spend her time wiping baby's bottoms. Without one or the other she will always be unhappy, unfulfilled . . ."

"Who will play Christine?"

"Nora Gregor. Christine thinks that the solution to her problems is clear-cut. She thinks that everything is simple, as long as she follows her heart. But things are much more complicated than that."

"And who will play her husband, the baron?"

"Dalio."

"Did you say that he 'brings Stiller to Paris'?"

A lover of art who fancies people more than ideas; a romantic lover, a flirtatious chambermaid, and other matters.

"The baron is a patron of the arts. He became one more or less from idleness. The son of a very wealthy man, he is a member of a few boards of directors. He decides to take up the arts. But does he understand them? A little. For him, Stiller represents music. That is why he brings him to Paris. Later, when

Stiller dies, he loses his interest in music and turns to painting. In short, he fancies people more than ideas."

"Are there any other major characters?"

"Yes, there is a romantic lover, who will be played by Roland Toutain. Don't be surprised. I am sure that it is precisely the role for him. There will also be a chambermaid, married to Ledoux,* who has Carette the poacher for her lover."

"Who will play that part?"

"I don't know yet. Because I haven't decided if she will be tall and blond, or brunette and plump . . ."†

"And what role will you take yourself?"

"A failure. I would like to have been a musician, but I am too lazy. So I satisfy myself with being a music critic. And I give advice to everyone, which leads to the worst problems and the most impossible complications."

"How long will you be shooting?"

"About eight weeks, if I count the shooting on location in Sologne."

"And afterward?"

"Afterward . . . there will be the editing. I'm planning to present *The Rules of the Game* at the World's Fair in New York. And then? A little rest, before starting a new film."

* Fernand Ledoux was replaced by Gaston Modot. F.T.
† It turned out to be a small, plump blonde: Paulette Dubost. F.T.

An Early Scenario for
The Rules of the Game *(extracts)*

●

This early treatment of The Rules of the Game *is closer to Renoir's idea of the film at the time of the* Pour Vous *interview than to the final script, which can be found in its entirety in a volume of Simon and Schuster's Classic Film Scripts Series, or in an excellent summary by Claude Beylie in the Filmography of this book.*

If The Rules of the Game *is the most exciting of Renoir's films, the history of the film—before, during, and after its conception—is no less so and would undoubtedly be worth a whole book (along the lines of Lillian Ross's* Picture, *on the making of John Huston's* The Red Badge of Courage).

This extract from the early draft of the screenplay that we discovered stops before the great hunting scene, but it illustrates, in terms of details which were forgotten, abandoned, or modified, in terms of its differences with the final version, what Jean Renoir's intentions were.

François Truffaut

Prologue
The Paris Opéra. A great concert is being given by Paul Stiller. It was his friend Robert Monteux who convinced the great conductor to come to Paris and who financed this sensational performance. Monteux is very proud, and he accepts

the congratulations as if he had composed the music himself. Great enthusiasm from the audience. Monteux decides to follow up this triumph by asking for the hand of Christine, Stiller's daughter.

Conversation between Christine and André Cartier,* a flyer. André Cartier loves Christine, but he loves flying even more, and the young girl feels unable to enter into a world so foreign to her. She assists her father, and by marrying Monteux, a prominent antique collector but also a patron of music, she will not have to change her activities. Only one person is not enthusiastic about the marriage. It is Octave, forty-five years old, a friend of Stiller's for the past twenty-five years, an unsuccessful musicographer, who knows Christine like a daughter, having often stayed at Stiller's in Vienna, more or less sponging off him. He likes Monteux, but he likes Christine more, and he thinks that the newlyweds will not get along with each other for long because Christine is more intelligent and Monteux, despite all the money he has earned, is a fool. People make fun of him. But the marriage is set.

Scene I

At the airport. The "Marseillaise" fills the air and the crowd is enthusiastic. André Cartier has just landed, having smashed all the world aviation records. Description of the kind of insanity that takes possession of a euphoric crowd.

The most eminent public figures congratulate Cartier. The most beautiful women throw kisses to him. Finally he manages to reach his car. It is a beautiful automobile in which his chauffeur whisks him away. To get back to Paris he will have to take an extensive detour since the heavy traffic has blocked the direct route.

Scene II

Cartier reaches home. A lovely apartment with a view of the Palais-Royal. His chauffeur and servants succeed in pull-

* In the film André Cartier becomes André Jurieu. F.T.

ing him away from the crowd of admirers waiting in front of his door.

Finally he is home. His luxurious apartment is filled with flowers. Almost all of them come from stage and film actresses.

Exhausted, he lets his valet undress him. The telephone rings. It is his friend Octave, who had gone to meet him at the airport but was unable to get near him. He is calling from a nearby bar. Cartier tells him to come up right away.

Cartier's first question to Octave is, "Was she at the airport?" She, we realize, is a woman whom Cartier must love very much. Octave replies that she was not there because it is "her day." Tea, cocktails, petits fours, important people, etc. Impossible to miss such a ceremony, even to watch a friend's spectacular triumph.

Cartier tells his friend of his definite intention to declare his love to the woman in question. Octave tells him that he is wrong and that he does not have a chance. He knows Aline* well because she is his goddaughter. Her father, Colonel de Brienne, was his best friend. They were in the war together. But Aline is a very proper person, who agreed loyally and without enthusiasm to marry her husband and who will probably remain faithful to him.

André is not discouraged by his friend's warnings. He picks up the telephone and calls Aline to make a date with her for the next day.

Then, exhausted, he starts to go to sleep. Octave rouses him for an instant to announce that he is going to spend the night. He doesn't have a cent right now, and he has just been kicked out of his hotel. André acquiesces, and Octave, as he prepares himself a generous Scotch and soda, announces that he is going to get his suitcase.

* Between the prologue and this second scene the heroine has changed names as well as fathers and husbands, but she is still the same woman who will finally be called Christine (Nora Grégor) in the film. F.T.

Scene III

The next day. We are at Aline's. The women are having a party. Aline's husband, Robert Dunoyer, is at work. He is a successful lawyer. He is very wealthy and very busy. The husbands of all these women are important people either in industry or business. In reality, all these men lead completely separate lives, and their wives see rather little of them. The principle behind all this is that the men of a certain milieu have wives in the same way they might have collections of paintings, or stables of race horses, or beautiful automobiles.

What can such a woman of the world do, if she has no children? If she does not want to die of boredom, have her mind stultify, or sink into pettiness, she has only one recourse: to take a lover.

Other outlets are mentioned: religion, charity work, music.

A lover is better. It is a far more spirited enterprise, and from the point of view of the husband, the taking of a lover by the wife is a means of extending and strengthening one's social ties.

The world is made up of clans which elbow and fight their way toward material success, and it is in the interest of the members of these clans to be united by strong bonds. One must only remember to keep up appearances and to observe the rules of the game.

The rules of the game infuriate Aline, and she insists that if she ever loved anyone but her husband, she would not hesitate to give herself to him without thinking about it. At this point a visitor is announced, and Aline leaves her friends.

Scene IV

It is André Cartier, who following up his telephone call of yesterday, has come to declare his love.

He has prepared a long speech on the way over, but once in the presence of the young woman he no longer knows what to say. Aline starts by congratulating him on his exploit and then puts him at ease by telling him that she knows very well what he wants to tell her.

Before his flight they had seen each other several times, and one evening at a party he had even spoken to her very tenderly and she had let him go on. But now she tells him that the secret rendezvous in a bachelor's apartment, however elegant, and the series of lies and hypocrisies that such an undertaking involves are not for her. He protests the purity of his intentions. Then if his intentions are pure, he must want to take her away and settle down with her. She imagines the hostility that would arise between her husband and him. Perhaps the two would fight a duel? She would be the heroine of a public scandal. But she does not feel at all cut out for such a role. She has a husband who satisfies her very well, and she is quite happy as she is.

André cannot believe that she really loves her husband, a remarkable but authoritarian and self-centered man.

For one thing, if Aline had really wanted to rebuff him strongly, why had she let him make advances before, and why had she almost encouraged him?

Aline mentions the natural flirtatiousness of women. Does it constitute a promise just to allow a man to say pleasant things to you?

André still insists. He is jealous of everyone who approaches her. He is jealous of her husband. He wants to have her for himself.

She ends the conversation by telling him that she is very flattered to be loved by a hero, by a great man whom she respects more than anyone in the world, but that love is out of the question. Friendship, companionship, camaraderie, as much as he likes, but no more. He leaves, crushed, and she goes back to the room where her friends are waiting for her.

Scene V

Looking out the window, one of Aline's friends sees Cartier walking away. She realizes what Aline's visit must have been about. Immediately all the ladies, not without a certain jealousy, congratulate Aline on her brilliant catch. They suppose that she too has found a pleasant arrangement without compromising her position and that, in spite of what she says, she, like the others, observes the rules of the game.

Scene VI

André rejoins Octave, who has been waiting for him not far from Aline's on a path in the Bois du Boulogne. He tells him of his failure. Octave becomes furious and declares that nothing in the world works, because people are not well matched.

The person he loves most in the world is Aline. Her father was his best friend. Even now he is inconsolable over his death. When she was little her mother neglected her, and it was he who took her out and entertained her. Thursdays he would pick her up at the convent and take her to the theater, the movies, or simply to the merry-go-round. He would like to see her happy, and he deplores her marriage with this ridiculous lawyer. If she accepted him, it was only to rescue her mother from misery. On the other hand, he likes and admires André. And now he has become a national hero. These two would be a perfect couple.

But things will not work out that way naturally. So Octave decides to make it his business. The union of André and Aline will henceforth be his goal in life, and as he leaves his friend he swears to dedicate himself to this mission.

Scene VII

At Dunoyer's. The end of a business lunch. Except for Aline, there are only men. At first they talked of Dunoyer and Aline's departure in a week or so on a hunting trip; otherwise the conversation is entirely about business. Aline is bored. Dunoyer is informed that Octave is asking for him. Irritated, Dunoyer asks his wife to take care of this dubious character, whose role in Aline's life he himself has taken over since his marriage. Aline agrees and goes to receive Octave.

Scene VIII

Aline greets Octave in a way which makes it clear that she does not share her husband's sentiments. She rushes to him enthusiastically and asks him what he wants. He is a little embarrassed because he would have preferred to ask Dunoyer. What he wants is simply to come and stay at the home of his goddaughter. Right now there are money problems; he has been kicked out of his hotel. All this is temporary. It is just a matter of weathering a few bad days, but he would like, even for such a short period, to avoid sleeping under bridges. Aline is very amused at the idea that her old godfather has not changed, that he is just as crazy and carefree as ever. She kisses him affectionately, and without giving it another thought, leads him to a room and starts to unpack his things.

As she arranges the contents of his suitcase in a wardrobe, Aline reproaches Octave vigorously for not having asked her for money. But Octave points out that if he had money he would feel obliged to pay his hotel bill, and that would not please him at all.

He is a little worried about how Dunoyer will take his arrival in the house. But she reassures him. Dunoyer himself arrives, surprised by his wife's prolonged absence. He looks unpleasantly at Octave, but Aline reminds him of a promise he made to her during their engagement that he would give her a room in which she could put up anyone she wanted. Rather gracelessly, Dunoyer assents and goes back to his guests.

Continuing to arrange his things, Aline suggests a rendezvous at lunch the day after next. Until then she is the prisoner of the inexorable schedule of her dreary life: dinner at an embassy, a golfing date, etc.

Scene IX

So it is two days later that Françoise,* Robert, and Octave are brought together over lunch. This first meal is rather awk-

* Aline turns into Françoise, but it is still Christine! F.T.

ward, and to enliven the conversation Françoise proposes a game of Philippine* to Octave.

Françoise reminds her husband of the story of the guest room which she had been promised during their engagement. She congratulates herself on this arrangement which enables her to receive Octave. Robert asks Octave to what he owes the honor of his visit. Octave explains that it is because he is out of money. Great theorizing about the sanctity of familial relations, and then he starts to talk about parasites. In Octave's perverse view, it is Robert who is the parasite, not him.

The conversation about games has taken place previously between Octave and Françoise. The audience must understand quickly the nature of the ties which unite the young woman and her old friend. One might follow the remark about parasites with one about appearances. For example, many people are parasites without appearing to be so, but they are in that they perform jobs created for no real purpose except to provide them with a livelihood. One can imagine, for example, that the legal profession—judges, lawyers, and others—have deliberately complicated the society with their absurd laws simply to justify their existence. Another example: one can imagine a doctor who has no customers conceiving the idea of persuading rich families to engage him to check their diets. Everyday he would stop by their kitchens and check the menus, comparing them to yesterday's and tomorrow's and keeping track of the number of calories. After a short while this post would become indispensable, and rich families would not dare to think of living without such a specialist. In addition, the cooks would go along readily, out of respect for science.

Robert replies to Françoise and Octave in the same ironic tone, but being very busy, he has to leave. He is hardly gone when Françoise and Octave begin to play at chasing each other around the room. Suddenly Françoise stops. She asks Octave

* A French game, traditionally played for almonds. The winner is the first to say "Good morning, Philippine" to the other after a minimum wait. Trans.

why he has really come. She does not believe a word of his story about sleeping under bridges. He promises to tell her the real reason, if she will answer one question. She agrees. The question is: "Are you happy?" The young woman begins to cry, huddles in his arms, and confesses all the emptiness and boredom of her upper bourgeois existence.

Description of the dreary servitude which is the life of an upper-class woman.

At this moment, we hear the sound of the organ grinder in the street. Françoise opens the window, and Octave asks him to play a certain tune. There are several people standing around the organ grinder, among them a laborer who works in the neighborhood whose wife has just brought him a snack. They seem quite close as they listen happily to the music.

Françoise tells Octave that of course she can imagine the difficult life of these poor people, but that she would give anything to be in the place of this woman whose husband greets her with such appreciation.

The music continues. It is Octave's turn to explain himself. He asks for a reprieve until the next morning.

Scene X

The morning of the next day. Octave is still sleeping in the much-discussed guest room. Françoise wakes him to win the game of Philippine. She begins by taking away the bottles which crowd Octave's bedside table. He has been drinking heavily. Then she tells him that as her reward for having won the game, she is going to ask him to get married. After all, he has talent; what does he need to succeed? The opportunity to write in peace, free from financial worries. She has a friend with an independent income who would make an excellent wife. She would not make great demands on him and would never interfere with their beautiful friendship by feeling jealous. She is rich, and she knows how to cook. He would be sitting pretty, free to turn out one masterpiece after another. Octave agrees to meet the friend in question, on the condition that

Françoise agree to meet André and consider his proposition.

At last they have a basis for agreement, and it is decided to invite André to the hunting party at Sologne.

Octave continues with his propaganda, severely denigrating her husband and falsely portraying the impending meeting with André as a casual affair. After all, what does it amount to? An experiment. They are going to get to know each other. There's no commitment involved. In two weeks André will have forgotten her; she will be no more unhappy for having seen him, and will have avoided being unnecessarily cruel.

She agrees on the condition that Octave also come to the hunt. He tries to beg off because he loathes that type of thing, but in the end he gives in. Françoise leaves. Enter the chambermaid bringing breakfast. Mistaken identity scene between the chambermaid and Octave. Octave talks gaily about going off to Sologne to meet a lover. The chambermaid thinks this means her, since, while she is married to the gamekeeper, she is also the mistress of a poacher in the area.

This scene will have to be moved along by innuendo; for example, suggesting Françoise's unhappiness, to give everyone else an idea of what the situation is. The scene will end with Octave and the maid in perfect understanding.

Scene XI

At Sologne. All the guests are standing on the steps of the château around Dunoyer, Françoise, and Octave. They are very excited about the arrival of André, the great aviator, the national hero. They are puzzled that he has not yet arrived, particularly since an automobile company has given him its latest model sports car.

Octave, dubious, expounds his ideas on sports cars. He himself has an old four-cylinder Citroën; not too exciting, but it gets him where he's going on time. Françoise expresses her complete agreement and starts to ridicule André. Turnabout by Octave, who contradicts himself. His new line of argument is supported by the arrival of André.

Françoise is annoyed by the adulation with which André

is greeted. Octave does his best to assuage her. Brief description of the evening meal at which everyone talks about André's flight and about the hunt. Françoise finds it idiotic. André senses the young woman's reticence and is embarrassed. Octave tries to straighten things out.

After the meal the older men play Ping-Pong. André agrees to be a fourth at bridge. Françoise is occupied with her duties as mistress of the house. Octave jokes with the maid, and the gamekeeper, husband of the maid, comes to find out his orders for tomorrow.

Night.

We see the poacher coming out of the house of the gamekeeper's wife. The guard comes back from his duties at the same moment and fires on the poacher as he flees into the shadows.

A hallway on the second floor of the château. A door opens. The guests bustle about in their night clothes and go down to the foyer. The guard arrives and explains that the poacher has come again to steal pheasants. What audacity, just when the château is full of people. He tried to stop him. The poacher fired at him, and he fired back.

Dunoyer proclaims that this is intolerable, that such an act is larceny pure and simple. If it happens again he will organize a posse to track down the culprit. Everyone approves except Françoise and Octave, who couldn't care less, and André, who, noticing Françoise's attitude, prudently remains silent.

The excitement of this event having died down, everyone goes back to bed.

•

PART THREE

•

Filmography

FILMOGRAPHY

●

This filmography is probably the most complete to date, but it is not necessarily definitive or free from errors. Some directors are less formal in their working arrangements than others, and Jean Renoir is a man for whom the dividing line between comrade and collaborator is seldom clearly drawn. In a list of credits for *Toni*, for example, we find "Mechanics: Bébert." We will never know which Bébert, or for that matter, which mechanics.

Some people who observed the making of *A Day in the Country* remember a certain Italian errand boy named Luchino Visconti; others say he was in charge of costumes. The filmographers usually list him with the assistant directors, and Claude Beylie mentions him as an apprentice prop man. In any case, we know that Renoir was drawn to the young man and suggested he read *The Postman Always Rings Twice*, the novel which became the source of Visconti's first film, *Ossessione*, five years later.

Thus a crew assembled around Renoir is less a stratified team than it is a little group of friends. Renoir himself has suggested that one should organize films "like pranks: by surrounding oneself with good accomplices." That is why the credits can never be as definitive as for a Hollywood production.

The filmography which follows is essentially the one published in the Christmas 1957 issue of *Cahiers du Cinéma*. It was put together by André Bazin, who described it as "a preliminary effort for a work on Jean Renoir." (He was referring to this book.) Each list of credits is followed by interpretive notes written in 1957 by Jacques Doniol-Valcroze, Claude de Givray, Jean-Luc Godard, Louis Marcorelles, Jacques Rivette, Eric Rohmer, myself, and of course André Bazin. To these notes we have added unpublished texts by Bazin and (for the more recent films) Jean Douchet and Michel Delahaye. All the technical credits have been checked and completed by Janine Bazin, Claude Beylie, and Jean Kress, who also wrote the synopses.

This collective work does not pretend to be definitive. It remains open to addition and correction, as probably all work of this nature must.

FRANÇOIS TRUFFAUT

N.B. The filmography often gives the lengths of films in meters. There are approximately 27.4 meters to each minute of sound film, and 18.3 meters to each minute of silent film. A "reel" is about 305 meters, or 16.6 minutes at silent speed and 11 minutes long at sound speed. Trans.

Catherine, or *Une Vie sans Joie* (1924)

DIRECTOR: Albert Dieudonné
SCREENPLAY: Jean Renoir, from a story by Jean Renoir and Pierre Lestringuez
CAMERAMEN: Jean Bachelet and Gibory
SHOOTING: March-May 1924 at Gaumont Studios and on location at Cagnes-sur-Mer, St-Paul-de-Vence
PRODUCER: Jean Renoir
LENGTH: 1,800 meters
DISTRIBUTOR: Films Jean Renoir, then Pierre Braunberger (after 1927)
FIRST SHOWING: November 9, 1927, at the Max Linder

ACTORS: Catherine Hessling (Catherine Ferrand); Albert Dieudonné (M. Mallet); Pierre Philippe, pseudonym for Pierre Lestringuez (Adolph the pimp); Pierre Champagne (the younger Mallet); Eugénie Naud (Mme. Laisné); Oléo (a prostitute); Jean Renoir (the subprefect); Georges Terof (Gédéon Grané); Louis Gauthier (Georges Mallet)

Catherine Ferrand, a young servant girl in Nice, is in love with the tubercular son of her employer. The father is a solid citizen, the deputy from St-Paul-de-Vence. His political rivals see the affair between the son and the maid as an opportunity for an odious blackmail campaign, which forces Catherine to run away and take refuge in a railroad car. The car is on a siding, but a switchman's error sends it rolling toward a cliff. The son manages to stop the car in time and brings Catherine back to the house. But the political rivals resume their efforts, and she takes flight again. She goes to the city, where she falls into the clutches of a notorious pimp. After numerous and varied adventures she finds the son once again, and they live happily ever after.

Jean Renoir wrote and financed this film, which introduced Catherine Hessling to the screen. He also participated in the shooting under Albert Dieudonné's direction with the hope of learning the trade. Apparently the young backer did not find his director as sympathetic as he had hoped, judging by a rather imperious letter Dieudonné wrote to *Cinéa-Ciné* on January 5, 1926: "I am the only director of a scenario which I wrote from a story created by Jean Renoir . . . with my collaboration. Moreover, M. Jean Renoir was my backer and my pupil. I shall see by his future productions whether or not I should be satisfied with him."

Pierre Lestringuez, who wrote Renoir's first scenarios, plays the role of the pimp under the name of Pierre Philippe. He will appear frequently in Renoir's films, even playing several roles in one film, *Nana*, and showing up as a priest in *A Day in the Country*.

ANDRÉ BAZIN

La Fille de l'Eau (1924)

DIRECTOR: Jean Renoir
SCREENPLAY: Pierre Lestringuez
ASSISTANT DIRECTOR: Pierre Champagne
SETS: conceived by Renoir
DIRECTORS OF PHOTOGRAPHY: Jean Bachelet and Gibory
SHOOTING: summer 1924 at G.M. Films studios and on location at Marlotte, "La Nicotière" (Cézanne's estate), and the Bon Coin Café
PRODUCER: Jean Renoir; Maurice Rouhier in France, Films Renoir and subsequently Studios Films abroad
LENGTH: 1,700 meters, cut to 1,600 meters on its first release
RUNNING TIME: 1 hour 10 minutes
FIRST SHOWING: April 1925 at the Ciné Opéra
ACTORS: Catherine Hessling (Virginia Rosaert); Pierre Philippe, pseudonym for Pierre Lestringuez (Jef, Virginia's uncle); Pierre Champagne (Justin Crépoix); Maurice Touzé (Bouche, or La Fouine, the little vagabond); Georges Terof (M. Raynal); Mme. Fockenberghe (Mme. Raynal); Harold Lewingston (Georges Raynal); Henriette Moret (La Roussette, an aging bohemian); Charlotte Clasis (Mme. Maubien, the miller); Pierre Renoir (a peasant); André Derain (the owner of the Bon Coin Café); Van Doren (the leading man)

Virginia is cooking on a river barge. Her Uncle Jef is leading a horse along the tow path. Her father is busy on the boat. From the bank M. Raynal and his son Georges watch Virginia. They are amused and charmed. They take a picture. She makes a face at them.

Reaching down to get some water, the father slips and falls. When Virginia realizes what has happened, it is too late. The search for the body with poles and lanterns continues into the night. When the body is finally found, it is a horrible sight.

Later, the uncle has squandered his inheritance on drink. The barge is going to be sold. Virginia scolds her uncle. He tries to rape her. She hides under the bed—a fairly impressive scene which foreshadows *Toni*. Eventually, she escapes with her dog. She encounters a young gypsy, who takes her to the trailer where he lives with his mother.

The gypsy makes his living stealing and poaching fish. He laughs contemptuously when a local hick discovers and breaks his fish traps and swears angrily to ruin him for his thieving. The gypsy gets his revenge by setting fire to a haystack. The firemen come to put out the blaze, and the hick convinces them to punish the gypsy by burning down his trailer. Foreseeing the disaster, the mother and son have taken flight by the time an angry crowd of peasants (among them Pierre Renoir) arrive to confront a terrified Virginia. They set fire to the trailer.

Once again abandoned and frightened, Virginia lives like a wild animal. Raynal's son brings her things to eat. One stormy night, sleeping in the rain, Virginia has a nightmare: Dressed in a white veil, she is at the foot of a tree where her uncle is hanged. The hanged man descends from the tree and comes to life. The rope around his neck becomes a snake. She runs away and takes refuge on the branch of a tree, only to find her uncle and the hick. Next, she is trapped in a gallery of columns over which the faces of her uncle and the peasant are superimposed. A monster (a chameleon with wings and a little makeup) makes his way through the colonnade. Finally, she sees a door at the end of the gallery and escapes. On the other side of the door she finds Raynal's son, dressed as a knight and riding a white charger. He carries her off. (This sequence, shot in slow motion, contains several special effects—for example, a horse riding through the clouds—which prefigure the dream sequence in *La Petite Marchande d'Allumettes*.)

The storm over, M. Raynal discovers Virginia the following morning. He takes her to the mill, where the farmers will care for her. She recovers rapidly. A romantic stroll with the younger Raynal. He is too shy to declare his love.

Later, Virginia goes to town to do some errands and runs into her uncle, who has become a railwayman. He forces her to give him the money she has in her purse and demands that

she bring more. The same afternoon M. Raynal sends Virginia
to the village to pay the harness maker, and she gives the
money to her uncle.

The inevitable occurs. M. Raynal learns that the harness
maker has not been paid, and naturally he suspects Virginia.
Desperate, she decides to confess, but as she is going to M. Raynal's château, her uncle accosts her and intimidates her further.
Virginia cries out her hatred of her uncle, telling him he is
making her lose her only friend by turning her into a thief.
Luckily, M. Raynal happens to be on the other side of the wall
and hears the whole exchange. He leaps over the wall and
grapples with the despicable uncle. A fairly long fight scene on
the riverbank. M. Raynal finally manages to throw the uncle
in the water, and he swims off. All's well that ends well.

The theme of *Orvet* is already apparent in this first film.
The water is of course significant, as is the role of poaching.
There is a brief shot of the gypsy, up to his thighs in water,
holding a fish in his hand, which reminds me of a similar shot
of Zachary Scott in *The Southerner*.

Renoir's realism is already well developed. There is physical realism (nature, shot on location) and human realism
(close-ups of the peasants of Marlotte). The fire sequence reminds one of Stroheim—for example, the diabolical shot of
Pierre Renoir, seen through the tongs of his pitchfork.

The scenario is obviously melodramatic, but with some
very cruel elements. The only good characters are the Raynals.
Even the gypsies are not sympathetic.

ANDRÉ BAZIN

Nana (1926)

DIRECTOR: Jean Renoir
SCREENPLAY: Pierre Lestringuez, from the novel by Émile Zola,
    adapted by Jean Renoir
TITLES: Mme. Leblond-Zola

ASSISTANT DIRECTORS: André Cerf, Pierre Lestringuez (?)
SETS: Claude Autant-Lara, executed by Robert-Jules Garnier
COSTUMES: Claude Autant-Lara
DIRECTORS OF PHOTOGRAPHY: Edmund Corwin and Jean Bachelet
CAMERAMEN: Ralleigh and Gibory
ASSISTANT CAMERAMEN: Holski, Asselin, Perie
STAGE MANAGER: R. Turgy
SOUND: R. Turgy
EDITOR: Jean Renoir
SHOOTING: from the end of October 1925 to February 1926, on location in the Paris area (the race-track scene), at Montigny, and at the Gaumont studios in Paris and the Grunewald studios in Berlin
PRODUCER: Films Jean Renoir
DISTRIBUTOR: Aubert–Pierre Braunberger
LENGTH: 2,700 meters
FIRST SHOWING: Aubert Palace
ACTORS: Catherine Hessling (Nana); Jean Angelo (Count de Vandeuvres); Werner Krauss (Count Muffat); Raymond Guérin-Catelain (Georges Hugon); Jacqueline Forzane (Countess Sabine Muffat); Valeska Gert (Zoé, Nana's chambermaid); Harbacher (Francis, Nana's hairdresser); Pierre Philippe, pseudonym of Pierre Lestringuez, (Bordenave); Claude Moore, pseudonym for Claude Autant-Lara (FaucHery); Nita Romani (Satin); Jacqueline Ford (Rose Mignon); Pierre Champagne (La Faloise); René Koval (Fontan); Marie Prévost (Gaga); André Cerf ("Le Tigre"); Pierre Braunberger and R. Turgy (spectators at the Théâtre des Variétés)

Nana is an ambitious young actress. After some success in earthy roles, she suffers a total failure when she attempts to play a respectable lady. She decides to become a prostitute and is kept by a series of lovers, whom she more or less drives to suicide. She finally dies herself, of smallpox.

Nana is the first of his films which Renoir considers worthy of discussion. It cost exactly one million francs, and although fairly well received, it was a financial failure. It was the first of Renoir's films in which acting took predecence over the story and the plastic elements. It was made under the influence of

Foolish Wives, which accounts for the emphasis on the heroine's cupidity. This influence also explains why *Nana* is the only one of Renoir's films in which money plays an important role. The most original and personal element in the film is the parallel treatment of masters and servants. (Renoir will think back to *Nana* when he makes *The Rules of the Game* and *Diary of a Chambermaid*.)

Probably reacting against the stiffness of his preceding film, Renoir brings his characters close together in *Nana*, constantly shooting them in American-style two-shots. Only in the four very long dolly shots (for which he used the chassis of an old Ford) does one become aware of the splendor and the (partly illusory) size of the sets, designed by Claude Autant-Lara. There are various characteristic themes here: the love of spectacle, the woman who chooses the wrong vocation, the actress trying to find herself, the lover who dies of his sincerity, the distracted politician, the showman. In short *Nana* rhymes with *Eléna (Paris Does Strange Things)*.

FRANÇOIS TRUFFAUT

Renoir had financed Nana *himself, and its failure at the box office ruined him. He directed* Marquitta *to earn money while he was working on* Charleston *for his own pleasure.*

Charleston, or *Sur un Air de Charleston* (1926)

ALTERNATE TITLE: *Charleston-Parade*
DIRECTOR: Jean Renoir
SCREENPLAY: Pierre Lestringuez, from an idea by André Cerf
ASSISTANT DIRECTOR: André Cerf
DIRECTOR OF PHOTOGRAPHY: Jean Bachelet
MUSIC: Clément Doucet

SHOOTING: autumn 1926 (in a few days) at the Epinay studios
DISTRIBUTOR: Néo-Film
LENGTH: 600 meters, cut to 29 minutes
FIRST SHOWING: March 19, 1927, at the Artistic or the Pavillon (later the Palais Berlitz)
ACTORS: Catherine Hessling (the dancer); Johnny Huggins (the black explorer); Pierre Braunberger and Pierre Lestringuez (two angels). (Johnny Huggins was a famous tap-dancer in "La Revue Nègre" on the Champs-Elysées.)

Glaciers have descended on Europe and thrown it into disorder. A black scholar, who has come to explore the continent, discovers a savage white woman, who introduces him to the barbaric dances of the day, notably the Charleston. Needless to say, the woman is none other than Catherine Hessling, hips swaying and more provocative than ever. She emerges from the billboard column on which the scholar's flying ship has landed.

At the end of the film the elegant Negro invites the naked white woman to come away with him. A fur coat and an umbrella appear from a manhole. Equipped for the voyage, she climbs aboard the space ship with Johnny Huggins and they leave France, now *terra incognita*.

Because its humor was strictly burlesque, *Charleston* had no success at all, but what remains of its original 1,200 meters is zany, spontaneous, and very amusing. Taking advantage of the freedom the film gave them, Catherine Hessling and Johnny Huggins threw themselves into it wholeheartedly. Catherine Hessling's eroticism, evident in *Nana*, is here systematically exploited. It is not surprising that this orgy of thighs displayed by a dancer wearing nothing but panties and a half-open corset caused some scandal. Only the silent version survives, but apparently the film was once accompanied by some fine music written for it by Doucet.

FRANÇOIS TRUFFAUT

Marquitta (1927)

ORIGINAL TITLE: "Marcheta," from the name of a song by Saint-Granier

DIRECTOR: Jean Renoir

SCREENPLAY: Pierre Lestringuez, from an adaptation by Jean Renoir

SETS: Robert-Jules Garnier

DIRECTORS OF PHOTOGRAPHY: Jean Bachelet and Raymond Agnel

SHOOTING: winter 1926–27 at the Gaumont studios and on location at Nice (Moyenne Corniche)

PRODUCER: Artistes Réunis (Marie-Louise Iribe*)

DISTRIBUTOR: Jean de Merly

LENGTH: 2,400 meters, cut to 2,200 meters

FIRST SHOWING: September 13, 1927, at the Aubert Palace

ACTORS: Marie-Louise Iribe (Marquitta); Jean Angelo (Prince Vlasco); Henri Debain (the chamberlain, Count Dimitrieff); Lucien Mancini (the adoptive father); Pierre Philippe, pseudonym of Pierre Lestringuez (the manager of the casino); Pierre Champagne (a taxi driver)

The film itself has been lost, but three different accounts of it survive:

"A Russian prince has a particularly exasperating mistress. One day in front of the Barbès metro station he sees a Piaf-style street singer and says to his mistress: 'You are not irreplaceable. I'll bet that in a year I can make a star of that beggar.' He undertakes the project, but the street singer proves to be ten times more unbearable than the old mistress. She forces him to leave restaurants in the middle of meals and humiliates him so much and in so many ways that the prince finally throws her over and returns to his old lover, who takes him back with open arms."

This summary was dictated to me in 1949 by Pierre Les-

---

* La Société des Artistes Réunis was founded by Marie-Louise Iribe, sister-in-law of Pierre Lestringuez and at the time the wife of Pierre Renoir. F.T.

tringuez. André Bazin left a note which summarizes the film in a different way:

"A little street singer is noticed by a Russian prince, who takes her on as his protégée. This lower-class woman accustoms herself to the prince's elegant life style without difficulty, but her adoptive father, who has also been taken in by the prince, steals an enormous sapphire from their benefactor. The prince has the innocent Marquitta kicked out. The little singer becomes famous singing her street songs in elegant dance halls. One day she runs into the prince, who, having lost his fortune in a revolution, has joined a Russian dancing troupe. The stolen sapphire saves the prince from a life of misery and assures the happiness of the reunited lovers."

In his pamphlet *Jean Renoir*, published in the series *Albums Diapositives*, Claude Beylie tells the tale in yet a third fashion:

"The prince, the heir of Décarlie, falls for a little street singer on a trip to Paris. In spite of the warnings of his chamberlain, he goes off to the Riviera with her, where they live in high style. They cause a scandal at Cannes. The rest of the film is comprised of a series of adventures—the arrival of the singer's father (a crafty thief); an affair involving the dynastic legacy of the Soviet crown; the sudden return of the prince, fed up with the excesses of his mistress, to his native land; his exile following a palace revolution; their reunion in Nice; an automobile chase along the cliffs."

We know that to make the film Renoir had to construct a miniature of the Barbès metro station, which appeared life size when reflected in a mirror. The actors worked in front of the mirror. It was a variation of Abel Gance's "pictograph."

FRANÇOIS TRUFFAUT

Back on his feet, Renoir joined with Jean Tédesco, manager of the Théâtre du Vieux-Colombier, and set up a tiny studio in the attic of

the Theater. It was under these primitive conditions that he made
La Petite Marchande d'Allumettes.

La P'tite Lili* (1927)

DIRECTOR: Alberto Cavalcanti
SCREENPLAY: Alberto Cavalcanti, suggested by a 1900 song by Louis
    Branch
SETS: Eric Aes
DIRECTOR OF PHOTOGRAPHY: Rogers
EDITOR: Marguerite Renoir
MUSIC: Max de la Casinière (for the silent version†)
SHOOTING: 1927 at the Boulogne-Billancourt studios
PRODUCER: Néo-Film (Braunberger), Albatros (?), Armor (?)
LENGTH: 300 meters
FIRST SHOWING: October 1, 1927, at the Ursulines theater along with
    NJU by Paul Czinner
ACTORS: Catherine Hessling (La P'tite Lili); Jean Renoir (the
    pimp); Guy Ferrand (the singer); Roland Caillaux (the woman
    concierge); Eric Aes, Rogers, Dido Freire (silhouettes)

La P'tite Lili was shot in three days under cloudy skies in
an outdoor set at Billancourt. They were able to use the Paris
street set precisely because of the bad weather; no one else
wanted it. The idea of shooting the film through a sort of burlap
cloth provided the artistic justification for the dull gray photography.

* Renoir acted in this film and *Le Petit Chaperon Rouge*, both of which
were directed by Alberto Cavalcanti, the Brazilian-born director who was
associated with the French avant-garde at the end of the silent era, then
with the English documentarists for many years, and with the brief
flowering of the Brazilian cinema in the early 1950s. His films include
Rien que les Heures (1927), *En Rade* (1928), *Went the Day Well?*
(1942), *Simao o Caolho* (1952), *O Canto do Mar* (1954). Trans.
† Darius Milhaud produced a sound track for it in 1930 for the Festival
of Baden-Baden. This sound version was very successful in Germany, but
was never presented in France. F.T.

The title, taken from a popular song already twenty years old and forgotten when the film was made, was chosen because Catherine Hessling often sang such popular tunes. Among the other players were Renoir, Guy Ferrand, Roland Caillaux, Eric Aes, Rogers, Dido Freire (Cavalcanti's niece and the future Mme. Jean Renoir).

The film cost 7,100 francs. It had two runs at the Ursulines theater and was distributed throughout the world after Darius Milhaud added the sound track.

Apparently Jean Cocteau stormed out of the opening, furious that someone had had the bad taste to make fun of the song "La P'tite Lili."

ANDRÉ BAZIN

La Petite Marchande d'Allumettes (1928)

ORIGINAL TITLE: "La Petite Fille aux Allumettes," designed to avoid confusion with an American film starring Mary Carr which was released in Paris in 1926 under the title *La Petite Marchande d'Allumettes*

DIRECTORS: Jean Renoir and Jean Tédesco

SCREENPLAY: Jean Renoir, from the story by Hans Christian Andersen ("The Little Match Girl")

ASSISTANT DIRECTORS: Claude Heymann and Simone Hamiguet

SETS: Eric Aes

DIRECTOR OF PHOTOGRAPHY: Jean Bachelet

MUSIC: (added in 1930): a potpourri of Mendelssohn, Strauss, Wagner, etc.

ARRANGEMENTS: Manuel Rosenthal

SHOOTING: August 1927 to January 1928 at the Théâtre du Vieux-Colombier and on the sands of Marly

PRODUCERS: Jean Renoir and Jean Tédesco

DISTRIBUTOR: S.O.F.A.R.

LENGTH: 29 minutes (considerably cut from its original length)

FIRST SHOWING: March 31, 1928, at the Alhambra in Geneva and June 1928 at the Vieux-Colombier in Paris. (The original Paris run was interrupted and the film seized when Edmond Rostand's widow brought suit against the film makers for plagiarism. The second release, with a sound track added, took place in February 1930.)

ACTORS: Catherine Hessling (Karen, the little match girl); Manuel Raabi (the policeman and the Hussar of Death); Jean Storm (the rich young man and the cavalier); Anny Xells (Amy Wells?; the mechanical doll)

It is a cold winter's night in a distant northern city. A little girl dressed in rags and tatters tries in vain to sell her matches to passers-by hastening to the warmth of their homes. Knocked about, ignored, and a bit frightened by the watchful eye of a nearby policeman, she had sold nothing and dares not return to her squalid shanty. She falls asleep on the snow-covered ground beside a fence, and begins to dream . . .

She enters a toy store, where she recognizes one of the men from the street as the lieutenant commanding a platoon of wooden soldiers. The policeman is a jack-in-the-box dressed to look like the "Hussar of Death." Chased by the hussar, the little match girl and the lieutenant flee into the clouds. But Death has the last word. Karen comes slowly back to reality, but not to wake up. Passers-by gather around her frozen, lifeless body.

CLAUDE BEYLIE

La Petite Marchande d'Allumettes stands apart from the rest of Renoir's silent work. Its tragic fairy-tale subject and its fantastic technical effects place it, superficially at least, in the French avant-garde at the end of the silent era. It blatantly contradicts the fallacious notion of Renoir as essentially a realist. Still, his choice of subject seems to have been determined much less by the influence of an "avant-garde" expressionism than by his admiration for Andersen and his taste for rigging up special effects (cf. the metro scene in *Marquitta*).

La Petite Marchande gave Renoir his first opportunity to make a film indoors with panchromatic film. In order to do this, after consultation with the Philips Company, Renoir and Jean Bachelet decided to use supercharged lamps backed by metal reflectors. This technique—the forerunner of the modern floodlight—was to have an important future.

The film required the use of several special technical effects. Along with *Nana* it is probably the most interesting and instructive of Renoir's silent films. In spite of the avant-garde technique, however, *La Petite Marchande* has none of the expressionist dreaminess of some of the cinema of its day. Its technique is expressionist, but its style is impressionist. More precisely, it amused Renoir to superimpose impressionism on expressionism. The special effects were not created for the sake of fantasy but as ends in themselves, as games to amuse their inventor.

As for the style of acting and its general sensibility, they clearly derive directly from Chaplin. His influence is particularly noticeable in Catherine Hessling's acting and in the street scenes preceding Karen's dream.

ANDRÉ BAZIN

The "silly lawsuit" resulted in an order enjoining the showing of the film, but Renoir remained in the good graces of the producers by agreeing to make the kinds of military comedy and pseudo-historical film which were popular at the time (Tire au Flanc *and* Le Bled).

Tire au Flanc (1929)

DIRECTOR: Jean Renoir
SCREENPLAY: adapted by Jean Renoir, Claude Heymann, and André Cerf from the comedy by A. Mouézy-Eon and A. Sylvane
TITLES AND DRAWINGS: André Rigaud
ASSISTANT DIRECTORS: André Cerf and Lola Markovitch

SETS: Eric Aes

DIRECTOR OF PHOTOGRAPHY: Jean Bachelet

STAGE MANAGER: Pascal

SHOOTING: at Billancourt studios and on location at a military barracks at St-Cloud and at the Bois de St-Cloud

PRODUCER: Néo-Film–Pierre Braunberger

DISTRIBUTOR: Armor

LENGTH: 2,200 meters

FIRST SHOWING: December 1928 at the Electric

ACTORS: Georges Pomiès (Jean Dubois d'Ombelles); Michel Simon (Joseph Turlot, the servant); Fridette Fatton (Georgette, the soubrette); Félix Oudard (Colonel Brochard); Jeanne Helbling (Solange Blandin); Jean Storm (Lieutenant Daumel); Paul Velsa (Corporal Bourrache); Manuel Raabi (the adjutant); Maryanne (Mme. Blandin); Esther Kiss (Mme. Flechais); Catherine Hessling (the teacher [?]); André Cerf (a soldier); Max Dalban (a soldier); Zellas (Muflot); Kinny Dorlay (Lili, Solange's sister)

Jean Dubois d'Ombelles is a poet by profession, and he is not in the least looking forward to his imminent induction into the army. His aunt, Mme. Blandin, does her best to make things easy for him by pulling strings with Colonel Brochard and sending her servant, Joseph, along with him to training camp. Jean immediately becomes the butt of the classic barracks pranks, while Joseph, a gregarious soul and an enthusiastic womanizer, feels completely at home. The fiancées of these two young soldiers are also on the scene: Jean's, a capricious young lady, flirts with a dashing lieutenant; Joseph's, a sprightly waitress in the canteen, is everybody's sweetheart. Jean's instinctive eccentricities get him into a little scrape with the police. But he stands up heroically to adversity, and during a wild masquerade party, organized to celebrate the anniversary of the regiment, he and Joseph succeed in eliminating any vestiges of civil or military propriety still vaguely observed by the stunned gathering.

CLAUDE BEYLIE

This comedy by Mouézy-Eon and Sylvane has been brought to the screen on three different occasions, with Jean Bachelet as director of photography. A fourth version was made by Claude de Givray in 1961 with Raoul Coutard as cameraman.

If the film historians are to be believed, *Tire au Flanc* is nothing but a shabby vaudeville show of no interest whatever. If we are to judge by the enthusiastic reaction of contemporary audiences at the Paris Cinémathèque, however, it is one of the funniest films ever made in France and one of the greatest silent comedies.

Certainly *Tire au Flanc* is the Renoir film which owes the most to Chaplin. Quite probably, it in turn had considerable influence on Jean Vigo's *Zéro de Conduite*. Renoir's film is to life in the barracks what Vigo's is to life in boarding school. The structures—short sketches of eight or ten shots—are similar too. The arrival at the barracks, the inoculations, the tryout of the gas masks in the forest, are among the hilarious scenes. The film, which was obviously shot as rapidly as possible and was clearly completely improvised, is a masterpiece of "living cinema" in the tradition of Chaplin's *Shoulder Arms* and *A Night in the Show*.

The camera work in *Tire au Flanc* is a *tour de force*. Triumphing over technical limitations, the camera pivots, pans, spins around, pulling close-ups from crowd scenes, coming to a halt only when the two comrades fall exhausted to the floor. When the hilarity starts again, Renoir brings a new sketch to a quick climax in four or five shots.

There are few films in which the tension between a director anxious for movement and equipment with a tendency for static recording is so obvious, few films where the director's triumph over circumstances is so complete.

Michel Simon's mugging foreshadows some of the greatest faces in the French cinema, which will come in his creations of Bruel, Caussat, Boudu, and Père Jules.

FRANÇOIS TRUFFAUT

Note the extraordinary liberty with which Renoir, royally indifferent to verisimilitude, pushes situations to outrageous limits in *Tire au Flanc*. Keep in mind in particular the sequence à la Stroheim: Pomiès, in prison, glued to the window, his body against the wall like a great nailed bird. The gracefulness of this farcical appearance is incredible; meanwhile below in the courtyard the lieutenant and Pomiès's fiancée are kissing in the midst of a forest of men's trousers hung out on the lines to dry.

As for themes, note the "Cytherian" ending, which foreshadows the triumph of love in *Paris Does Strange Things*.

ANDRÉ BAZIN, manuscript notes

Le Tournoi, or *Le Tournoi dans la Cité* (1928)

DIRECTOR: Jean Renoir
SCREENPLAY: Henry Dupuy-Mazel and André Jaeger-Schmidt
ADAPTATION: Jean Renoir
ASSISTANT DIRECTOR: André Cerf
TECHNICAL ADVISER (for the cavalry): Colonel Wemaere
SETS: Robert Mallet-Stevens
COSTUMES: Georges Barbier
DIRECTORS OF PHOTOGRAPHY: Marcel Lucien and Maurice Desfassiaux
CAMERAMAN: J.-L. Mundwiller
STAGE MANAGER: Pierre Belmonde
EDITOR: André Cerf
SHOOTING: summer-autumn at the St-Maurice studios and on location at Carcassonne
PRODUCTION: Société des Films Historiques
PRODUCERS: M. de Maroussem and François Harispuru
DISTRIBUTOR: Jean de Merly and Fernand Weil
LENGTH: 2,400 meters, cut to 2,000
FIRST SHOWING: December 1928 at the Agora in Brussels and February 9, 1929, at the Marivaux in Paris
ACTORS: Aldo Nadi (François de Baynes); Jackie Monnier (Isabelle

Ginori); Enrique Rivero (Henri de Rogier); Blanche Bernis (Catherine de' Medicis); Suzanne Desprès (Countess de Baynes); Manuel Raabi (Count Ginori); Gérard Mock (Charles IX); Vivian Clarens (Lucrèce Pazzi, the Florentine); Janvier (the guard officer); William Aguet (the Master of the Horse); the dwarf Narval (Antonio, the jester); Max Dalban (Captain du Guet); and with the participation of the black cadre of Saumur

The action takes place in the South of France, where Queen Catherine de Medicis and Charles IX have come to try to smooth over the tensions between the Catholics and the Protestants. In honor of the queen, a tournament has been organized (despite the royal edict outlawing hand-to-hand combat).

The Protestant nobility is represented by the Countess de Baynes, who has lost her husband and her two sons in the war. Her only surviving son, François de Baynes, is a courageous fellow, but he is thoroughly profligate. In love with Isabelle Ginori, he provokes a duel with her father, in spite of the royal ban, and kills him.

Isabelle, however, is secretly engaged to Henri de Rogier.

Queen Catherine gives Isabelle in marriage to François de Baynes as a peace offering to the Protestants. François organizes a great Florentine-style engagement party. At the banquet Henri de Rogier appears to rescue Isabelle. The guards intervene, and de Rogier is wounded in the left arm and then taken to the queen. He resolves to decide the affair before God in the course of the tournament, which is set for the next day. De Baynes returns to the château, and Isabelle takes refuge in the apartments of the Countess de Baynes.

De Rogier is handicapped by the injury to his arm. He will fight under Isabelle's colors. Blades break at the third or fourth pass, and de Rogier is knocked from his saddle. Swordplay ensues on the ground. Meanwhile Lucrèce Pazzi (de Baynes's mistress), jealous of Isabelle, has denounced de Baynes as the man responsible for the death of Count Ginori. Soldiers break up the fight to arrest de Baynes. He defends himself to the death with his mace. Mortally wounded by a sword thrust through his breast plate, he is left alone on the battlefield. His mother runs from the sidelines to hear his last words. He begs her forgiveness and dies.

This résumé is sketchy because of the disastrous condition of the surviving copy of the film.

Le Tournoi is a little boring, but more because of the limitations of the genre than because of the filming, which is rather successful. The evocation of the period is by no means naïve, and the costumes in particular suggest that some serious historical research was done. The duels and the tournament are technically very well done.

As for the style, we noticed an attempt at realism and psychological depth which is rare in films of this type. The ambiguous character of François de Baynes is exceptionally well drawn. His mixture of vice and perfidy with the virtues of nobility is shown in an interesting fashion, and when he dies we find him quite sympathetic.

Perhaps even more noteworthy are the many details which reveal a desire to present realistically the violence and cruelty of the period: the duel, the blood from the sword wiped on Lucrèce's hair, eroticism and death. The conventional plot unfolds against a disturbing background of brutality.

Also interesting are the mundane details revealed beneath the military pomp and ceremony; for example, at the end of the film, when Lucrèce denounces François to Captain du Guet, the captain is still in his night cap.

ANDRÉ BAZIN

Le Bled (1929)
(*Le Bled* 1929)

DIRECTOR: Jean Renoir
SCREENPLAY: Henry Dupuy-Mazel and André Jaeger-Schmidt
ADAPTATION: Jean Renoir

TITLES: André Rigaud
ASSISTANT DIRECTORS: André Cerf and René Arcy-Hennery
TECHNICAL DIRECTOR: J.-L. Mundwiller
SETS: William Aguet
DIRECTORS OF PHOTOGRAPHY: Marcel Lucien and Morizet
CAMERAMEN: Boissey and André Bac
EDITOR: Marguerite Renoir
SHOOTING: February-March 1929 at the Joinville studios and on location in Algeria
PRODUCTION: Société des Films Historiques
DISTRIBUTOR: Mappemonde-Film
LENGTH: 2,400 meters
FIRST SHOWING: May 11, 1929, at the Marivaux
ACTORS: Jackie Monnier (Claudie Duvernet); Diana Hart (Diane Duvernet, Claudie's cousin); Enrique Rivero (Pierre Hoffer, the nephew); Alexandre Arquillère (Christian Hoffer); Manuel Raabi (Manuel Duvernet); Berardi Aïssa (the Algerian, Zoubir, friend of Pierre); Jacques Becker (laborer); Hadj Ben Yasmina (the chauffeur); M. Martin (Ahmed, the falconer); Mme. Rozier (Marie Jeanne)

The film opens with a series of documentary shots of Algeria as a prologue.

A young man (Pierre Hoffer) and a girl (Claudie Duvernet) meet on the boat to Algeria. He is broke and has come to try to wheedle some money from his uncle, Christian Hoffer. The girl is going to Algeria for the reading of her uncle's will. At the dock the young man meets an Arab, a comrade from his army days. The girl is met by her cousins, who are also vying for the inheritance.

The opening of the will, at the notary's office. Claudie is the sole heiress. Manuel Duvernet and his sister, Diane, leave.

Pierre Hoffer arrives at the house of his uncle, whom he thinks a peasant. That evening he comes down to dinner in a tuxedo, to the great amusement of the rest of those present, who are all wearing country clothes. Among those around the table: Jacques Becker.

The following day the uncle takes his nephew around to see the property. They walk on ground that his ancestors reclaimed from the marshes. The uncle, who has immediately realized the purpose of Pierre's visit, asks him outright how much he wants. Pierre suggests 100,000 francs. The uncle does not say no, but takes Pierre to the edge of the sea. It was here that the French troops landed in 1830. The event materializes in their imagination, and the two men, inspired by the memory of this historic event, march at the head of the landing troops. Then the tractors arrive (one thinks of Eisenstein's *General Line*). Finally the uncle announces that he will give Pierre the money on one condition: that he work at the farm for six months to learn the value of money.

A few days later Claudie, out horseback riding, asks directions from a laborer. It is Pierre. A storm comes up. They run for shelter. Declaration of love among the sheep and the shepherds. Pierre hurries to tell the good news to his uncle, who is not at all pleased. "You will go back to Paris as soon as she has sold her property," he predicts. The Arab friend appears, to tell Pierre that he is leaving for the south. His destination is near the place where Claudie has to go to inspect the land she has inherited. Pierre convinces his uncle to let him go with his friend, on the pretext that he is going to buy sheep from him.

Everyone is together again in the south. The Algerian friend organizes a gazelle hunt, to which he is going to invite Claudie and her cousins. Diane Duvernet decides that she would like to get rid of Claudie so that she can have the inheritance after all. She convinces her brother to set up an ambush. The chauffeur will help out in the scheme. While they are chasing a herd of gazelles, the chauffeur draws Claudie away from the rest of the group to pursue a single animal, which they end up killing. Claudie cries, upset by the cruelty of the hunt. The chauffeur suggests that they go rest at the oasis. It is there that Manuel, the murderous cousin, is waiting for them, having come directly in his car. He explains the situation to Claudie without beating around the bush: she must marry him or die. Claudie refuses; he takes her off in the car.

Meanwhile Manuel's sister has taken a fall from her horse. She is seriously injured. Feeling the need to unburden her conscience, she reveals her brother's plans to Pierre. Pierre and several other riders take off after Manuel.

Manuel's car has broken down at a ford, but he has continued into the desert on camelback with his hostage. It will be difficult for the horses to follow them in the sand. Pierre orders the falconers to send their birds after the camel. The falcons attack the beast and blind it. Manuel is obliged to give himself up. Pierre Hoffer brings back the girl.

An epilogue shows the engagement dinner at the farm. This time everyone is in evening clothes, and Pierre shows up dressed for work!

ANDRÉ BAZIN

Here is another commissioned work, taken in the same light spirit as *Le Tournoi*. Since the simplicity of the script gave him a good deal of latitude, Renoir took the opportunity to make an adventure film in the style of the American pictures he had enjoyed so much in his youth. *Le Bled*, following the healthy tradition of Douglas Fairbanks in his Triangle days, starts out as comedy, comes to a climax of high adventure, and turns toward the sentimental at the end. Pierre (Enrique Rivero) himself, the inexperienced and awkward fellow inspired at the last minute by a threat to his loved one, is reminiscent of Fairbanks. It is all carried off with verve, the more serious scenes being slipped in without breaking the rhythm: the traditional love scene (this time in the rain, among the shepherds) glistens already with a few droplets from *Le Fleuve;* and the punishment of the villain, blinded by the falcons, allows Renoir to let another, more pungent liquid flow: "this precious blood" which still obsesses him.

JACQUES RIVETTE

Le Petit Chaperon Rouge (1929)

DIRECTOR: Alberto Cavalcanti
SCREENPLAY: adapted by Alberto Cavalcanti and Jean Renoir from a
    story by Charles Perrault ("Little Red Riding Hood")
DIRECTOR OF PHOTOGRAPHY: Marcel Lucien (or René Ribaud?)
CAMERAMAN: Rogers
ASSISTANT CAMERAMAN: Eli Lotar
EDITOR: Marguerite Renoir
MUSIC (added later): Maurice Jaubert; words of the song "La Java
    du Loup" by Claude André Puget
SHOOTING: summer 1929 at Billancourt studios and on location at
    Bourbon Marlotte (property of Renoir) and Forêt de Fontaine-
    bleau
PRODUCTION: Jean Renoir
PRODUCER: M. Guillaume
FIRST SHOWING: May 14, 1930, at the Tribune Libre du Cinéma
ACTORS: Catherine Hessling (Little Red Riding Hood); Jean Renoir
    (the wolf); André Cerf (the notary); Pierre Prévert (a little
    girl); Pablo Quevedo (the young man); La Montagne (a
    farmer); William Aguet (an old Englishwoman); Viviane Clar-
    ens, Pola Illery, Mme. Nekrassof, Raymond Guérin (the sil-
    houettes)

A Sunday entertainment in the tradition of *Charleston*;
which is to say that Renoir's Sundays would be likely to terrify
any hapless weekend artists who might come around to set up
their easels on his property. More than a risqué tale, the aesthetic is that of debauchery or an orgy done à la Mack Sennett.
Renoir or Cavalcanti? The question is an idle one, or at least
it answers itself. Let us say that one held the camera while the
other ran in the buff after a rather scantily clad Catherine
Hessling. The character is a lusty cousin of the hussar in *La
Petite Marchande* who carries her off in a balloon by the seat
of her pants.

JACQUES RIVETTE

La Chasse à la Fortune, or La Chasse au Bonheur (Die Jagd nach dem Glück 1930)

DIRECTOR: Rochus Gliese (set designer of Murnau's *Sunrise*)

SCREENPLAY: Lotte Reiniger and Carl Koch, from an idea by Alex Trasser

SPECIAL EFFECTS: Théâtre d'Ombres and Lotte Reiniger

DIRECTOR OF PHOTOGRAPHY: Fritz Arno Wagner

MUSIC: Theo Mackeben

SHOOTING: late 1929 and early 1930 on location in Germany and at Toulon

PRODUCTION: Comenius Films

FIRST SHOWING: May 25, 1930, in Berlin at the Marmorhaus

ACTORS: Jean Renoir (a businessman); Bertold Bartosch (the peddler); Catherine Hessling (Fortune[?]); Mme. Jean Tedesco, Alexander Murski, Anny Xells (Amy Wells?)

La Chasse à la Fortune was apparently a film which used real actors along with silhouettes in the tradition of *ombres chinoises*. The director of the Théâtre d'Ombres, Lotte Reiniger, later collaborated with Renoir on *La Marsellaise* (the scene in the theater where the entertainer presents the royal family in silhouette).

A Frankfurt newspaper published an account of the film on May 30, 1930. The following is an extract from that report:

"*La Chasse au Bonheur* was presented at the Marmorhaus amidst much publicity. A parade of famous names: Lotte Reiniger wrote and directed, along with Carl Koch and Rochus Gliese. The principal actors are the French Jean Renoir and Catherine Hessling, the Russian Alexander Murski, and the American Amy Wells. An international group, and as a subject something right up to date: a mixture of a sound and a silhouette film."

JEAN KRESS

Renoir went for two years without filming. It was the advent of the talkie. On Purge Bébé *would be a sort of "test." Thanks to the success of this film, he was able to make* La Chienne *a year later. During the filming he was "pitiless and intolerable" and had numerous quarrels with his producers.*

On Purge Bébé (1931)

DIRECTOR: Jean Renoir
SCREENPLAY: adapted by Jean Renoir from a play by Georges Feydeau
ASSISTANT DIRECTORS: Claude Heymann and Pierre Schwob
SETS: Gabriel Scongnamillo
DIRECTORS OF PHOTOGRAPHY: Theodore Sparkuhl and Roger Hubert
STILL PHOTOGRAPHY: Roger Forster
SOUND: D. F. Scanlon
RECORDING: Western Electric
STAGE MANAGER: Gaillard
ASSISTANT: Gaillard
EDITOR: Jean Mamy
SHOOTING: quickly—the end of March 1931 at Billancourt studios
PRODUCTION: Pierre Braunberger and Roger Richebé
PRODUCER: Charles David
EXECUTIVE PRODUCER: Roger Woog
ORIGINAL LENGTH: 2,000 meters.
FIRST SHOWING: end of June 1931 at the Roxy
ACTORS: Marguerite Pierry (Julie Follavoine); Louvigny (Follavoine); Michel Simon (Chouilloux); Olga Valéry (Mme. Chouilloux); Nicole Fernandez (Rose); Fernandel (Truchet); Little Sacha Tarride (Toto)

A little domestic drama in the Follavoine household: baby Toto refuses to take his medicine, much to his mother's dismay, just as his father is about to receive an important visitor. The influential guest, M. Chouilloux, is to help M. Follavoine sell his unbreakable chamber pots to the army. Greeted brusquely by the frantic mother, offended by the obstreperous baby, apprised that the chamber pots do indeed break, and annoyed by the arrival of his coquettish wife, Chouilloux finally leaves in a huff.

CLAUDE BEYLIE

La Chienne (1931)

DIRECTOR: Jean Renoir

SREENPLAY: adapted by Jean Renoir and André Girard from a novel by Georges de la Fouchardière

DIALOGUE: Jean Renoir

ASSISTANT DIRECTORS: Pierre Prévert, Pierre Schwob, Jacques Becker (?), Claude Heymann(?)

SCRIPT GIRL: Suzanne de Troye

SETS: Gabriel Scongnamillo

DIRECTOR OF PHOTOGRAPHY: Theodore Sparkuhl

CAMERAMAN: Roger Hubert

ADVISERS (sound): Hotchkiss and Bell

SOUND: Joseph de Bretagne and Courme

RECORDING: Western Electric

STAGE MANAGER: Gaillard

EDITORS: Denise Batcheff-Tual under the direction of Paul Fejos (rough cut), Marguerite Renoir and Jean Renoir (final version)

MUSIC: song by Eugénie Buffet, "Sois Bonne, O Ma Belle Inconnue," sung by Toselli (at the piano) and "Malbrough S'en Va-t-en Guerre," sung by M. Simon

SHOOTING: summer 1931 at Billancourt studios and on location at Montmartre, Nogent(?), Avenue Matignon

PRODUCTION: Films Jean Renoir, later Braunberger-Richebé

PRODUCER: Charles David

EXECUTIVE PRODUCER: Roger Woog

ART DIRECTOR: Courme

DISTRIBUTOR: Braunberger-Richebé, then Europa-Film (C.S.C.)

LENGTH: 3,000 meters, cut to 1 hour 40 minutes

FIRST SHOWING: November 19, 1931, at the Colisée (preview at the Nancy)

ACTORS: Michel Simon (Maurice Legrand); Janie Marèze (Lulu

Pelletier); Georges Flammand (André Jauguin, called Dédé);
Magdeleine Berubet (Mme. Adèle Legrand); Gaillard (Sergeant
Alexis Godard); Jean Gehret (M. Dagodet); Alexandre Rignault
(Langelard, the art critic); Lucien Mancini (Walstein, the art
dealer); Courme (the colonel); Max Dalban (Bonnard, a col-
league of M. Legrand); Romain Bouquet (M. Henriot, Legrand's
boss); Henri Guisol (Amédée, the waiter at the café); Pierre
Destys (Gustave, the pal of Dédé); Jane Pierson (the concierge);
Argentin (the magistrator); Mlle. Doryans (Yvonne); Sylvain
Itkine (Dédé's lawyer); Colette Borelli (Lily, Lulu's friend)

As *Paris Does Strange Things* was a homage to Venus–
Ingrid Bergman, *The Golden Coach* a homage to Columbine-
Magnani, *Orvet* to the young Leslie Caron, so *La Chienne* was
made for Michel Simon.

Renoir, who excels at depicting the exceptional individuals
who sacrifice their comfort for their liberty, shows us here a
strictly ordinary Frenchman. Not only is Legrand a cashier, but
he has received an award reserved for the most faithful of employees. In this exemplary but dismal existence there is only
one means of escape: painting. When he encounters the possibility of adventure in the person of Lulu Pelletier, he is seduced
by the idea of the perfect model as much as by the tempting
flesh-and-blood of the woman. And if the little apartment
rented with stolen money gives him a place for his illicit trysts,
it will also be the home for his beloved paintings, so despised
by his wife.

An artist without knowing it and an assassin without
meaning it, Legrand will follow the example of his wife's first
husband and become a bum. The freedom of a good rogue is
better than the servitude of an *honnête homme*. Note that the
myth of *Simon–Boudu–La Chienne* was completed twenty years
later in Sacha Guitry's *La Vie d'un Honnête Homme*.

CLAUDE DE GIVRAY

After La Chienne, *Renoir acquired a reputation for being temperamental and, he says, he made "some infrequent and poor films." But this remark is unjust, and not only to* Madame Bovary.

La Nuit du Carrefour (1932)
(*Night at the Crossroads,* 1932)

DIRECTOR: Jean Renoir
SCREENPLAY: adapted by Jean Renoir and Georges Simenon from a novel by Georges Simenon
DIALOGUE: Jean Renoir
ASSISTANT DIRECTORS: Jacques Becker and Maurice Blondeau
SCRIPT GIRL: Mimi Champagne
SETS: William Aguet, assisted by Jean Castanier
DIRECTORS OF PHOTOGRAPHY: Marcel Lucien and Asselin
ASSISTANT PHOTOGRAPHER: Fabian
SOUND: Bugnon, Joseph de Bretagne
RECORDING: Western Electric
STAGE MANAGER: Gaillard
EDITOR: Marguerite Renoir, assisted by Suzanne de Troye, with the participation of Walter Ruttmann
SHOOTING: January-March 1932 or winter 1931–32 at Billancourt studios and on location at La Croix Verte à Bouffemont (at the intersection of Routes N 1 and N 309)
PRODUCTION: Europa-Films
PRODUCER: Jacques Becker
DISTRIBUTOR: C.F.C.
ORIGINAL LENGTH: 2,000 meters
FIRST SHOWING: April 18, 1932, at the Théâtre Pigalle
ACTORS: Pierre Renoir (Inspector Maigret); Georges Terof (Lucas, his assistant); Winna Winfried (Else Andersen); Georges Koudria (Carl Andersen, Else's brother, the jailer); Dignimont (Oscar); G. A. Martin (Grandjean); Jean Gehret (Emile Michonnet); Jane Pierson (Mme. Michonnet, Emile's wife); Michel Duran (Jojo, the garage attendant); Jean Mitry (Arsène); Max Dalban (the doctor); Gaillard (the butcher); Boulicot (a policeman); Manuel Raabi (Guido); Lucie Vallat (Mme. Oscar)

Three houses at an intersection in Avrainville: the undistinguished villa of the insurance agent, Michonnet, M. Oscar's garage, and an old home set back from the street belonging to two rich foreigners of Danish origin, Carl Andersen and his sister, Else.

Inspector Maigret, who has come to investigate the theft of Michonnet's car, finds the automobile in question in Andersen's carriage house, a dead man at the wheel. The victim is the diamond merchant Goldberg. Andersen, who denies any knowledge of the crime, is released for lack of evidence. The intersection is placed under twenty-four-hour surveillance. A car pulls to a stop in the middle of the night, a woman leans out, shots are heard, Mrs. Goldberg rolls dead to the street. The following night the mysterious assassin seriously wounds Andersen, as Maigret is questioning his beautiful and enigmatic younger sister. The inspector is not altogether insensitive to her charms. Suddenly she collapses into his arms. She has been poisoned and is only brought around with considerable difficulty. Giving her first aid, Maigret notices that Else has a small scar on her left breast—rather surprising on a girl of noble birth who claims to have led an uneventful existence in a Danish château.

Maigret gradually begins to solve the mystery after he happens upon a fight between Else and Michennet. Else has tried to kill Michennet, who is puny but spirited. In self-defense he has practically strangled her. The inspector learns that the woman who was passing as a rich heiress is really nothing more than a common prostitute, daughter of an executed murderer, and sought by the Danish police for various armed robberies. Carl Andersen is not her brother at all, but a respectable man who has fallen for her, helped her to escape, and married her in the hopes of making her go straight. But he underestimated her violent instincts. More at home with the local hoods than with her rich husband, it is she who set up the Goldberg murders, providing one of Oscar's mechanics with the gun.

JEAN KRESS

Renoir's most mysterious film. Perhaps an involuntary obscurity, since Jean Mitry lost three reels after the film had been shot and Renoir had to do without them, but mysterious all the same, to wit: characters from Dostoevsky in the sets from *Une Ténébreuse Affaire*. Maigret fans will say, "Of course, because Simenon = Dostoevsky + Balzac." I say that *La Nuit du Carrefour* proves that this equation is only true insofar as Renoir *verifies* it.

We are frightened by this strange and poetic film. It is a fear which is not quite fear and yet is nonetheless the justification for it. Moreover, Pierre Renoir/Maigret finds the solution to the problem before it has even been presented. And we finally understand the exclamation that Simenon puts in Maigret's mouth at the end of every case: "Why didn't I think of it sooner?" *Clair-obscur* is half *clair*. Thanks to Renoir, we realize this right away.

The shots which ring out in the night, the roar of a Bugatti racing after the smugglers (a brilliant sequence speeding through the streets of the slumbering village), the dazed or shady looks of the inhabitants of the godforsaken hamlet. Winna Winfried's English accent and her old-fashioned eroticism. Pierre Renoir's drooping falcon's eye, the smell of the rain and the fields soaked by the mist, every detail, every second of every shot, makes *La Nuit du Carrefour* the only great French detective movie—in fact, the greatest of all *adventure* movies.

JEAN-LUC GODARD

Chotard et Cie. (1932)

DIRECTOR: Jean Renoir
SCREENPLAY: adapted by Jean Renoir from a play by Roger Ferdinand
DIALOGUE: Roger Ferdinand
ASSISTANT DIRECTOR: Jacques Becker

SCRIPT GIRL: Suzanne de Troye
TECHNICAL DIRECTOR: Ralleigh
SET: Jean Castanier
DIRECTOR OF PHOTOGRAPHY: J.-L. Mundwiller
CAMERAMEN: Claude Renoir and R. Ribault
SOUND: Kalinowski
RECORDING: Tobis Klangfilm
EDITORS: Marguerite Renoir and Suzanne de Troye
PRODUCTION: Films Roger and Ferdinand
DISTRIBUTOR: Universal
ORIGINAL LENGTH: 2,125 meters, cut to 1 hour 23 minutes (?) or 1 hour 13 minutes
FIRST SHOWING: March 1933
ACTORS: Ferdinand Charpin (François Chotard); Jeanne Lory (Marie Chotard, François's wife); Georges Pomiès (Julien Collinet); Jeanne Boitel (Reine Chotard, Collinet's wife); Mme. Treki (Augustine, the maid); Max Dalban (an employee of Chotard, the grocer); Luis Tunc, or Tunk (the subprefect); Louis Seigner (the police captain); Dignimont (Julien's friend); Robert Seller (the police chief); Fabien Loris (a guest at the masquerade ball)

The masquerade ball with its revealing disguises and delightful mix-ups, the "resistible rise" of the captain of police, the narcissistic posing of the dancer-poet Pomiès in the seclusion of his room, Chotard's predictable metamorphosis (he dresses up as a *bourgeois gentilhomme* and then in fact becomes one; in other words, no one can escape his destiny, no one can refuse the role he has to play), a sort of simultaneous rejection of both Poujadism and what we would call today the spirit of protest, all this makes *Chotard et Cie.* a strangely deceptive film. It does not suffer from the "filmed theater" syndrome, but has the same high-spirited style which marks *Tire au Flanc* and *Boudu.* In short, the film seems to live up to Renoir's wish "to make something comparable to a nice American comedy."

CLAUDE BEYLIE

Boudu Sauvé des Eaux (1932)
(*Boudu Saved from Drowning*, 1967)

DIRECTOR: Jean Renoir
SCREENPLAY: adapted by Jean Renoir from a play by René Fauchois
ASSISTANT DIRECTORS: Jacques Becker and Georges Darnoux
SCRIPT GIRL: Suzanne de Troye
SETS: Jean Castanier and Laurent
DIRECTOR OF PHOTOGRAPHY: Marcel Lucien
CAMERAMEN: Jean-Paul Alphen and Asselin
SOUND: Kalinowski
RECORDING: Tobis Klangfilm
EDITORS: Marguerite Renoir and Suzanne de Troye
MUSIC: Raphael and Johann Strauss; flute, Jean Boulze; choir, Edourad Dumoulin; song "Sur les Bords de la Riviera" by Léo Daniderff (Danidoff?)
SHOOTING: summer 1932 at Epinay studios and on location at Chennevières, the Seine quais, and the Pont des Arts
PRODUCTION: Société Sirius
PRODUCERS: Jean Gehret and Le Pelletier
DISTRIBUTOR: Jacques Haik
ORIGINAL LENGTH: 1 hour 23 minutes
FIRST SHOWING: mid-November 1932 at the Colisée
ACTORS: Michel Simon (Boudu); Charles Granval (Lestingois); Marcelle Hainia (Mme. Lestingois); Séverine Lerczinska (Anne-Marie); Jean Dasté (the student); Max Dalban (Godin); Jean Gehret (Vigour); Jacques Becker (the poet on the bench); Jane Pierson (Rose, the neighbors' maid; Georges Darnoux (a marriage guest)

Disappointed by society, Boudu, a rather appealing Paris bum, has thrown himself into the Seine from the Pont des Arts. Lestingois, who runs a bookstore overlooking the river and claims various liberal views, saves Boudu and wants to reform him. But Boudu, bored by the bourgeois life, spends most of his time causing trouble. He scandalizes clients in the store, seduces the maid, and audaciously satisfies the repressed desires of Lestingois's wife at the very moment that the bookseller is receiving a medal for his bravery in saving Boudu. To "comply with the morality of the day" and "respect the laws of divine nature," Boudu is married to the spirited and obliging maid. It is too much for a congenital anarchist. The very day of the wedding Boudu escapes during an outing on the river, letting himself be carried away by the current. Society, shaken momentarily, can breathe easily again.

CLAUDE BEYLIE

Boudu is the archetypal hobo, the model for 99 percent of the real and would-be bums. If the type had not existed, Boudu would have invented it. He is a perfect specimen of the species. Seeing him for the first time, we can only express our admiration, much as Lestingois does when he spies him through his telescope. This perfectly natural being is also a perfect comedian, comedy being a natural thing. He could only have been created by a great actor. Renoir gives Michel Simon free rein; and, not having to worry about the acting, he is free to concentrate on filming. He uses his camera unerringly, whether shooting deep-focus scenes in Lestingois's apartment or filming the outing on the Marne. The use of liaisons (the trumpet), even though this technique is unfashionable now, has not lost any of its comic effectiveness. If Renoir lets Simon/Boudu wander around free, it is because he expects pleasant surprises from him. He does not want to restrict the actor any more than the character. Also, he discovers in Boudu too much of his own philosophy not to let him speak as he pleases. If "philosophy" is saying too much, we can say at least that Boudu has all the charming capital vices enumerated in Renoir's Album de Famille: lust, gluttony, hypocrisy, and above all, sloth, the famous laziness celebrated in entirely different terms in The River and Paris Does Strange Things. Only envy and avarice are missing, saved for The Diary of a Chambermaid.

With Boudu Renoir revealed a good half of himself in a single, clear stroke. The rest, timid and hidden, will take longer to emerge.

ERIC ROHMER

Madame Bovary (1933)
(Madame Bovary, 1934)

DIRECTOR: Jean Renoir

SCREENPLAY: adapted by Jean Renoir from the novel by Gustave Flaubert

DIALOGUE: Jean Renoir

ASSISTANT DIRECTORS: Pierre Desouches and Jacques Becker

SETS: Robert Gys and G. Wakewitch(?)

COSTUMES: Medgyes (Valentine Tessier's clothes by Mme. Cassegrain)

DIRECTOR OF PHOTOGRAPHY: Jean Bachelet

CAMERAMEN: Gibory and Claude Renoir

SOUND: Courme and Joseph de Bretagne

MUSIC: Darius Milhaud, "Le Printemps dans la Plaine"; Orgue de Barbarie, "Lucie de Lammermoor" (Donizetti)

SHOOTING: autumn 1933 at Billancourt studios and on location in Normandy (Rouen, Rys, Lyons-la-Fôret)

PRODUCTION: N.S.F. (Gaston Gallimard)

PRODUCER: Jaspar or Jaspard

EXECUTIVE PRODUCER: Robert Aron

DISTRIBUTOR: C.I.D. (Cie. Indépendante de Distribution)

ORIGINAL LENGTH: 3 hours 30 minutes, cut to 3,200 meters

FIRST SHOWING: January 4, 1934, at the Ciné Opéra

ACTORS: Pierre Renoir (Charles Bovary); Alice Tissot (Mme. Bovary, his mother); Valentine Tessier (Emma Bovary); Héléna Manson (the first Mme. Bovary); Max Dearly (M. Homais, the pharmacist); Daniel Lecourtois (Léon); Fernand Fabre (Rodolphe); Léon Larive (the prefect); Pierre Larquey (Hipollyte, the clubfoot); Florencie (Father Bournisien); Le Vigan (Lheureaux, the cloth merchant); Romain Bouquet (Master Guillaumin, the notary); Georges Cahuzac (old Rouault); Alain Dhurtal (the surgeon); André Fouché (Justin, the chemist); Georges de Neubourg (the marquis de Vaubyessard); Edmond Beauchamp (Binet); Robert Moor (the footman); Henri Vilbert (Canivet); Monette Dinay (Félicité); Marthe Mellot (Nicaise, the old woman); Maryanne (Mme. Homais); René Bloch (the coachman); and Pierre Bosy, Max Tréjean, Albert Lambert, Christiane Dor, Odette Dynès, and Paulette Elambert.

Flaubert's masterpiece is one of the five or six novels which most stubbornly defy adaptation to the screen. Renoir, without abandoning a strict fidelity to the dialogues and scenes from the novel (the original version, never shown, was over three hours long), does not let himself be intimidated by Flaubert's golden pen. Instead he concentrates on the characters, doing his best to help them realize a wish at least half-consciously conceived by their creator: to escape forever the confines of literature.

One consistent stylistic touch is used to check the novelist's dogmatic realism: perspective, in the material sense of the word. Strictly speaking, this does not mean the use of depth of field, as we have seen previously in *La Chienne* and *Boudu*, because the foregrounds in *Madame Bovary* are only fragments (furniture, window and door casements), while the essential action takes place in the background. These "frames within the frame" indicate (and the ball at Rouen affirms it beyond a doubt) that the heroes of the story are acting out a play for themselves that even the pangs of death cannot interrupt. The doors which close on the loge prefigure the final curtain of *The Golden Coach*.

For Renoir, Madame Bovary's syndrome is only another form of the uncertainty that will plague Camilla: "Where does the comedy begin? Where does life end?" Madame Bovary is real even when she is the most contrived, artificial even in her moments of truth. In her comportment everything is composed and stilted except those elements which are so basic as to be by nature beyond artifice: the quality of her flesh and her expression, which cannot lie, at least in front of the camera. With wonderful assurance Valentine Tessier reveals only those techniques of acting which can be imputed to the character of Emma Bovary. At a respectful distance, Pierre Renoir and Max Dearly follow her lead.

What was natural in 1850 is not natural in the twentieth century. *Madame Bovary* scrupulously takes notice of this fact, and everything—text, intonation, movement, behavior—combines to re-create the earlier reality. It may be said that in Renoir's other "period" films, from *The Lower Depths* to *Paris*, he opted consciously for an anachronistic style. But the roads that lead to Art and Truth are different, and it is the point where they cross which has always fascinated Renoir. Each perspective is true, each is false. They complement one another.

ERIC ROHMER

Madame Bovary, a misunderstood film, was also a commercial failure. Even so, Renoir got the opportunity, thanks to Marcel Pagnol among others, to undertake a project close to his heart: Toni, *which today appears as the glorious precursor of Italian neorealism. It is only fair to add that the Italians later credited Pagnol as much as Renoir. And Renoir himself declared in* Pour Vous, *"I consider Marcel Pagnol the greatest contemporary cinematic author."*

Toni (1934)
(*Toni*, 1968)

DIRECTOR: Jean Renoir
SCREENPLAY: Jean Renoir and Carl Einstein, based on research by Jacques Mortier suggested by a newspaper article
DIALOGUE: Jean Renoir and Carl Einstein
ASSISTANT DIRECTORS: Georges Darnoux and Antonio Canor
ASSISTANT: Luchino Visconti
SCRIPT GIRL: Suzanne de Troye
TECHNICAL DIRECTOR: Albert Ausouad
SETS: Léon Bourelly and Marius Brauquier
DIRECTOR OF PHOTOGRAPHY: Claude Renoir
CAMERAMAN: Roger Ledru
SOUND: Barbishanian, assisted by Sarrazin
RECORDING: R.C.A.
MECHANICS: Bébert
EDITORS: Marguerite Renoir and Suzanne de Troye
MUSIC: guitar and popular songs by Paul Bozzi

SHOOTING: summer 1934 on location in Martigues and at Marcel
    Pagnol's studio (Marseille) for several retakes
PRODUCTION: Films d'Aujourd'hui
PRODUCER: Pierre Gault
EXECUTIVE PRODUCER: E. Boyer
DISTRIBUTOR: Films Marcel Pagnol
ORIGINAL LENGTH: 1 hour 40 minutes, cut to 2,600 meters
FIRST SHOWING: February 22, 1935, at the Ciné Opéra and at the
    Bonaparte
ACTORS: Charles Blavette (Antonio Canova, called Toni); Jenny
    Helia (Marie); Celia Montalvan (Josepha); Edouard Delmont
    (Fernand); Andrex (Gaby); André Kovachevitch (Sébastian);
    Max Dalban (Albert); Paul Bozzi (Jacques Bozzi, the guitarist)

The film's prologue: "The action takes place in the South
of France, where nature, destroying the spirit of Babel, knows
how to bring the different races together."

Toni, a foreign worker, arrives in Martigues and soon be-
comes the lover of his young landlady, Marie. A few months
later he falls in love with a beautiful Spaniard, Josepha, who
lives with her father, Sébastian, at the home of their cousin,
Gaby. Toni's foreman, a greedy and lecherous boozer named
Albert, rapes Josepha in a ditch just as Toni has received per-
mission to marry her from the aging Sébastian. Albert marries
Josepha. She has his child and names Toni the godfather. After
Sébastian dies, Toni leaves Marie with the hope of convincing
Josepha to go off with him to start their life anew elsewhere.
Albert surprises Josepha as she is stealing all the money from
the farm in preparation for her escape. She kills her husband.
Gaby, who suggested the theft, disappears. Toni is discovered
by a gendarme as he is burying Albert's body. He confesses to
the murder, runs away, and is shot down by a man from the
town. Meanwhile Josepha has turned herself in.

Renoir likes to point out that *Toni*, shot entirely against
real backgrounds mostly with nonprofessional actors, is the first
neorealist film. In fact, what is striking about *Toni* is its dreamlike quality, the fantasy-like atmosphere surrounding the
rather ordinary drama. The *mise en scène* is entirely "in-

vented," and particularly disconcerting and primitive when compared to *La Chienne*, for example. One gets the impression that *Toni* was made in an improvised, even disorderly way.

The most remarkable thing about the movie is not the contrast of the characters of the two women but the delineation of the two distinct stages in the life of one woman, Josepha. Before her marriage to Albert she is a seductive tease, exciting, irresistible. Afterward, she becomes just another poor victimized woman, like Marie. The scene where Josepha, stung by a wasp, implores Toni to suck out the poison, *all* the poison, is unforgettable.

In every gesture of Max Dalban in the role of Albert one can recognize Renoir caricaturing himself as he directs his lookalike. *Toni* is one of the five or six most beautiful of Renoir's films, a tragedy in which the sun takes the place of Fate.

FRANÇOIS TRUFFAUT

The following year saw the first and only collaboration of Jean Renoir and Jacques Prévert. It turned out to be a very fruitful one. The Crime of M. Lange *marks a turning point in Renoir's work. It begins a period in which social preoccupations will color his films up to* The Rules of the Game *(not counting* A Day in the Country*). It was the time of the triumph of the Popular Front. Renoir "committed himself."* La Vie Est à Nous *was made to order for the Communist Party,* La Marseillaise *for the Confédération Générale de Travail. It was then that Renoir became "famous" to the mass audience and acquired an international reputation with* The Lower Depths, Grand Illusion, *and* The Human Beast.

Le Crime de M. Lange (1935)
(The Crime of M. Lange, 1964)

EARLY TITLES: "L'Ascension de M. Lange," "Sur la Cour," "Dans la Cour," "Un Homme Se Sauve"

DIRECTOR: Jean Renoir

SCREENPLAY: Jacques Prévert and Jean Renoir, adapted by Jacques Prévert from a story by Jean Castanier and Jean Renoir

DIALOGUE: Jacques Prévert and Jean Renoir

ASSISTANT DIRECTORS: Georges Darnoux and Jean Castanier

SCRIPT GIRL: Marguerite Renoir

SETS: Jean Castanier and Robert Gys, assisted by Roger Blin

DIRECTOR OF PHOTOGRAPHY: Jean Bachelet

CAMERAMAN: Champion

STILL PHOTOGRAPHY: Dora Maar

SOUND: Moreau, Louis Bogé, Loisel, Robert Teisseire (continuity)

RECORDING: the first Marconi sound track belonging to Vaison and Moreau

EDITOR: Marguerite Renoir

MUSIC: Jean Wiener and a song by Joseph Kosma, "Au Jour, le Jour, à la Nuit, la Nuit"

ORCHESTRA: under the direction of Roger Désormières

SHOOTING: October-November 1935 at Billancourt studios and on location in Paris–Le Tréport

PRODUCTION: Obéron

PRODUCER: André Halley des Fontaines

ART DIRECTOR: Marcel Blondeau

DISTRIBUTOR: Minerva

ORIGINAL LENGTH: 2,200 meters

FIRST SHOWING: January 24, 1936, at the Aubert Palace

ACTORS: Jules Berry (Batala); René Lefèvre (Amédée Lange); Florelle (Valentine); Nadia Sibirskaïa (Estelle); Sylvia Bataille (Edith); Henri Guisol (young Meunier); Marcel Levesque (the concierge); Odette Talazac (the concierge's wife); Maurice Baquet (their son, Charles); Jacques Brunius (M. Baigneur); Marcel Duhamel (a worker); Jean Dasté (a worker); Paul Grimault (a typesetter); Guy Decomble (a worker); Claire Gérard (the prostitute); Edmond Beauchamp (the priest in the train); René Génin (a customer at the inn at the border); Paul Demange (a creditor); Sylvain Itkine (Batala's cousin); Fabien Loris, Janine Loris, Bremaud, Henri Saint-Isles, Lupovici

Monsieur Amédée Lange works for Batala's publishing house, feverishly writing adventure novels which Batala publishes in a desperate attempt to escape bankruptcy. One day,

Batala leaves town to elude his creditors. Following a train wreck he is believed dead. His company, taken over and run cooperatively by the workers, begins to prosper. Lange has an idyllic love affair with Valentine, a laundress who lives in the courtyard and was previously Batala's mistress. Charles, the son of the concierge, is going to marry another of the laundresses whose baby by Batala is stillborn.

It is at this moment that the ignoble Batala, disguised as a priest, returns with the intention of resuming control of his company and dissolving the cooperative. Lange guns him down and runs away to Belgium with Valentine. Recognized by the peasants at the border, they are not turned in, thanks to Valentine's eloquent recounting of the events leading up to the murder. The film takes the form of a single flashback which is Valentine's story.

The Crime of M. Lange being an *unanimiste** work, this brief précis of the story does not do justice to the ensemble of the actors. Batala's secretary (Sylvia Bataille), the little laundry girl (Nadia Sibirskaïa), the concierge (Marcel Levesque), M. Meunier's son (Henri Guisol), the printers (Jean Dasté, Paul Grimault, Marcel Duhamel) all play important roles in the action.

The poetic force of the film seems to stem not only from the combined talents of Renoir and Prévert, but also from the disparity of its several intentions.

"Who paid when Estelle had her baby? The co-op! Who paid for Charles' doctor's fees? The co-op!" This bit of dialogue from the middle of the film reminds us of the authors' social intentions. Yet in spite of the perfection of the scenario, which emphasizes love as a social force, these polemical intentions remain in the background, simply because the characters are so vital and healthy. Here is another example of a phenomenon common in Renoir's work: in his concern for human truth, he creates a film which quickly enters into the realm of fantasy. Jules Berry plays an ignoble and treacherous Batala, but Prévert and Renoir have so much fun developing and fooling

* See footnote on page 45.

around with his character that he becomes a baroque figure, almost sympathetic in the complex machinations of his dark spirit. This petty publisher is suspiciously reminiscent of the film producers who plagued Renoir. Perhaps one of those who obliged him to make *On Purge Bébé* in four days?

Of all Renoir's films *M. Lange* is the most spontaneous, the richest in miracles of camera work, the most full of pure beauty and truth. In short, it is a film touched by divine grace.

FRANÇOIS TRUFFAUT

La Vie Est à Nous (1936)
(*People of France*, 1937)

DIRECTORS: Jean Renoir, André Zwoboda, Jean-Paul Le Chanois

SCREENPLAY: Jean Renoir, Paul Vaillant-Couturier, Jean-Paul Le Chanois, André Zwoboda, and others

ASSISTANT DIRECTORS: Jacques Becker, Marc Maurette, Henri Cartier-Bresson, Maurice Lime, Jacques B. Brunius, Pierre Unik

SCRIPT GIRL: Renée Vavasseur (called Ritou)

DIRECTORS OF PHOTOGRAPHY: Louis Page, Jean Isnard, Jean-Serge Bourgoin, A. Douarinou, Claude Renoir

EDITOR: Marguerite Renoir (à Aubervilliers)

MUSIC: the "Internationale"; Ronde des Saints-Simoniens, and songs of the Popular Front sung by the Chorale de Paris; songs of the Komsomol (by Shostakovich); "Auprès de Ma Blonde"; "La Cucaracha," hummed; choruses under the direction of Suzanne Conte

SHOOTING: at Francœur studios and on location in Porte de Montreuil, Marlotte

DISTRIBUTOR: Cinémas Associés

LENGTH: 1 hour 6 minutes

FIRST PUBLIC SHOWING: November 12, 1969

ACTORS: Jean Dasté (the teacher); Jacques B. Brunius (president of the Conseil d'Administration); Simone Guisin (a lady at the casino); Teddy Michaux (a Fascist); Pierre Unik (the secretary of Marcel Cachin); Max Dalban (Brochard); Madeleine Sologne (a factory worker); Fabien Loris (a worker); Emile Drain (old

Gustave Bertin); Charles Blavette (Tonin); Jean Renoir (the bistro owner); Madeleine Dax (a secretary); Roger Blin (a sailor); Sylvain Itkine (the bookkeeper); Georges Spanelly (the factory manager); Fernand Bercher (the secretary); Eddy Debray (the usher); Henri Pons (M. Lecocq); Gabrielle Fontan (Mme. Lecocq); Gaston Modot (Philippe, the Lecocqs' nephew); Léon Larive (the customer at the auction); Pierre Ferval (second customer); Julien Bertheau (René, unemployed engineer); Nadia Sibirskaïa (Ninette, René's friend); Marcel Lesieur (the garage owner); O'Brady (Mohammed, the North African); Marcel Duhamel (M. Moutet, a Volontaire National); Tristan Sevère (an unemployed worker); Guy Favières (the old unemployed worker); Muse d'Albret (?) (an unemployed working woman); Jacques Becker (the young unemployed worker); Claire Gérard (a bourgeois woman in the street); Jean-Paul Le Chanois (Little Louis); Charles Charras (a singer); Francis Lemarque (another singer). *In the final parade*: Vladimir Sokoloff, François Viguier, Yolande Oliviero, Madeleine Sylvain, and appearing as themselves: Marcel Cachin, André Marty, Paul Vaillant-Couturier, Renaud Jean, Martha Desrumeaux, Marcel Gitton, Jacques Duclos, Maurice Thorez, and the involuntary participation of Colonel de la Rocque.

The film was not approved by the censors, but it was nevertheless shown with great success before the war in neighborhood theaters. The audience did not pay at the entrance but instead subscribed to a short-lived program called *Ciné Liberté*, which was created especially for the occasion. The real commercial career of the film began in 1969 (probably thanks to the student-worker revolt of 1968) at the Studio Git-le-Cœur.

The film opens with a close-up of the faces of a man and a woman. The camera moves back to reveal their miserable living conditions. Political statements, read by Maurice Thorez, Marcel Cachin, and Jacques Duclos, follow. Renoir's style is evident in the camera work used for these opening scenes. The speeches are filmed as at the beginning of *The Lower Depths* when the minister is lecturing Jouvet: the camera wheels slowly around the speaker on a circular track. The procedure is the same for all three talks.

La Vie Est à Nous ends exactly like *Boudu*. The camera is in a ditch, shooting up at a parade of militants singing no longer "Sur les Bords de la Riviera," but the "Internationale." Among the "comrades" we recognize a few pals as well: Julien Bertheau, Itkine, Roger Blin, Gaston Modot, Brunius, Loris, Jacques Becker, and, for the first time on the screen, Madeleine Sologne, who was at the time the wife of A. Douarinou, one of the film's cameramen.

FRANÇOIS TRUFFAUT

Une Partie de Campagne (1936)
(*A Day in the Country*, 1950)

DIRECTOR: Jean Renoir

SCREENPLAY: adapted by Jean Renoir from the story by Guy de Maupassant

DIALOGUE: Jean Renoir

ASSISTANT DIRECTORS: Jacques Becker, Claude Heymann, Jacques B. Brunius, Yves Allégret, Henri Cartier-Bresson, Luchino Visconti (props)

SETS: Robert Gys

DIRECTOR OF PHOTOGRAPHY: Claude Renoir

CAMERAMEN: Jean-Serge Bourgoin, A. Viguier, Eli Lotar

SOUND: Courme(?) and Joseph de Bretagne

MAKE-UP: Gaidaroff

EDITOR: Marguerite Renoir (final version, Marinette Cadix, under the direction of Marguerite Renoir, assisted by Marcel Cravenne)

MUSIC: Joseph Kosma and Germaine Montero

ORCHESTRA: under the direction of Roger Désormières

SHOOTING: July-August 1936 on location near Montigny and Marlotte

PRODUCTION: Pierre Braunberger–Films du Panthéon

PRODUCER: Roger Woog

EXECUTIVE PRODUCER: Jacques B. Brunius

DISTRIBUTOR: Panthéon (1946)

ORIGINAL LENGTH: 1,232 meters, cut to 1,100 meters

FIRST SHOWING: May 8, 1946, at the Raimu

ACTORS: Jeanne Marken (Mme. Juliette Dufour); Gabriello (M. Cyprien Dufour); Sylvia Bataille (Henriette Dufour); Georges Darnoux (Henri); Jacques Borel, pseudonym for Jacques Brunius (Rodolphe); Paul Temps (Anatole); Gabrielle Fontan (the grandmother); Jean Renoir (old Poulain); Marguerite Renoir (the servant); Pierre Lestringuez (an old priest)

In *A Day in the Country* comedy is constantly dissolving into emotion: emotion before nature, emotion of the senses, romantic emotion. It is useless to consider the film as a short subject or as a pictorial film (even though at least three of Auguste Renoir's paintings are re-created in it: "La Grenouillère," "La Balancoire," and "Le Déjeuner des Canotiers"). Useless also to say that the movie is not complete. The various problems Renoir had to face, his indecision about the final length, the long time between the film's completion and its release, the loss of the first version to the Germans, the fact that the second version was edited in Renoir's absence, the exterior scene which was not shot and had to be replaced by a backdrop, the failure to shoot any of the studio scenes (for the boutique), all this finally does not affect the film in the slightest. Whether its director and producer know it or not, *A Day in the Country* was finished the day somebody wound the camera for the last time. Not a frame is missing.

The film is a romantic dialogue between Renoir and nature, a conversation now gay, now serious, at which de Maupassant is only a spectator. Nature responds to Renoir's love for her by cooperating with his filming: during a long scene in which the mother and the daughter are talking about spring ("a sort of vague desire . . .") a butterfly is flying back and forth between the two, darting in and out of the camera's range.

JACQUES DONIOL-VALCROZE

Les Bas-Fonds (1936)
(The Lower Depths, 1937)

DIRECTOR: Jean Renoir

SCREENPLAY: Eugène Zamyatin and Jacques Companeez, adapted by Charles Spaak and Jean Renoir from the play by Maxim Gorki

DIALOGUE: Charles Spaak and Jean Renoir

ASSISTANT DIRECTORS: Jacques Becker and Joseph Soiffer

SETS: Eugène Lourié and Hugues Laurent

DIRECTORS OF PHOTOGRAPHY: Fedote Bourgassoff (?) and Jean Bachelet

CAMERAMAN: Jacques Mercanton

SOUND: Robert Ivonnet

STAGE MANAGER: Koura

EDITOR: Marguerite Renoir

MUSIC: Jean Wiener, song (words by Charles Spaak) sung by Irène Joachim

SHOOTING: August-October 1936 at Eclair à Epinay studios and on location along the Seine (between Epinay and St-Denis)

PRODUCTION: Albatros–Alexandre Kamenka

PRODUCER: Vladimir Zederbaum

ART DIRECTOR: Alexandre Kamenka

DISTRIBUTOR: Les Distributeurs Français, S.A.

LENGTH: 1 hour 30 minutes

FIRST SHOWING: December 1936 at the Max Linder; awarded the Prix Louis-Delluc, 1936

ACTORS: Louis Jouvet (the baron); Jean Gabin (Pepel); Suzy Prim (Vasilissa); Vladimir Sokolov (Kostileff); Junie Astor (Natacha, sister of Vasilissa); Robert Le Vigan (the actor); Camille Bert (the count); Léon Larive (Félix, servant of the baron); Gabriello (the police chief); René Génin (the old man); Maurice Baquet (the accordion player); Lucien Mancini (owner of the outdoor café); Paul Temps, Henri Saint-Isles, René Stern, Sylvain, Robert Ozenne, Alex Allin, Fernand Bercher, Annie Ceres, Nathalie Alexieff, Jacques Becker (silhouette); Jany Holt (the prostitute)

The two masters of the silent cimena who impressed Jean Renoir the most and are in a way responsible for his vocation are Erich von Stroheim and Charlie Chaplin. Just as *Nana* was a friendly hello to the author of *Foolish Wives*, *The Lower Depths* is a knowing wink directed at Chaplin. Not only does the last sequence of *The Lower Depths* refer directly to *Modern Times*, but Junie Astor's acting is entirely inspired by Paulette Goddard, whom Renoir himself will have the opportunity to direct in *The Diary of a Chambermaid*.

It is clear what Renoir found attractive in Gorki's play. It is something we find throughout his films: a remarkable gallery of dissatisfied, fiercely individualistic, nicely revolutionary characters, more sociable than socialist, whose unusual situations allow us to experience, if not to judge, the human condition. For Renoir's characters live as they think, and they recreate in the midst of their dissatisfaction a community more pure than ours.

CLAUDE DE GIVRAY

La Grande Illusion (1937)
(*Grand Illusion*, 1938)

DIRECTOR: Jean Renoir
SCREENPLAY: Charles Spaak and Jean Renoir
DIALOGUE: Charles Spaak and Jean Renoir
ASSISTANT DIRECTOR: Jacques Becker
SCRIPT GIRL: Gourdji (Françoise Giroud)
TECHNICAL ADVISER: Carl Koch
SETS: Eugène Lourié
COSTUMES: Decrais
WARDROBE: Suzy
DIRECTOR OF PHOTOGRAPHY: Christian Matras
CAMERAMEN: Claude Renoir, Ernest Bourreaud, Jean-Serge Bourgoin
STILL PHOTOGRAPHY: Sam Levin
SOUND: Joseph de Bretagne
MAKEUP: Raphaël
PROPS: Alexandre and Pillon
STAGE MANAGER: Pierre Blondy

EDITOR: Marguerite Renoir, assisted by Marthe Huguet (1958: Renée Litchtig*)

MUSIC: Joseph Kosma; the song "Si Tu Veux, Marguerite" (Fragson) by Vincent Telly and A. Valsien

ORCHESTRA: under the direction of Emile Vuillermoz

SHOOTING: winter 1936–37 at Billancourt-Eclair studios and on location in Alsace, in the vicinity of Neuf-Brisach in the Haut-Koenigsburg and the Colmar barracks

PRODUCTION: R.A.C. (Réalisation d'Art Cinématographique), Frank Rollmer, Albert Pinkovich, and Alexandre

PRODUCER: Raymond Blondy

DISTRIBUTOR: R.A.C. (1937), then Cinédis, Film-Sonor Gaumont

LENGTH: 3,542 meters

FIRST SHOWING: June 1937 at the Marivaux; awarded the prize for the best artistic ensemble at the Film Festival, Venice 1937†

ACTORS: Erich von Stroheim (von Rauffenstein); Jean Gabin (Maréchal); Pierre Fresnay (de Boïeldieu); Marcel Dalio (Rosenthal); Julien Carette (the actor); Gaston Modot (the engineer); Jean Dasté (the teacher); Georges Peclet (a French soldier); Jacques Becker (an English officer); Sylvain Itkine (Demolder); Dita Parlo (Elsa, the farm widow); Werner Florian, Claude Sainval, Michel Salina

I will not be so perverse as to belittle the one Renoir film which has been understood and loved by audiences all over the world. I think simply that *Grand Illusion* is just as good a film as *Toni*, or *The Lower Depths*, or *The Southerner* and that its great success is based, if not on a misunderstanding, on appearances. Everything that we love in Renoir's work (and everything for which he is usually criticized)—the changes of tone, the casualness, the frivolity, the digressions, the crudity, the preciousness—are all here. This time, however, they are serving a patriotic theme, and everyone knows that movies about

---

* The film was mutilated during its original distribution. In 1958 Renée Lichtig edited under Jean Renoir's direction a new version conforming to the master print. Renoir had an introductory sequence made for this version, in which he speaks a commentary he wrote for the occasion. F.T.

† It was banned before the war by the Fascists in Italy and was called by Joseph Goebbels "cinematographic enemy No. 1."

the war, the resistance, and prison escapes succeed automatically, be they baroque (*Open City*), lyrical (*J'Accuse*), pseudo-poetic (*Quelque Part en Europe*), literary (*La Bataille du Rail*), romantic (*Kanal*), comic (*Stalag 17*), intelligent (*Man's Hope*), demagogical (*Vivre en Paix*), abstract (*Un Condamné à Mort S'est Echappé*), or totally without interest (*La Dernière Chance*).

In short, any excess is permitted within the genre, and *Grand Illusion*, acclaimed by Roosevelt, Céline, and Field Marshal Goering, is no exception to the rule. Banned in Belgium by the minister Henri Spaak, brother of the co-writer, mutilated in Germany by Goebbels, who deleted all scenes in which the Jew is sympathetic, *Grand Illusion* was boycotted at the Venice Film Festival. Il Duce had the Grand Prix bestowed on *Carnet de Bal*. In France the critic Georges Altman protested against the movie's anti-Semitism.

The fundamental idea in this film, a concept which will reappear in *La Marseillaise* and of course in *The Rules of the Game*, is that the world is divided horizontally rather than vertically. Renoir explains very clearly that the idea of class should remain, all the more since certain classes disappear on their own. On the other hand, the idea of national boundaries, the source of all misunderstanding among men, should be abolished.

Another reason that this film is so popular is that it is one of the few Renoir pictures where psychology takes precedence over poetry. It is perhaps the least eccentric of all of Renoir's French movies.

FRANÇOIS TRUFFAUT

La Marseillaise (1937)
(*La Marseillaise*, 1939)

DIRECTOR: Jean Renoir
SCREENPLAY: Jean Renoir, with the collaboration of Carl Koch,

N. Martel Dreyfus, and Mme. Jean-Paul Dreyfus (historical consultants)

DIALOGUE: Jean Renoir

ASSISTANT DIRECTORS: Jacques Becker, Claude Renoir, J.-P. Dreyfus (J.-P. Le Chanois), Demazure, Marc Maurette, Tony Corteggiani; Lotte Reiniger (of the Théâtre d'Ombres)

SETS: Léon Barsacq, Georges Wakhevitch and Jean Périer

CAMERAMEN: Jean-Serge Bourgoin, Alain Douarinou, Jean-Marie Maillols, Jean-Paul Alphen, J. Louis

SOUND: Joseph de Bretagne, Jean-Roger Bertrand, J. Demede

RECORDING: Western Electric

STAGE MANAGERS: Edouard Lepage, Raymond Pillon, Barnathan, Veuillard, Henri Lepage, Decrais, Deffras

EDITOR: Marguerite Renoir, assisted by Marthe Huguet

MUSIC: Lalande, Grétry, Rameau, Mozart, Bach, Rouget de l'Isle, Kosma, Sauveplane

ORCHESTRA: under the direction of Roger Désormières

SHOOTING: summer-autumn 1937 at Billancourt studios and on location in Fontainebleau, Alsace, Haute-Provence, Antibes, Place du Panthéon

PRODUCTION: Société de Production et d'Exploitation du Film *La Marseillaise*

PRODUCERS: A. Zwoboda and A. Seigneur

EXECUTIVE PRODUCER: Louis Joly

DISTRIBUTOR: R.A.C. in 1938, Compagnie Jean Renoir since 1967

LENGTH: 2 hours 15 minutes

FIRST SHOWING: February 9, 1938, at the Olympia

ACTORS: *The court*: Pierre Renoir (Louis XVI); Lise Delamare (Marie Antoinette); Léon Larive (Picard, the king's valet); William Aguet (La Rochefoucauld-Liancourt); Elisa Ruis (Mme. de Lamballe); G. Lefebure (Mme. Elizabeth); Pamela Stirling, Genia Vaury (two servants)
Civil and Military officials: Louis Jouvet (Roederer); Jean Aquistapace (the mayor); Georges Spanelly (La Chesnaye); Pierre Nay (Dubouchage); Jaque Catelain (Captain Langlade); Edmond Castel (Leroux)
The aristocrats: Aimé Clariond of the Comédie Française (M. de Saint-Laurent); Maurice Excande (lord of the village); Zibral (M. de Saint-Méry); Jean Aymé (M. de Fougerolles); Irène Joachim (Mme. de Saint-Laurent)

The Marseillaise: Andrex (Honoré Arnaud); Charles Blavette, later Edmond Ardisson (Jean-Joseph Bomier), who replaced Blavette in the course of the shooting; Paul Dulac (Javel); Jean-Louis Allibert (Moissan); Fernand Flament (Ardisson); Alex Truchy (Cuculière); Georges Peclet (Lieutenant Pignatel); Geo-Dorlys (a Marsielle leader); Jo Lastry (Captain Massugue); Adolphe Autran (the drummer); Edouard Delmont (Cabri, the farmer)

The people: Nadia Sibirskaïa (Louison); Jenny Helia (the interpellant); Gaston Modot, Carette (two volunteers); Séverine Lerczinska (a farm woman); Marthe Marty (the mother of Baumier); Edmond Beauchamp (the priest); and Roger Pregor, Pierre Ferval, Fernand Bellon, Jean Boissemond, Blanche Destournelles, and Lucy Kieffer

Louis XVI is a regular fellow, not too upset by the fall of the Bastille. Marie Antoinette is beautiful, but something of a sourpuss. In the mountains, peasants aroused against the nobles are cooking their food over camp fires. In Marseille a voluntary batallion is organized to go up to Paris. Louis is interested in "this new dish," tomatoes. He does not like the "style" of this Brunswick fellow, but Marie Antoinette forces his hand. The militiamen from Marseille adopt the song of the Army of the Rhine: "Allons, enfants de la patrie . . ." (familiar tune). Louis against Marie Antoinette's wishes, approves of the new hygienic practice which consists of brushing one's teeth: "I will gladly attempt this brushing." The émigrés from Coblenz are discontented. The soldiers from Marseille have arrived in Paris and attacked the Tuileries Palace, crushing the Swiss guards. Tomorrow, Valmy . . .

Renoir, faithful to his principle of balance and careful to avoid the artifice and stiffness inherent in a period film with costumes and historic characters, succeeds perfectly in humanizing the thirty or so major characters in this neorealist fresco by using details from everyday reality. The dialogue of *La Marseillaise*, for example, is the richest in culinary vocabulary of any of Renoir's films; and real cuisine is echoed by the political potpourri. We are moved by the Swiss guards as much as by the troops from Marseille, by the emigrant courtiers as much as by the oppressed peasants. We note much nobility in the revolutionaries, much ingenuity and honesty in the nobles. Renoir serves up an entire world, where all causes are presented with the objectivity, generosity, and intelligence which mark all his work.

Renoir is above the struggle; he observes. *La Marseillaise* has more than anything the look of newsreels culled from the French Revolution. Only Renoir could make a film about cavemen and have it look like an authentic documentary!

FRANÇOIS TRUFFAUT

La Bête Humaine (1938)
(*The Human Beast*, 1939)

DIRECTOR: Jean Renoir
SCREENPLAY: adapted by Jean Renoir from the novel by Émile Zola
DIALOGUE: Jean Renoir
ASSISTANT DIRECTOR: Claude Renoir and Suzanne de Troye
SETS: Eugène Lourié
DIRECTOR OF PHOTOGRAPHY: Curt Courant
CAMERAMAN: Claude Renoir (senior) and Jacques Natteau
ASSISTANT CAMERAMEN: Maurice Pecqueux, Guy Ferrier, Alain Renoir (apprentice)
STILL PHOTOGRAPHER: Sam Levin
SOUND: Robert Teisseire
RECORDING: R.C.A.
EDITOR: Marguerite Renoir (railway sequences: Suzanne de Troye)
MUSIC: Joseph Kosma; "Le P'tit Cœur de Ninon," Italian song, hit in 1920
SHOOTING: August-September 1938 at Billancourt studios and on location in Gare St-Lazare, Le Havre and surroundings
PRODUCTION: Paris Film Production–Robert Hakim
PRODUCER: Roland Tual
DISTRIBUTOR: Paris Film

LENGTH: 1 hour 45 minutes, cut to 2,400 meters (Cinémathèque Française copy)

FIRST SHOWING: December 29, 1938, at the Madeleine (first run: 13 weeks)

ACTORS: Jean Gabin (Jacques Lantier); Simone Simon (Séverine); Fernand Ledoux (Roubaud, Séverine's husband); Julien Carette (Pecqueux); Jenny Halia (Philomène, Pecqueux's friend); Colette Régis (Victoire, Pecqueux's wife); Gérard Landry (the Dauvergne son); Jacques Berlioz (Grand-Morin); Léon Larive (Grand-Morin's servant); Georges Spanelly (Camy-Lamothe, Grand-Morin's secretary); Jean Renoir (Cabûche, the poacher); Emile Genevois and Jacques B. Brunius (farm hands); Marcel Perez (the lamp maker); Blanchette Brunoy (Flore); Claire Gérard (the traveler); Tony Corteggiani (the supervisor); Guy Decomble (the gatekeeper); Georges Peclet (railway worker); Charlotte Clasis (Aunt Phasie, the godmother); Marceau (a mechanic)

Engineer of the locomotive *La Lison*, Jacques Lantier, a hereditary epileptic, is infatuated with Séverine, the exceedingly young wife of the assistant stationmaster, Roubaud. Insanely jealous of the well-to-do Grand-Morin for having once seduced his wife, Roubaud has murdered him on the Paris–Le Havre run with the aid of Séverine. The crime, to which there were no witnesses, is attributed to a poacher. But Lantier, who was in the same car as the couple on the day of the crime, suspects Roubaud. He keeps quiet because of his love for Séverine, who has succumbed readily to his advances, even suggesting that he get rid of her husband, who oppresses and disgusts her. But it is she whom Lantier kills in a fit of insanity, after which he kills himself, leaping from the speeding train.

The film is preceded by a short passage taken from the text of Zola's work recounting Jacques Lantier's alcoholic heredity. This is followed by a portrait of the novelist.

If *The Golden Coach* is a triangle film and *The River* a circle film, then *The Human Beast* is a straight-line film. That is to say, it is a tragedy. Between the credits and the admirable sequence without dialogue of Gabin and Carette driving their locomotive, a signed photograph of Zola appears, along with a quotation from the novel: "Sometimes he had the feeling of suffering for all the fathers and mothers, for the generations of alcoholics who had rotted his blood." Jacques Lantier's fate is determined by a material, or rather physiological, destiny. The ancient gods would strike down the different branches of a genealogical tree with bolts of lightning. The modern gods have reserved a far more horrible fate for the Rougon-Macquarts*: they have spilled poison in their veins. The laws of heredity have been substituted for divine vengeance, but the forces of destiny remain the same.

"Jacques Lantier interests me as much as Oedipus Rex," wrote Jean Renoir in *Cinémonde* in 1938. "This train engineer carries a curse as heavy as that of any of the ill-fated Atrides."

Gabin in *The Human Beast*, like Claude Laydu in *Diary of a Country Priest*, like Humphrey Bogart in *In a Lonely Place*, carries his own drama, his own suspense, within him. His problem becomes clear to us in the first minutes of the film: Can Lantier's undermined constitution stand up to the test? From then on, every move he makes takes on added value for us: the way he eats, works, speaks, makes love, and stops making love. Love is Simone Simon, the most charming provincial coquette imaginable. She expresses herself in awkward clichés ("I have lived my whole life in this one minute") which are rendered insurpassably precious by the peculiar affectation of her voice. She is profoundly evil. She plays on the nerves of her lover like a cat with a ball of yarn. For that matter, she is a cat herself. In her first appearance we see her empathizing with a white Angora. In Renoir's mythology Simone Simon takes her rightful place between Catherine Hessling and Leslie Caron. No one has ever been more sensitive to the dangers of woman.

CLAUDE DE GIVRAY

* Rougon-Macquart: the French family whose various branches and generations provide the characters for the twenty-novel cycle by Zola which includes *The Human Beast*. Trans.

After The Human Beast, *a new direction in Renoir's work, a desire to get away from naturalism toward a more classical, more poetic genre: the great experiment of* The Rules of the Game, *which Renoir fully expected to be controversial for a long time.*

La Règle du Jeu (1939)
(*The Rules of the Game,* 1951)

EARLY TITLES: "Les Caprices de Marianne," "Fair Play," "La Chasse en Sologne"

DIRECTOR: Jean Renoir

SCREENPLAY: adapted by Jean Renoir with the collaboration of Carl Koch

DIALOGUE: Jean Renoir

ASSISTANT DIRECTORS: Carl Koch, André Zwoboda, Henri Cartier-Bresson

SCRIPT GIRL: Dido Freire

TECHNICAL ADVISER (for the hunt): Tony Corteggiani

SETS: Eugène Lourié, assisted by Max Douy

COSTUMES: Coco Chanel

DIRECTOR OF PHOTOGRAPHY: Jean Bachelet

CAMERAMAN: Jacques Lemare

ASSISTANT CAMERAMEN: Jean-Paul Alphen and Alain Renoir

STILL PHOTOGRAPHER: Sam Levin

SOUND ENGINEER: Joseph de Bretagne

RECORDING: Western Electric

MAKEUP: Ralph

STAGE MANAGER: Raymond Pillon

EDITOR: Marguerite Renoir, assisted by Marthe Huguet

MUSIC: Mozart ("Danse Allemande"), Monsigny, Sallabert, Johann Strauss ("La Chauve-Souris"), Saint-Saëns ("Danse Macabre"), Chopin ("Valse"), arranged by Roger Désormières and Joseph Kosma

ORCHESTRA: under the direction of Roger Désormières

SHOOTING: February-March 1939 at Joinville studios and on location in La Motte-Beuvron, Château de la Ferté Saint-Aubin, Aubigny, the surroundings of Brinon-sur-Sauldre

PRODUCTION: N.E.F.

PRODUCER: Claude Renoir (senior)

ADMINISTRATOR: Camille François

DISTRIBUTOR: N.E.F., Gaumont, Les Grands Films Classiques (1965), Marc Gelbart (in foreign countries)

LENGTH: 1 hour 53 minutes, cut to 3,006 meters or 1 hour 52 minutes

FIRST SHOWING: July 7, 1939, at the Aubert Palace and the Colisée

PARIS REVIVAL: cut version, September 26, 1945, at the Impérial Cinécran

REVIVAL OF INTEGRAL VERSION: April 23, 1965, at the Studio Médicis

ACTORS: Marcel Dalio (the marquis Robert de La Chesnaye*); Nora Grégor (Christine, La Chesnaye's wife); Roland Toutain (André Jurieu); Jean Renoir (Octave); Mila Parely (Geneviève de Marrast); Odette Talazac (Charlotte de La Plante); Pierre Magnier (the general); Pierre Nay (M. de Saint-Aubin); Richard Francœur (M. La Bruyère); Claire Gérard (Mme. La Bruyère); Anne Mayen (Jackie, Christine's niece); Roger Forster (the effeminate guest); Nicolas Amato (the South American); Tony Corteggiani (Berthelin); Paulette Dubost (Lisette, Christine's chambermaid); Gaston Modot (Lisette's husband, Schumacher, the gamekeeper); Julien Carette (Marceau, the poacher); Eddy Debray (Corneille, the steward); Léon Larive (the cook); Jenny Helia (the servant); Lise Elina (the radio reporter); André Zwoboda (the engineer from Caudron's, the airplane company); Camille François (the announcer); Henri Cartier-Bresson (the English domestic)

The pilot André Jurieu has just accomplished a stunning feat: he has crossed the Atlantic in twenty-three hours. He hopes in doing this to capture the love of a wealthy bourgeoise, Christine de La Chesnaye. But she has not even come to the airport to meet him. Piqued, he childishly proclaims his disappointment over the radio.

After Jurieu has tried to kill himself in his car, Octave, a mutual friend, in the hope of fixing things up, gets the La Chesnayes to invite Jurieu to a hunting party they are giving at their estate, La Colinière, in Sologne. Meanwhile Robert de La Ches-

* In the credits the name is spelled La Cheyniest. F.T.

naye, while touring his estate, engages the services of the poacher Marceau, despite the vigorous objections of his gamekeeper, Schumacher. During the hunt Christine discovers by chance that her husband has been having an affair with one of their friends, Geneviève de Marrast, just at the moment when he is in the process of breaking it off for good. Hurt, she allows Jurieu and another suitor, M. de Saint-Aubin, to declare their love. It is during a costume party that the masks will fall. Jurieu fights with Saint-Aubin, then La Chesnaye with Jurieu, while in the midst of the guests the gamekeeper Schumacher pursues Marceau with a gun, having surprised him making advances to his wife, Lisette.

A brief lull follows. Jurieu and Robert, reconciled, discuss Christine's future. Marceau consoles Schumacher, who has been fired. Meanwhile Octave, who has long been secretly in love with Christine and feels his hour has come, declares his love and convinces her to go away with him. But Schumacher, confused by a double change of costume and urged on by Marceau, kills Jurieu. Before their disbelieving guests, who have gathered at the sound of gunfire, La Chesnaye and his wife go back into the house trying to maintain their dignity.

CLAUDE BEYLIE

At the time of its release: the greatest failure of Renoir's career. In retrospect: his masterpiece! Renoir had aimed too high, for although many of his films have taken a few years to find a broad audience, this one for decades was appreciated only by film buffs. Two re-releases of *The Rules of the Game*, in 1945 and 1948, met with complete commercial failure before the great success of the release of the definitive version in 1965.

After *Grand Illusion* and *The Human Beast*, Renoir was tired of psychology in movies. Undoubtedly he felt the need to show instead of to analyze, to move instead of to touch. As he explained in an interview, the "rules of the game are those which must be observed in society if one wishes to avoid being crushed." The problem is that of sincerity in love: "Dishonesty is a garment which weighs heavily . . . Earnest people are so boring . . . I would like to disappear, my friend, to see nothing more . . . Then I would no longer have to try to figure out what is good and what is bad; because you see in this world there is one awful thing, and that is that everyone has his reasons . . . I am suffering, and I can't stand that." These comments suggest the tone of the film and show how important the moral element is.

The nine principal characters of *The Rules of the Game* have a sentimental problem to resolve, and since the film shows them on the eve of a crisis, we will see them behave at their worst. The only sincere person—the pilot André Jurieu—awkward in an unfamiliar milieu, unleashes a tragicomedy in which he is the only victim, precisely because he has not followed the rules of the game.

Ludicrous skeletons, the characters of *The Rules of the Game*, viewed at a critical moment in their decay, forsake the farandole ("It's nice, but it's a little old-fashioned") for a *danse macabre* which assaults the senses. For the ostensible purpose of a party, they are led to disguise themselves, which is to say, to take off their masks. The shadows of the masters and servants mingle and merge in an image of a sybaritic life style which cannot last: man is imperfect, he is a born liar, and besides, "If love is endowed with wings, is it not to flutter?" *The Rules of the Game* is a profoundly pessimistic film, a bitter and prophetic carnival in which friendship itself is exposed as just another empty game. "I don't believe in much, but I am beginning to believe in friendship," La Chesnaye confides to Jurieu, speaking of Octave, their mutual friend, who at that very moment is getting ready to carry off the woman they both love.

After the hunt Christine de La Chesnaye follows through a small spyglass the activities of a little squirrel perched on the branch of a tree. Then comes a tribute to the optics of the glasses, which one would like to think was meant as well as a definition of the camera and a homage to the cameraman: "Its lens is so powerful and it is so well made that, from a short distance, you see all of the animal's private life, without his knowing it."

Personally, I cannot think of another film maker who has put more of himself—and the best of himself—into a film than Jean Renoir has into *The Rules of the Game.*

FRANÇOIS TRUFFAUT

As everyone knows, The Rules of the Game *was a total commercial failure. A few days after the opening, Renoir agreed to make a dozen important cuts, mostly affecting the role of Octave, which he played himself. Shortly afterward the film was withdrawn from circulation because it was anticommercial and thought to be "demoralizing" for the French public. Renoir left for Italy to make* La Tosca, *but Italy's entry into the war prevented him from going beyond the first five shots.*

La Tosca (1940)

DIRECTOR: Carl Koch (Jean Renoir: five shots)
SCREENPLAY: Luchino Visconti, Jean Renoir, and Carl Koch from the play by Victorien Sardou
DIRECTOR OF PHOTOGRAPHY: Ubaldo Arata
EDITOR: Gino Bretone
MUSIC: Giacomo Puccini
ORCHESTRA: under the direction of Fernando Previtali
MUSICAL ARRANGEMENT: Umberto Mancini
SONGS: Mafalda Favero and Ferruccio Tagliavini
SHOOTING: winter 1939-40 at the Scalera studios, Rome, and on location in Rome, Palais Farnèse, and Château St-Ange
PRODUCTION: Scalera-Films
LENGTH: 2,500 meters
FIRST SHOWING: September 30, 1942, in Paris at the Lord Byron (dubbed version)
DISTRIBUTOR (in France): Scalera-Films
ACTORS: Imperio Argentina (Tosca); Michel Simon (Scarpia); Rossano Brazzi (Mario Cavaradossi); Massimo Girotti (Angeloti); Clara Candiani, Adriano Rimaldi, Juan Calvo, Nicolas Perchicot

Or the aborted masterpiece. No, there is no point in denigrating Carl Koch, whose direction, whether or not it follows Renoir's plan, is consistently elegant and sometimes has great allure. He is responsible for those broad movements in the chapel and the final execution scene, where a brief dolly shot, following Tosca to where she throws herself into the void, leaves us face to face with Rome. There is nothing in this well-crafted work which is unworthy of the opening, but neither is there anything which attains the enchantment of the five or six opening shots of nocturnal riding, where the magical baroque spectacle suddenly comes to life. Under the close scrutiny of the camera the stones seem to pulsate and merge with the movement of the drama. *La Tosca* is no longer a realistic opera; it is reality become opera.

JACQUES RIVETTE

Jean Renoir returned to Paris, then, after a few jobs for the Army Film Service, left for the South of France. A long letter from Robert Flaherty convinced him to come to America. In the autumn of 1940 he embarked for the United States, bringing with him Dido Freire, Cavalcanti's niece and the script girl on The Rules of the Game, *whom he married shortly thereafter, not realizing that his divorce from Catherine Hessling, although recognized in America, was not valid elsewhere, and thus becoming an unintentional bigamist. (Renoir has often wrongly been credited with a third wife: Marguerite Mathieu, one of the best French editors, known as Marguerite Renoir, who lived with him from 1935 to 1940.) Renoir divides his American period in two: "a few short efforts in the big studios and some others with the independents." Hired by Fox, he chose a Dudley Nichols script and made* Swamp Water.

Swamp Water (1941)

DIRECTOR: Jean Renoir
SCREENPLAY: Dudley Nichols, from a story by Vereen Bell

SETS: Thomas Little
COSTUMES: Gwen Wakeling
DIRECTORS OF PHOTOGRAPHY: Peverell Marley and Lucien Ballard
MAKEUP: Guy Pearce
ART DIRECTOR: Richard Day
EDITOR: Walter Thompson
MUSIC: David Rudolph
STUDIO: 20th Century–Fox
LOCATIONS: Georgia
PRODUCTION: 20th Century–Fox
PRODUCER: Irving Pichel
ASSOCIATE PRODUCER: Len Hammond
DISTRIBUTOR: 20th Century–Fox
LENGTH: 2,535 meters (86 minutes)
FIRST SHOWING: December 5, 1941
ACTORS: Dana Andrews (Ben Ragan); Walter Huston (Thursday
    Ragan); John Carradine (Jesse Wick); Eugene Palette (Sheriff
    Jeb MacKane); Ward Bond (Tim Dorson); Guinn Williams
    (Bud Dorson); Virginia Gilmore (Mabel MacKenzie); Walter
    Brennan (Tom Keefer); Anne Baxter (Julie); Mary Howard
    (Hannah); Russell Simpson, Joseph Sawyer, Paul Burns, Dave
    Morris, Frank Austin, Matt Williams

The vast swampy expanses of Georgia have often attracted
adventurers and hunters, many of whom have never returned.
A group of men—Ben Ragan, his father. Thursday, Jesse Wick,
Sheriff Jeb MacKane—have gone to search for two hunters lost
in the swamp; after many hours of searching, they decide that
their friends must be dead. Later, when Ben's dog, Trouble, runs
off into the swamp in pursuit of a deer, Ben jumps into his boat
and heads out to look for him, despite the warnings of his father
and the pleas of his fiancée, Mabel.

Watching out for crocodiles, Ben penetrates farther and
farther into the swampy forest. He leaves his boat and sets out
on foot. When night falls he lights a fire and sets up camp.
While sleeping, he is struck on the head with a club.

Coming to, he finds himself, along with his dog, prisoner of
an escaped criminal, Tom Keefer. Tom refuses to let them go,
fearing that Ben will reveal his hideout, but after Ben nurses

him and cures him of a snake bite, Tom agrees to let him leave on condition that he take care of his daughter Julie, who lives in the same town.

On returning, Ben finds Jesse Wick making advances to his stepmother in his father's absence. Later Ben argues with his father and leaves the house to live on his own.

Mabel is furious about his prolonged absence, and when Ben lets it slip that he was not alone in the swamp, she becomes suspicious.

Jesse continues to pursue Hannah when Thursday goes off hunting. Although she resists him, Jesse is not discouraged. One day he has to take off in a hurry when Thursday comes back unexpectedly. Hannah refuses to reveal the name of her visitor for fear that Thursday will kill him, and distrust begins to grow between them.

Seeing Ben taking Julie to a dance, Mabel becomes angry. After Ben refuses to see her, she guesses that he is hiding someone in the swamp, and that it is Tom Keefer.

Ben, having learned that Tom is really innocent of the murders, threatens Jesse with telling his father everything unless he reveals the truth, and Jesse admits that the Dorsons are the real killers.

Ben goes off into the swamp to find Tom, but the Dorsons prepare an ambush on his way back. Their plan fails, and they pursue Ben and Tom. Tom leads them into a particularly dangerous swamp. Bud Dorson disappears in the quicksand, and his brother Tim is set free on condition that he go through the fatally dangerous section.

Thursday and Hannah are reconciled. Tom is vindicated. Ben and Julie can at last be happy.

JEAN KRESS

The second of Renoir's films to be shown after the Liberation, *Swamp Water* caused the misunderstanding which was to turn the most admired of French film makers into the most widely scorned. The supreme irony was that it was Renoir's warmest partisans who cast the first stone, the same stone previously cast at *The Rules of the Game*, which even after five years of world-wide chaos, had not won comprehension or acceptance.

Swamp Water can be credited with having, over the long run, revolutionized Hollywood. For the first time a major company accepted the idea of not shooting the exterior shots in the studio. The principle of *Swamp Water* is that of *Toni*, but with twenty years of experience behind it. It represents no longer the taste for risk, but the assurance of confident audacity.

Jeered in Biarritz before its Paris opening, *Swamp Water* is one of the seven or eight decisive turning points in Renoir's work. The difficulty is that it is not the beginning of the turn but the end of it. And everyone knows that as he comes out of a curve, the champion driver floors the accelerator to take off at full throttle. This is what Renoir does on the aesthetic plane.

Genius, Malraux wrote somewhere, is born like a fire: in the destruction of what it consumes. If *The Rules of the Game* was not understood in its time, it was because it burned, destroyed, *The Crime of M. Lange*. And *Swamp Water* because it consumed in its turn *The Rules of the Game*. In the same way *Paris Does Strange Things* will be disdained by those who applauded *French CanCan*. And wrongly, because Renoir proves to us continually that the only way not to lag behind is to be always ahead. Just as one is admiring the rashness of his creation, he is already destroying it.

JEAN-LUC GODARD

After Swamp Water, *which had some success in America, Renoir broke amicably with Darryl Zanuck. Universal proposed a film with Deanna Durbin, which he started but did not finish. He thought of making Saint-Exupéry's* Wind, Sand, and Stars, *but the project was never realized. He made two propaganda films,* This Land Is Mine *and* Salute to France. *Then Robert Hakim allowed him to make* The Southerner, *an independent production distributed by United Artists.*

This Land Is Mine (1943)

DIRECTOR: Jean Renoir
SCREENPLAY: Dudley Nichols and Jean Renoir
DIALOGUE: Dudley Nichols
DIALOGUE DIRECTOR: Leo Bulgakov
ASSISTANT DIRECTOR: Edward Donohue
SPECIAL EFFECTS: Vernon L. Walker
CHIEF STAGE DESIGNERS: Eugène Lourié, Albert d'Agostino, Walter F. Keeler
SETS: Darrell Silvera and Al Fields
DIRECTOR OF PHOTOGRAPHY: Frank Redman
EDITOR: Frederic Knudtsen
SOUND: Terry Kellum and James Stewart
MUSIC: Lothar Perl
ORCHESTRA: under the direction of Constantin Bakaleinikoff
PRODUCTION: R.K.O.
PRODUCERS: Jean Renoir and Dudley Nichols
DISTRIBUTION: R.K.O.
LENGTH: 2,847 meters
FIRST SHOWING: March 17, 1943
ACTORS: Charles Laughton (Albert Lory); Kent Smith (Paul Martin); Maureen O'Hara (Louise Martin, Paul's sister); George Sanders (George Lambert); Walter Slezack (Major von Keller); Una O'Connor (Mrs. Lory, Albert's mother); Philip Merivale (Professor Sorel); Thurston Hall (the mayor); Nancy Gates (Julie Grant); Ivan Simpson (the judge); Wheaton Chambers (Mr. Lorraine); John Donnat (Edmund Lorraine); Franck Alten (Lieutenant Schwartz); Leo Bulgakov (Little Man); Cecile Weston (Mrs. Lorraine)

Albert Lory, a schoolmaster of uncertain age and a shy, fearful man, secretly loves his colleague Louise Martin. Louise is engaged to George Lambert, a railway engineer who is an avid partisan of the Nazi regime. Following an assassination attempt, the German authorities take a group of hostages, including Lory, who will be shot if the real culprits are not denounced. Mrs. Lory, who loves her son with a fierce possessiveness and who is very jealous of Louise, had seen the girl's brother, Paul, in compromising circumstances immediately following the attempt. She denounces Paul Martin to Lambert, who in turn tells Commandant von Keller. But at the last minute Lambert realizes the monstrousness of what he has done. He tries to warn Paul of the danger—but the young man is shot down by the Nazis.

Lory is released, but when he learns the truth he rushes, crazed with rage and despair, to have it out with Lambert. He arrives too late. Tormented by guilt, Lambert has just killed himself. Lory, who arrives at the engineer's office moments after the suicide, is accused of murder.

During the trial von Keller comes to see Lory in prison. Singing the praises of the Nazi regime, von Keller promises Lory his freedom. A letter of farewell supposedly written by Lambert will be produced in court, and Lory will be vindicated. The timid schoolmaster is almost convinced, but when he looks out his window and sees the other hostages being executed, he understands what is behind von Keller's friendly words. In the course of the trial, the weakling finds the moral courage to publicly denounce the oppressor and his allies, to proclaim his love for Louise, and to face death bravely, not for the crime he did not commit, but for having pleaded the cause of liberty.

JEAN KRESS

The most scorned of Jean Renoir's American films. The action unfolds (like that of *Diary of a Chambermaid*) in a small French town reconstructed in a Hollywood studio. This little bit of France, made of plaster and stucco, is really an imaginary country, the country of Verdoux as well, and of certain Fritz Lang films such as *Hangmen Also Die*.

"With *This Land Is Mine* I wanted to show the Americans a less conventional view of occupied France . . . Perhaps I was unskillful, perhaps I didn't understand the state of mind that reigned in France after the Liberation. In any case, I was inundated with insulting letters from France and was castigated by the Parisian press. For once, I was sincerely distressed not to have been understood." (Jean Renoir, "My American Experience," *Cinémonde*, 1946)

This Land Is Mine, in spite of its classical *mise en scène*, which is unusually restrained for Renoir (but of course he had to satisfy the American public at any cost), is a very beautiful film in which we can immediately recognize the author if only in the character and acting of Charles Laughton, who resembles the director as much as Pierre Renoir did in *La Marseillaise*.

It is also, whether one likes this or not, a typically French film, and it is not by coincidence that one thinks constantly of Daudet in *La Dernière Classe*. Maurice Bardèche, who achieved new heights of critical insouciance by giving in one of the editions of his *History of the Cinema* an account of an American film by Renoir which was never made—*Wind, Sand, and Stars* from Saint-Exupéry—redeems himself with this very accurate analysis of *This Land Is Mine:*

> Although it contains the same type of errors (as other American-made films depicting wartime conditions in Europe), it is less shocking than many to the Europeans invited to watch themselves portrayed on the screen. Laughton makes an admirable schoolmaster who is very afraid of the bombardments, who likes his comforts, his meals, his aging mother; who feels great respect for the Inspector of the Academy and the occupation authorities; and who at the end becomes an enraged sheep. The sessions of the military court are conducted in public like a municipal police court; the patriotism is in flamboyant style; the teachers cry as they tear out pages from history texts about Joan of Arc, the public school and Jules Ferry; and the film ends with choirs of students singing from the Declaration of the Rights of Man as if it were the Book of Psalms. These exalted republican displays cause one to smile a little, and the film was severely criticized in France. It was a rather unjust reception, because, inevitable omissions notwithstanding, Renoir had honestly tried to come to terms with the situation of an occupied country. It is the film of an intelligent man which fails because of conditions under which it was made, but all in all, there is certainly less stupidity and vulgarity in this film than there was in the films made in France shortly afterward on similar themes.

We agree with Maurice Bardèche's judgment.

FRANÇOIS TRUFFAUT

Salute to France (1944)

DIRECTOR: Jean Renoir, in collaboration
SCREENPLAY: Philip Dunne, Jean Renoir, Burgess Meredith
DIRECTOR OF PHOTOGRAPHY: Army Pictorial Service
EDITING: under the supervision of Helen Van Dongen
MUSIC: Kurt Weill
PRODUCTION: Office of War Information
DISTRIBUTOR: United Artists
LENGTH: 540 meters (20 min.)
FIRST SHOWING: December 1944 or January 1945 in Paris (without credits)
ACTORS: Burgess Meredith (Tommy); Garson Kanin (Joe); Claude Dauphin (Jacques, the narrator and multiple roles: the soldier, the peasant, the intellectual, the guerrilla, etc.)

Presented in France in complete anonymity a year after the end of the war, *Salute to France* was not, as far as I know, honored with the slightest notice from the Parisian press. However, in America it had had a handsome measure of success, which, though not equal to that of his great previous film *This Land Is Mine*, proves that Renoir, when he wants to express certain elemental truths, knows how to reach a large audience. The point was, in Renoir's words, "to explain France to the Americans who are going to land there."

On the bridge of a troop transport headed for the continent, a little group, including a French soldier, an English soldier, and an American soldier, discuss the country they are about to discover or rediscover. Claude Dauphin, naturally, is the spokesman for the charms of the French way of life. But he wonders, along with his interlocutors, what kind of a country he shall return to after the terrible years of occupation. Renoir

—whose participation in this unsigned collaborative work must not be overestimated, or even more, underestimated—demonstrates once again, without fanfare but with the straightforward good sense of a man who is utterly French to the tips of his toes, his confidence in the land of "red wine and Brie cheese." The style of the film—simple, haphazard, close to the unceremoniously made films which Renoir favored before the war—is completely different from that of the usual run of propaganda films (particularly the Anglo-Saxon ones). Even in this occasional work, Renoir indulges once again his taste for superficially incongruous casting. Burgess Meredith, for example, with his overly subtle smile of the Broadway intellectual. And yet how could one forget the shot of him by the bridge weighed down with all his gear?

LOUIS MARCORELLES

The Southerner (1945)

DIRECTOR: Jean Renoir
SCREENPLAY: Jean Renoir, from the novel by George Sessions Perry, *Hold Autumn in Your Hand*, adapted by Hugo Butler
DIALOGUE: Jean Renoir, advised by W. Faulkner
ASSISTANT DIRECTOR: Robert Aldrich
SETS: Eugène Lourié
DIRECTOR OF PHOTOGRAPHY: Lucien Andriot
SOUND: Frank Webster
EDITOR: Gregg Tallas
MUSIC: Werner Janssen
ORCHESTRA: Janssen Symphony Orchestra
PRODUCERS: David L. Loew and Robert Hakim
ASSOCIATE PRODUCER: Samuel Rheiner
DISTRIBUTOR: United Artists
LENGTH: 2,586 meters (92 minutes)
FIRST SHOWING: April 30, 1945, at the Four-Star Theater in Beverly Hills
ACTORS: Zachary Scott (Sam Tucker); Betty Field (Nana Tucker);

J. Carrol Naish (Devers); Beula Bondi (the grandmother); Percy Kilbride (Harmie); Blanche Yurka (Mom); Charles Kemper (Tim); Norman Lloyd (Finley); Estelle Taylor (Lizzie); Noreen Nash (Becky); Jack Norworth (the doctor); Paul Harvey (Ruston); Nestor Paira (the bartender); Jay Gilpin (Jot); Jean Vanderbilt (Daisy, Sam's daughter); Paul Burns (Uncle Pete); Dorothy Granger (young girl at the party); Earl Odgkins (guest at the wedding); Almira Sessions (customer at the store); Rex (Zoonie)

This film, Renoir assures us, was made with complete freedom. There is no trace in this quasi-documentary of the customary Hollywood production. The director assumes full responsibility for his actions, without pleading mitigating circumstances. Thus, if the film does not remain faithful to a certain image we have developed of Renoir, it is because he does not want it to do so. Renoir is always Renoir; that is why he does not need to imitate Renoir.

And for a new subject, a new style. Renoir presents these cotton farmers of Anglo-Saxon background and Protestant upbringing with entirely appropriate austerity. The solemnity of their actions demands a treatment different from what one accords a Parisian vagabond or a provincial laborer. There is something noble in their meager lives, something dramatic, to which Renoir gives an added dimension, as he has always enriched the characters he is given to work with.

That said, it should be noted that Renoir's outlook is no longer exactly the same. He is no longer content to marvel: he judges. In this rough country, this world of pioneers, the grandeur of man resides not in abandoning himself to nature but in defying it, dominating it. Under the surface—which seems grayer than usual—the shadow of a great moral or metaphysical idea takes shape, the idea of a *God* explicitly named, a God with whom Renoir's work up to this point has hardly been concerned at all.

This profession of spiritual faith might seem surprising. But let us content ourselves with noticing it, as we take note of *The River* or *Orvet*, without pretending to resolve a contradiction which Renoir likes to nourish in himself. Let us just say that this contradiction prevents us from interpreting in a very strict or easy fashion the materialism which is no less sincerely proclaimed in *Boudu* and *Paris Does Strange Things*.

ERIC ROHMER

The Diary of a Chambermaid (1946)

DIRECTOR: Jean Renoir
SCREENPLAY: Jean Renoir and Burgess Meredith, from the novel by Octave Mirbeau and the play by André Heuse, André de Lorde, and Thielly Nores
ASSISTANT DIRECTOR: Lamdew
SPECIAL EFFECTS: Lee Zavitz
SETS: Eugène Lourié (constructed by J. Heron)
COSTUMES: Barbara Karinska
DIRECTOR OF PHOTOGRAPHY: Lucien Andriot
EDITOR: James Smith
MUSIC: Michel Michelet
PRODUCERS: Benedict Bogeaus and Burgess Meredith
DISTRIBUTOR: United Artists
LENGTH: 2,350 meters (82 minutes)
FIRST SHOWING: 1948
ACTORS: Paulette Goddard (Célestine); Burgess Meredith (Captain Mauger); Hurd Hatfield (George); Reginald Owen (Mr. Lanlaire); Florence Bates (Rose); Francis Lederer (Joseph); Judith Anderson (Mrs. Lanlaire); Irene Ryan (Louise); Almira Sessions (Marianne)

The passage of time permits us to better assess the quality and importance of Renoir's next-to-last American film. For a long time appreciated for its "realism," *The Southerner* was the only one of the American films to be highly regarded. *The Southerner* is admirable, but *Diary*, I think, is even purer and more beautiful. Here Renoir attains without reserve and with a dazzling unity of style one of his fundamental creative goals:

the synthesis of the comic and the serious. *The Rules of the Game* is still only an amusing drama; *Diary* is a slapstick tragedy. It merges burlesque and atrocity.

With *Diary* Renoir completely abandoned the "realism" of his French work. It is significant that the film was shot in the studio in a strange, nightmare light far different from that of Sologne or even of the Georgia of *Swamp Water*. Everything, right up to the extraordinary, detailed accuracy of the costumes, is fused into a kind of cruel fantasy world, as disengaged from reality as a theater set. Perhaps here is the source of the obsession with the theater which will increasingly characterize Renoir's evolution. Up to now, the theater had hardly furnished the director of *Boudu* with so much as a pretext for a scenario. But perhaps for the first time we see in his work not the theater, but theatricality in its purest state.

ANDRÉ BAZIN

The Woman on the Beach (1946)

DIRECTOR: Jean Renoir
SCREENPLAY: Jean Renoir, Franck Davis, and J. R. Michael Hogan, from the novel *None So Blind* by Mitchell Wilson
DIALOGUE DIRECTOR: Paula Walling
ASSISTANT DIRECTOR: James Casey
SPECIAL EFFECTS: Russel A. Cully
SETS: Darrell Silvera and John Sturtevant
DIRECTOR OF PHOTOGRAPHY: Harry Wild
CAMERAMAN: Leo Trover
SOUND: Jean L. Speak and Clem Portman
ART DIRECTORS: Albert S. d'Agostino and Walter E. Keller
TECHNICAL ADVISER: Lt. Cmdr. Charles A. Gardiner, USCGR
EDITORS: Roland Gross (Cross?), and Lyle Boyer or (according to other sources) Harold Palmer
MUSIC: Hanns Eisler
ORCHESTRA: under the direction of C. Bakaleinikoff
ORCHESTRATION: Gill Grau

PRODUCTION: R.K.O.
PRODUCER: Jack J. Gross
ASSOCIATE PRODUCER: Will Price
LENGTH: 1,928 meters (71 minutes)
FIRST SHOWING: May 14, 1947
ACTORS: Joan Bennett (Peggy Butler); Robert Ryan (Lieutenant Scott); Charles Bickford (Butler); Nan Leslie (Eve); Walter Sande (Vernecke); Irene Ryan (Mrs. Vernecke); Glenn Vernon (Kirke); Franck Dorien (Lars); Jay Norris (Jimmy)

The first of the trilogy of great masterpieces. However mutilated it is in comparison with the original, it can still be as fairly judged as, say, von Stroheim's *Greed*.* And if there was ever a director, who, irrespective of the importance he attaches to composition, perceives each part as a microcosm of the whole, it is Renoir.

The Woman on the Beach, more than any other of Renoir's works, looks like a film made by Fritz Lang (and Lang was soon to return the compliment†), but it is close to Lang only in appearance. The tragedy of *The Woman on the Beach* does not stem from the inexorable movement of some force of destiny, as in Lang's films, but on the contrary, from fixation and immobility: each of the three characters is frozen in a false image of himself and his desire. Enclosed in a setting bound on one side by the rhythmic movements of the waves, the blind painter has lost himself in his canvasses, just as Ryan and Joan Bennett have lost themselves in a purely sexual obsession. The fire shatters the spell and brings them back to reality.

The Woman on the Beach represents the culmination of what might be called Renoir's second technical apprenticeship. Technical extravagance has been completely suppressed. Camera movements, few and brief, neglect the top of the frame in favor of eye-level shots edited for horizontal continuity and classical angle–reverse angle dialogues. Henceforth Renoir puts forth facts, one after another, and the beauty stems from the

* *Greed* was cut from ten hours to two. For a consideration of the cuts made in *The Woman on the Beach*, see *Cahiers du Cinéma* No. 34. Trans.
† By making *Human Desire* (1954). Trans.

inexorability with which they follow each other. There is nothing but a raw succession of actions; each shot is an event. Although they seem more richly adorned, Renoir's subsequent films use this simple structure as a framework, and in their more intense moments they put aside their elegant ornamentation and allow it to show through.

Must one prefer the great *Passions* to *The Well-Tempered Clavier?* Perhaps, but if there is such a thing as pure cinema, it is to be found in *The Woman on the Beach*.

JACQUES RIVETTE

The River (1950)

DIRECTOR: Jean Renoir
SCREENPLAY: Rumer Godden and Jean Renoir, from the novel by Rumer Godden
COMMENTARY: spoken by June Hillman
ASSISTANT DIRECTOR: Forrest Judd
SET DESIGNER: Eugène Lourié
SETS: Bansi Chandra Gupta
DIRECTOR OF PHOTOGRAPHY: Claude Renoir
CAMERAMAN: Romananda Sen Gupta
SOUND: Charles Paulton and Charles Knott
SOUND ASSISTANTS: Harishadnan J. das Gupta, Sukhano y Sen, Bansi Ashe
COLOR: Technicolor
EDITOR: George Gale
MUSIC DIRECTOR: M. A. Parata Sarathy; music recorded in India
SHOOTING: 1949–50 on location near Calcutta (banks of the Ganges)
PRODUCTION: Oriental International Film, Inc. (with the cooperation of the Theater Guild)
PRODUCERS: Kenneth McEldowney, Kalyan Gupta, Jean Renoir
DISTRIBUTOR: Associated Artists
LENGTH: 2,730 meters (99 minutes)
FIRST SHOWING: December 19, 1951, at the Madeleine and the Biarritz in Paris; won first prize at the Venice Film Festival, 1951

ACTORS: Nora Swinburne (the mother); Esmond Knight (the father); Arthur Shields (Mr. John); Thomas E. Breen (Captain John); Suprova Mukerjee (Nan); Patricia Walters (Harriet); Radha (Melanie); Adrienne Corri (Valerie); Richard Foster (Bogey); Penelope Wilkinson (Elisabeth); Jane Harris (Muffie); Jennifer Harris (Mouse); Cecilia Wood (Victoria); Ram Singh (Sahjn Singh); Nimai Barik (Kanu); Trilak Jetley (Anil)

Every great film is the story of an experiment. That is, it goes from the particular to the general. It does not sacrifice universality by starting with a particular conflict, for it carries this one destiny to its most crucial point where general truths far beyond the specific case become suddenly apparent.

The voyage to India has now replaced the traditional voyage to Greece. But it is not toward an exotic land that a Renoir or a Rossellini embarks, but rather toward the cradle of all the Indo-European civilizations. They ask India to give them back the fundamental note which now seems lost in the general cacophony.

With Rossellini's *Viaggio in Italia* and perhaps what Eisenstein's *Que Viva Mexico!* might have been, *The River* is the only example of a film which reflects rigorously on itself, in which the narrative content, the sociological description, and the metaphysical themes do not just respond to each other but are at every point interchangeable. "We are a part of the world." Three boats, three young girls simultaneously reach the central point where all contradictions cancel each other out, where death and birth, giving and refusing, possessing and taking away, have the same value and the same meaning. He who forgets himself finds himself; he who gives in, triumphs. Harriet's adventure is the story of a death which is also a birth; that is, of a metamorphosis, of an avatar. Thus the woodcutter becomes God; Krishna becomes the woodcutter. This film, so rich in metaphor, is ultimately only about metaphor itself, or absolute knowledge.

JACQUES RIVETTE

Le Carrosse d'Or (1952)
(The Golden Coach, 1954)

DIRECTOR: Jean Renoir
SCREENPLAY: Jean Renoir, Renzo Avanzo, Giulio Macchi, Jack Kirkland, and Ginette Doynel, freely adapted from the play by Prosper Mérimée, *Le Carrosse du Saint-Sacrement*
ASSISTANT DIRECTORS: Marc Maurette and Giulio Macchi
SCRIPT GIRL: Ginette Doynel
SETS: Mario Chiari, assisted by Gianni Polidori
COSTUMES: Mario de Mattëis
DIRECTORS OF PHOTOGRAPHY: Claude Renoir and H. Ronald
CAMERAMAN: Rodolfo Lombardi
ASSISTANTS (Technicolor): Ronald Hill, Ernest Tiley, Hubert Salisbury
STILL PHOTOGRAPHY: Studio Dial
SOUND: Joseph de Bretagne and Ovidio del Grande
RECORDER: Mario Ronchetti
RECORDING: Western Electric
COLOR: Technicolor
MAKEUP: Romolo de Martino and Alberto de Rossi
DESIGNER: Gino Brosio
STAGE MANAGER: Franco Palagi
EDITORS: Mario Serandrei and David Hawkins
MUSIC: Antonio Vivaldi, adapted by Gino Marinuzzi
SHOOTING: beginning February 4, 1952, at Cinecittá studios
PRODUCTION: Panaria Films, Hoche Productions
PRODUCER: Francesco Alliata
DIRECTORS OF PRODUCTION: Valentino Brosio and Giuseppe Bardogni
EXECUTIVE PRODUCER: Giovanni A. Giurgola
DISTRIBUTOR: Corona
LENGTH: 1 hour 40 minutes
FIRST SHOWING: February 27, 1953, at the Olympia and the Paris
ACTORS: Anna Magnani (Camilla); Duncan Lamont (the viceroy); Odoardo Spadaro (Don Antonio); Riccardo Rioli (Ramon); Paul Campbell (Felipe); Nada Fiorelli (Isabelle); George Higgins (Martinez); Dante (Arlequin); Rino (the doctor); Gisella Mathews (Marquise Altamirano); Lina Marengo (the old actress); Ralph Truman (Duke of Castro); Elena Altieri (Duchess

of Castro); Renato Chiantoni (Captain Fracasse); Giulio Tedeschi (Baldassare); Alfredo Kolner (Florindo); Alfredo Medini (Polichinelle); the Medini brothers (the four children); John Pasetti (captain of the guards); William Tubbs (the innkeeper); Cecil Mathews (the baron); Fedo Keeling (the viscount); Jean Debucourt (the bishop)

An American critic compared *The Golden Coach* to those boxes which you open to find another, smaller box inside, which in turn contains another box, and so on. Renoir tells us: "This critic pleased me very much by saying that. He thought that it was a flaw and that a film should not be made that way. Personally I find this box game very interesting."

The Golden Coach opens with a curtain which rises on a second curtain which rises on a staircase leading to three levels. The middle level is in fact the stage of a theater. At this moment we are in the audience. A traveling shot takes us from our seats onto the stage, then to the top floor, into the royal apartments. Only then are we at the movies. One thinks of Salvador Dali's quip: "An expectant hush falls over the audience. The curtain rises on a second curtain painted by Salvador Dali."

Since Prosper Mérimée's *Le Carrosse du Saint-Sacrement* is a play and La Perichole, the principal character in the play, is an actress, it seems natural that the film inspired by this work should take place in a dramatic climate which partakes both of life and of the theater. Here again Jean Renoir's comments are priceless: "As for the acting, I asked those who were playing the real-life roles to play with a little exaggeration so as to give real life a theatrical tone and create confusion between the stage and reality."

For this reason, *The Golden Coach* is constructed like a play in three acts. The first act ends with Camilla's curtsy to the viceroy. At the end of the second act we come back to the stairway-crossroads, which leads, according to the whim of the camera, to the court, into the town, or up on the stage, and infrequently, in front of the screen. After having humiliated her royal lover, Camilla is off to the bullfight, when addressing the court—facing stage left with an eye on the audience—she says:

"When the second act ends and Colombine* is alone, having been put out by her masters, there is a tradition of which you seem to be ignorant: the actors form a line and bow."

At this moment the ladies and gentlemen of the court bow to Camilla/Colombine. But the courtiers are really only film actors, not actors of the *commedia dell'arte*. Thus this time it is Jean Renoir who addresses the courtiers, through Anna Magnani. Just as through the courtiers we, the audience of the film, might address the author, who asks us to applaud the actors—the real ones and the false ones—who have served him so well.

The action of *The Golden Coach* reaches its climax on the stairway. After the bishop's little speech, the entire film is turned inside out like a glove, but since the glove had already been turned inside out in the opening minutes, it is now right side out, and everything is in order. A curtain falls in front of the actors and the court. A second curtain falls, leaving in front of it Don Antonio, the head of the *commedia dell'arte* troupe, "the delight of the crowned heads of old Europe."

Don Antonio greets us: "Ladies and gentlemen, to celebrate the triumphs of Camilla over the intrigues of the Court, I would have liked to offer you a melodrama in the Italian style, but Camilla is late . . . Camilla . . . Camilla on stage." Camilla arrives. Don Antonio addresses her: "You were not made for what is called life. Your place is among us, the actors, acrobats, mimes, clowns, jugglers. You will find your happiness only on stage each night for the two hours in which you ply your craft as an actress, that is, when you forget yourself. Through the characters that you will incarnate, you will perhaps find the real Camilla."

Anyone who knows Jean Renoir cannot fail to be struck by the extent to which these words constitute an "artistic testament." Before the war Renoir acted in some of his films. He has since given it up, but one might think he is present here as Don

---

* Colombine is a stock character of the *commedia dell'arte*. Usually a chambermaid prone to romantic misadventure, she figures in the on-stage acting of *The Golden Coach*, as she did in many French theatrical works of the seventeenth and eighteenth centuries. Trans.

Antonio. *The Golden Coach* is perhaps the only film to treat the perilous subject of the theater and the craft of entertainment as a whole from the inside. At the fall of the last curtain, the boxes are enclosed, one inside another: the "interesting box game" is finished. Renoir himself has given us the message of *The Golden Coach:* "The desire for civilization was the force which drove me during the making of *The Coach.*"

As André Bazin often pointed out, long before it came into general use in Hollywood, in the 1940s, depth of field was used to the greatest extent possible in Jean Renoir's films. This is not true in *The Golden Coach.* Although there are many similarities between *The Rules of the Game* and *The Golden Coach*—a woman and three men, a chase, masters and servants, etc.—the *mise en scène* is completely different. In *Coach* there are no traveling shots, or rather only imperceptible ones, and no pans. The camera is anchored in front of the theater stage or the movie scene, and it *records. The Golden Coach* is absolutely flat. (I mean that the *mise en scène* is in one plane.) It is a film in two dimensions. Everything is located and moved by *height*—thanks to the stairway—and by *width.* However, this *mise en scène* does not mark a return to the old technique, "cinema, the art of montage," as Malraux characterized it in his *Psychology of the Cinema.* On the contrary, in *Coach* the image is all, the shot stands on its own. For every gesture, every attitude, a shot. Renoir slides smoothly from one to another.

The message of *The Golden Coach* is also in its form. The "box game" is not superficial. It is true of *The Golden Coach* as it is for *Paludes.** One can propose any interpretation without being wrong. Everything is in *The Golden Coach.* For example, it is the story of four characters in search of their meaning who find it through suffering and appeasement: the viceroy will learn to suffer jealousy "like a normal man"; Felipe will find peace in voluntary exile; Ramon will return to the arena;

---

* *Paludes:* a novel by André Gide. The reference here is to *composition en abîme,* Gide's technique of writing novels about men writing novels about men writing novels. Trans.

and Camilla will understand that her place is on the stage because she is not made "for what is called life."

FRANÇOIS TRUFFAUT

The "open Sesame" of all Renoir's work. The two customary poles of his work—art and nature, acting and life—take
shape in two facing mirrors, which reflect each other's images
back and forth until it is impossible to tell where one ends and
the other begins. The critical question of all the films which
precede and follow—that of sincerity—here finds its most elegant answer and in turn a new formulation, as in a dialogue.
This *necessary* work (it had to be made, and everything in it
flows from its initial hypothesis) is a commissioned project,
taken from a play in which nothing seems to suggest such a
transformation (unless it is Mérimée's esoteric vein). It is a
rigorous game whose only rule is improvisation as a matter of
principle. It is an exquisite jewel box which had the good fortune to contain the priceless gems known as *commedia dell'arte*,
Vivaldi, and Magnani. If an author can claim to transfer the essence of his message into aesthetic form, it is because this message is so compatible with the art in which he practices.

All this concerns not only Renoir but the entire cinema,
for both of them have the same unique and profound object:
spectacle, or if you prefer, appearance.

And in this case, the appearances were not inherently propitious. This sort of presentation—the mime, the masquerade—
usually offers the greatest resistance to screen adaptation. But
Renoir was able to shape it to the demands of the cinema and
at the same time to use it as a foil, for the artificiality of attitudes is only there to better set off the natural, to make the in-
terventions of the real even more striking. Once the mask is removed, the human figure shines in its true splendor, freed from
the mud left by the age-old processes of life and of art. This
*chassé-croisé** of order and freedom ultimately finds its ana-

---

* *Chassé-croisé:* a dance figure in which the gentleman and his lady pass
alternately one in front of the other; hence a reciprocal exchange of position in general. Trans.

logue on the moral plane. The beautiful irresolution of a woman is presented to us as the most sublime of attitudes. If Renoir does not state his message boldly, it is not from caution. His work is perfect like the circle; and like the circle, it cannot be neatly framed.

ERIC ROHMER

The Golden Coach *was a commercial and even a critical failure. Jean Renoir went for two years without shooting. He planned to shoot* Les Braconniers (The Poachers) *in Burgundy with Danielle Delorme, as well as an adaptation of Turgenev's* First Love, *but finally it was a film initially intended for Yves Allegret,* French CanCan, *prepared during the summer of 1954 and shot in November and December, which marked Renoir's return to the Paris studios after fifteen years in Hollywood. Also, in July 1954, he made his debut as a theater director by staging Shakespeare's* Julius Caesar *in the arena at Arles.*

Julius Caesar (1954)

DIRECTOR: Jean Renoir
TRANSLATION AND ADAPTATION OF THE PLAY BY WILLIAM SHAKE-
    SPEARE: Grisha and Mitsou Dabat
STAGE MANAGER: Jean Serge
ACTORS: Jean-Pierre Aumont (Marc Antony); Loleh Bellon (Por-
    tia); Yves Robert (Cassius); Françoise Christophe (Calpurnia);
    Paul Meurisse (Brutus); Henri Vidal (Julius Caesar); Jean
    Parédès (Casca); Jean Topart (Octavius Caesar); François Vi-
    bert (the seer); Gaston Modot (Ligarius); Henri-Jacques Huet
    (Flavius); Jaque Catelain (Decius); sixteen other actors per-
    forming approximately thirty roles and 200 extras recruited on
    site (notably the guards of Camargue)
SOLE PRODUCTION: July 10, 1954 in the arena at Arles

French CanCan (1954)
(*French CanCan*, 1956)

DIRECTOR: Jean Renoir
SCREENPLAY: Jean Renoir, from an idea of André-Paul Antoine
DIALOGUE: Jean Renoir
ASSISTANT DIRECTORS: Serge Vallin, Pierre Kast, Jacques Rivette (trainee)
SCRIPT GIRL: Ginette Doynel
CHOREOGRAPHY: G. Grandjean
SETS: Max Douy
COSTUMES: Rosine Delamare, made by Coquatrix and Karinska
WARDROBE: Paulette Tentave, Elise Servet, Mariette Chabrol
MAKEUP: Yvonne Fortuna, assisted by Georges Klein
HAIRDRESSER: Huguette Lalaurette
DIRECTOR OF PHOTOGRAPHY: Michel Kelber
CAMERAMAN: Henri Tiquet
ASSISTANT CAMERAMEN: Vladimir Lang and Georges Barsky
STILL PHOTOGRAPHER: Serge Beauvarlet
SOUND: Antoine Petitjean
RECORDER: Jean Labussières
COLOR: Technicolor
RECORDING: Western Electric
PROPS: Daniel Lagille and Edouard Duval
STAGE MANAGER: Lucien Lippens
ASSISTANT STAGE MANAGER: René Forgeas
LOCATIONS MANAGERS: Robert Turlure and Charles Chieusse
EDITOR: Boris Lewin
MUSIC: Georges Van Parys (and an assortment of tunes from the "Cafés-Concert" of the turn of the century)
SHOOTING: October 4 to December 20, 1954, at Saint-Maurice–Francœur studios
PRODUCTION: Franco-London Films, Jolly Films
PRODUCER: Louis Wipf
EXECUTIVE PRODUCER: Georges Walon
DISTRIBUTOR: Gaumont
LENGTH: 97 minutes
FIRST SHOWING: April 27, 1955, at the Berlitz, the Paris, and the Gaumont-Palace

ACTORS: Jean Gabin (Danglard); Maria Félix (La Belle Abesse); Françoise Arnoul (Nini); Jean-Roger Caussimon (Baron Walter); Gianni Esposito (Prince Alexandre); Philippe Clay (Casimir); Michel Piccoli (Valorgueil); Jean Parédès (Coudrier); Lydia Johnson (Guibole); Max Dalban (manager of the Reine Blanche); Jacques Jouanneau (Bidon); Jean Marc Tennberg (Savate); Hubert Deschamps (Isidore, the waiter); Franco Pastorino (Paulo, the baker); Valentine Tessier (Mme. Olympe, Nini's mother); Albert Rémy (Barjolin); Annik Morice (Thérèse); Dora Doll (La Génisse); Anna Amendola (Esther Georges and the voice of Cora Vaucaire); Léo Campion (the commandant); Mme. Paquerette (Mimi Prunelle); Sylvine Delannoy (Titine); Anne-Marie Mersen (Paquita); Michèle Nadal (Bigoudi); Gaston Gabaroche (Oscar, the pianist); Jaque Catelain (the minister); Pierre Moncorbier (the bailiff); Jean Mortier (the hotel manager); Numes Fils (the neighbor); Robert Auboyneau (the elevator attendant); Laurence Bataille (La Pygmée); Pierre Olaf (Pierrot, the heckler); Jacques Ciron (first dandy); Claude Arnay (second dandy); France Roche (Béatrix); Michèle Philippe (Eléonore); R. J. Chauffard (the police inspector); Gaston Modot (Danglard's servant); Jacques Hilling (the surgeon); Patachou (Yvette Guilbert); André Claveau (Paul Delmet); Jean Raymond (Paulus); Edith Piaf (Eugénie Buffet); Jedlinska (La Gigolette); Jean Sylvère (the groom); Palmyre Levasseur (the laundry woman); André Philip, Bruno Balp, Jacques Marin, H. R. Herce, René Pascal, Martine Alexis, Corinne Jansen, Maya Jusanova, and the voice of Mario Luillard

CUT SCENES: François Joux (secretary to the businessman); Jean-Marie Amato (the worldly painter); Roger Saget (the businessman); Claude Berri (the hunter); Joelle Robin (the girl accompanying the military officer); Jean Castanier (Bordeau, manager of the Parvant Chinois); Léon Larive (a bourgeois)

Among the recent Renoirs, *French CanCan* is the best liked by the dilettantes, the least esteemed by the purists. One wonders why. Of course, it is a hastily shot, transitional film; one upset by massive cuts, and in which the principal actors were imposed on Renoir. But Renoir has made others under similar conditions. Certainly the constraints of assembly-line production are different from those of the small shop; expensive sets involve problems that tiny rooms do not; and big-name actors might pose greater difficulties than would personal friends; but all these impediments are swept away by the same rich current as always, and they are inevitably made to harmonize.

The grandeur of this ode to the physical pleasures lies first in its prodigious archaism, a vigorous, aggressive archaism. It was surprising, after the pure music of *The Golden Coach*, to hear these more popular strains; but two years later it was clear that this film was a necessary link between *The Golden Coach* and *Paris Does Strange Things*. And then it was only one step from "the holy prostitution of the theater" of which Baudelaire speaks, to the apotheosis of the bordello, and Renoir takes it gladly. There is immodesty in every great film. Renoir is inspired by it. He absolves the dancer as readily as he did the actress; the one for baring her legs, the other for baring her soul.

Like him, his heroes refuse to choose. Renoir's work constantly recalls these lines from "L'Après-Midi d'un Faune" by Mallarmé:

> My crime is that I, gay at conquering the treacherous
> Fears, the disheveled tangled divided
> Of kisses, the gods kept so well commingled.

(This will also be the crime of Eléna, who will be punished for it by ending up with a gypsy beau.) In short, a pantheism, one which teaches not to separate the sensual from the spiritual, nor *French CanCan* from *The Golden Coach*. All this is not without bitterness, but neither is pleasure gay, being only a half which tries to give the illusion of the whole.

No, Pan does not sleep. The feverish panic of the final cancan more than makes up for the lapses in the film. In this fury of girls and undergarments we can see the most triumphant hymn the cinema has ever dedicated to its own soul, the movement which by breaking the rules, creates them.

The art of life and of poetry, closely entwined, which was

in *The River* and *The Golden Coach*, is also in *French CanCan*. It merely wears a different mask. For *French CanCan* is intimate theater, the supreme comedy which Renoir plays for himself. And now everything is ready for the entrance of Eléna in *Paris Does Strange Things*, a melodrama in the French style, performed to celebrate the victory of desire over the intrigues of the heart . . . Do not worry. Eléna is not far behind.

JACQUES RIVETTE

Before the release of French CanCan, *which was to have great success in 1954, Renoir staged his first play,* Orvet, *written for Leslie Caron in 1953.*

Orvet (1955)
A Comedy in Three Acts by Jean Renoir

DIRECTOR: Jean Renoir
SETS: Georges Wakhevitch, painted by Laverdet
MUSIC: Joseph Kosma
TECHNICAL ASSISTANCE: Robert Petit
STAGE MANAGER: Maurice Fraigneau
COUTURIERS: Karinska and Givenchy
LIGHTING DIRECTOR: Albert Richard
STAGE SET: Alex Desbiolles
PREMIÈRE: March 12, 1955, at the Théâtre de la Renaissance
ACTORS: Leslie Caron (Orvet); Paul Meurisse (Georges); Michel Herbault (Olivier); Catherine Le Couey (Mme. Camus); Raymond Bussières (Coutant); Jacques Jouanneau (William); Marguerite Cassan (Clotilde); Yorick Royan (Berthe); Suzanne Courtal (Mother Viper); Pierre Olaf (Philippe, the clubfoot); Georges Saillard (the doctor); Georges Hubert (the first huntsman); Henry Charrett (the second huntsman)

"Is it necessary to shout about nothing, and is *Orvet* anything but the portrait of a failure?" (Guy Verdot)

"Here we have in the purest sense of the word a piece of childishness compounded by Pirandellism. We have seen too much of it. It would be unjust to blame Pirandello, since he never saw it." (Robert Kemp)

"A complex amalgam of good intentions, literary reminiscences, familiar themes, rustic poetry, homespun philosophy, kindness, ingenuity, clumsiness, perception, and ambition." (Claude Baignères)

"And there is something else: an absolutely ferocious healthiness, a taste for life, a naïve and rather cruel joy, an argumentative geniality which delighted me, a gentle drollness, an unfeigned ingenuousness, an honest vulgarity . . . Does not all that make a play?" (De Garambé)

Precisely, *Orvet* is a play, Jean Renoir's first play, mostly defended by film people:

"This is not literary theater. It is the work of a director who has built his play around his actors, who has been guided on the one hand by the sincerity of his inspiration and on the other by the surest instinct for theatrical effect." (André Bazin)

"The night before the première, I saw *Orvet*, and I came out at once conquered and overwhelmed." (Roberto Rossellini)

Let Jean Renoir conclude by means of this excerpt from a radio interview: "M. Stève Passeur has the right to find my play a failure. He knows the theater. But I deny M. Pavallelli has the right to criticize Leslie Caron, because he knows nothing about this. I can assure him that if my father had known Leslie, he would not have painted one portrait of her, nor even a hundred. He would have spent his life painting her."

CAHIERS DU CINÉMA

Eléna et les Hommes (1956)
(Paris Does Strange Things, 1957)

DIRECTOR: Jean Renoir
SCREENPLAY: Jean Renoir, adapted by Jean Renoir and Jean Serge

DIALOGUE: Jean Renoir
ASSISTANT DIRECTOR: Serge Vallin
SCRIPT GIRL: Ginette Doynel
SETS: Jean André
COSTUMES: Rosine Delamare and Monique Plotin
DIRECTOR OF PHOTOGRAPHY: Claude Renoir
COLOR: Eastmancolor
SOUND: William Sivel
STAGE MANAGER: Lucien Lippens
EDITOR: Boris Lewin
MUSIC: Joseph Kosma; song "Méfiez-Vous de Paris" by Léo Marjane, song "O Nuit" by Juliette Gréco; with songs of the period arranged by Georges Van Parys
SHOOTING: December 1, 1955, to March 17, 1956
PRODUCTION: Franco-London Films, Films Gibé, Electra Compania Cinematografica
PRODUCER: Louis Wipf
DISTRIBUTOR: Cinédis
LENGTH: 1 hour 35 minutes
FIRST SHOWING: September 12, 1956
ACTORS: Ingrid Bergman (Eléna); Jean Marais (Rollan); Mel Ferrer (Henri de Chevincourt); Jean Richard (Hector, Rollan's servant); Magali Noël (Lolotte, Eléna's waiting-maid); Juliette Gréco (Miarka); Pierre Bertin (Martin-Michaud); Jean Castanier (Isnard); Jean Claudio (Lionel); Elina Labourdette (Paulette); Frédéric Duvallès (Godin); Dora Doll (Rosa la Rose); Mirko Ellis (Marbeau); Jacques Hilling (Lisbonne); Jacques Jouanneau (Eugène Godin); Renaud Mary (Fleury); Gaston Modot (the leader of the gypsies); Jacques Morel (Duchêne); Michèle Nadal (Denise Godin); Albert Rémy (Buchez); Olga Valéry (Olga); Léo Marjane (the street singer); Léon Larive (Henri's domestic); Gregori Chmara (Eléna's domestic); Paul Demange (a spectator); Jim Gérald (café owner); Robert Le Beal (the doctor); Claire Gérard (the strolling woman); the Zavattas, Gérard Buhr, Jean Ozenne, René Berthier, Hubert de Lapparent, Pierre Duverger, Jaque Catelain, Simone Sylvestre, Corinne Jansen, Liliane Ernout, Louisette Rousseau, Palmyre Levasseur, Lyne Carrel

To say that Renoir is the most intelligent of film makers comes down to saying that he is French to the tip of his toes. And if *Paris Does Strange Things* is *the* French film *par excellence*, it is because it is the most intelligent film in the world. Art and at the same time the theory of art. Beauty and at the same time the secret of beauty. Cinema and at the same time the analysis of cinema.

Our beautiful Eléna is only a provincial muse.* But she is a muse in search of the absolute. In filming Venus among men, Renoir for an hour and a half superimposes the point of view of Olympus on that of the mortals. Before our eyes the metamorphosis of the gods ceases to be a cheap slogan and becomes a spectacle of searing comedy. In fact, by the most beautiful of paradoxes, the immortals in *Paris* aspire to die. To be sure of living, one must be sure of loving. And to be sure of loving, one must be sure of dying. This is what Eléna discovers in the arms of men. This is the strange and hard moral of this modern fable disguised as comic opera.

Thirty years of on-the-set improvisation have made Renoir the preeminent technician in the world. He does in one shot what others do in ten. And the others take shots to say things which Renoir can dispense with entirely. There has never been a more free film than *Paris*. But ultimately, liberty is necessity. And neither has there ever been a more logical film.

Paris is Renoir's most Mozartian film. Not so much in its exterior appearance, like *The Rules of the Game*, but in its philosophy. The man who finishes *French CanCan* and prepares for *Paris* is, morally, a little like the man who completes the Concerto for Clarinet and launches into *The Magic Flute*. In substance, the same irony and the same distaste. In form, the same brilliant audacity of simplicity. To the question, What is cinema? *Paris* replies: More than cinema.

JEAN-LUC GODARD

* The reference is to Balzac's novel *La Muse du département*.

L'Album de Famille de Jean Renoir (1956)

DIRECTOR: Roland Gritti
SCREENPLAY: Pierre Desgraupes
DIRECTOR OF PHOTOGRAPHY: Jean Tournier
SHOOTING: Studio Paris-Télévision (Boulogne)
PRODUCTION: Paris Télévision, then Franco-London Films
DISTRIBUTOR: Cinédis
PRESENTATION: on the same program with *Eléna et les Hommes*
LENGTH: 711 meters
ACTORS: Jean Renoir and Pierre Desgraupes

Even before the opening of Paris Does Strange Things *in Paris (where its success was modest) Jean Renoir returned to the United States, where the American version of* Paris *was a failure. He wrote a play,* Carola, *which was performed at the University of California, as well as an adaptation of Clifford Odets' play* The Big Knife, *which opened at the Théâtre des Bouffes-Parisiens on October 30, 1957, with Daniel Gélin, Claude Génia, Paul Cambo, Paul Bernard, Teddy Billis, France Delahalle, Andréa Parisy, Vera Norman, and Robert Montage. During this same period Renoir wrote the story for a short ballet on the war, "Le Feu aux Poudres," created by Ludmilla Tcherina, which was given as the first part of a dance program by Raymond Rouleau and Ludmilla Tcherina,* Les Amants de Teruel.

Le Testament du Dr. Cordelier (1959)

DIRECTOR: Jean Renoir
SCREENPLAY: Jean Renoir, freely adapted from R. L. Stevenson's *Dr. Jekyll and Mr. Hyde*
DIALOGUE: Jean Renoir
ASSISTANT DIRECTOR: Maurice Beuchey
SCRIPT GIRLS: Andrée Gauthey and Marinette Pasquet

TECHNICAL CONSULTANT: Yves-André Hubert
ARTISTIC CONSULTANT: Jean Serge
SETS: Marcel-Louis Dieulot
DIRECTOR OF PHOTOGRAPHY: Georges Leclerc
CAMERAMEN: Bernard Giraux, Jean Graglia, Pierre Guéguen, Pierre Lebon, Gilbert Perrot-Minot, Arthur Raymond, Gilbert Sandoz
SOUND: Joseph Richard
COSTUMES: Monique Dunand
EDITOR: Renée Lichtig
MUSIC: Joseph Kosma
SHOOTING: January 1959 at R.T.F. (rue Darducci) studios, on location in Paris (Montmartre and Avenue Paul-Doumer) and at Marnes-la-Coquette
PRODUCTION: R.T.F., Sofirad, Compagnie Jean Renoir
PRODUCER: Albert Hollebecke
DISTRIBUTOR: Consortium Pathé
ORIGINAL LENGTH: 1 hour 40 minutes, cut to 1 hour 35 minutes
FIRST SHOWING: November 16, 1961, at the George V in Paris
ACTORS: Jean-Louis Barrault (Dr. Cordelier and Opale); Teddy Billis (Master Joly); Michel Vitold (Dr. Séverin); Jean Topart (Désiré, the major-domo); Micheline Gary (Marguerite); Jacques Dannoville (Commissaire Lardout); André Certes (Inspector Salbris); Jean-Pierre Granval (the owner of the hotel); Jacqueline Morane (Alberte); Ghislaine Dumont (Suzy); Madelaine Marion (Juliette); Didier d'Yd (Georges); Primerose Perret (Mary); Gaston Modot (Blaise, the gardener); Raymond Jourdain (the invalid); Sylvianne Margolle (the little girl); Jaque Catelain (the ambassador); Régine Blaess (his wife); Raymone (Mme. des Essarts); Dominique Dangan (the mother); Céline Sales (a girl); Claudie Bourlon (Lise); Jacqueline Frot (Isabelle); Françoise Boyer (Françoise); Monique Theffo (Annie); Annick Allières (the neighbor); Jean Bertho and Jacques Ciron (two passers-by)

Made in the same year as *Picnic on the Grass*, *Le Testament du Dr. Cordelier* is at once its double and its opposite. The two films are complementary. To the heat, the color, the sensual, fleshy quality of *Picnic on the Grass*, *Testament* opposes the icy character of its black-and-white images and its lucid,

Jean-Louis Barrault in *Le Testament du Dr. Cordelier*

abstract style. Either film can be seen and admired separately, but each can be completely understood only in the presence of the other.

While *Picnic on the Grass* portrays the return of a way of life which moves with the flow of nature, *Le Testament du Dr. Cordelier* describes the effects of stemming this flow. *Picnic* focuses on the Greek materialist conception of nature; *Testament* shows the Christian idealist conception and at the same time expresses Renoir's idea on science and its relation to a certain type of society.

The film is a modern version of *Dr. Jekyll and Mr. Hyde.* It is worth noting that in departing from the letter of Stevenson's story, Renoir once again achieves a cinematic adaptation which is as close as one could possibly be to the spirit of the original work.

Dr. Cordelier, an eminent psychiatrist, seeks to prove the existence of the soul by causing it to materialize. Experimenting on himself, he creates the alter ego of Opale, who is bestial, cruel, and destructive. Less and less able to control his metamorphoses, Cordelier finally finds that suicide is the only way to suppress his monstrous second identity.

The interest and the novelty of this version lie in Renoir's masterful use of Jean-Louis Barrault, who was chosen for the contrasting qualities of his dry, icy classical acting and his light, nimble, ethereal miming. Thus the change in character is no longer the result of a change of makeup, but of a complete physical transformation. Barrault's abilities give Renoir wide latitude in expressing the intellectual thrust which informs his film.

On the one hand, there is Cordelier, whom a rigorous education in strict bourgeois, Christian principles, inculcated by an emasculating mother, has trapped in the rigid confines of a moral existence. He sacrifices his spirit in the quest for an absolute which would allow him to fulfill himself. But his confession reveals the failure of such an effort. He is nothing more than a hypocritical actor, a small man whose affected modesty masks an unbounded pride in his science, his privileges, his social class.

On the other hand, there is Opale, the incarnate projection of Cordelier's soul, whose very name evokes a substance which is translucent but murky. This soul is merely the materialization of repressed desires, of stifled tendencies, above all of the irresistible need for liberty and life which Cordelier's constrained existence has only exacerbated. And here is the soul reduced to its opposite: the sexual urge which is the primal force in the Dionysian universe. A perverted, deviant urge which changes the gentle, innocent Opale into a raging, sadistic satyr.

And yet, through a dialectical movement, Opale fulfills

Cordelier's spiritual quest by inverting and destroying it. Cordelier's quest for the soul is by its very nature an ethereal, spiritual undertaking, an ideal enterprise which tends to deny weighty materialism. But the only way ideal thought can prove itself is by first taking concrete form and subjecting itself to the laws of the physical world. Thus the contradiction arises that the very demonstration of abstract ideas destroys them. It is a quest for the impossible, a dream. Renoir's voice comes at the end to tell us that "in his search for the spiritual, Cordelier got the best of the bargain." But this does not mitigate the film's demonstration that true freedom can only follow from the natural movement of life toward its own fulfillment.

No adequate account of the film could omit mention of the fact that, just as fantastic and philosophical elements of Cordelier have their reflection in Opale, so his mundane and social aspects are reflected in the notary, Master Joly, and in his enemy, the psychiatrist Séverin. The notary, always anxious to close his shutters on anything that might disturb the tranquility of the wealthy and to silence scandals with money, defends the Christian, bourgeois order. (Note that there is a crucifix over the bed in his room, while there is none in Cordelier's.) He is all the more Cordelier's friend because he is the director of his considerable estate. He admires Cordelier as an aristocrat who can show—his class's finest trait—a complete disinterest in material wealth (cf. the irony of the will [testament], which, to the profound and sad amazement of Joly, Cordelier makes in favor of Opale).

Séverin is as excited as Cordelier seems calm. Like Professor Alexis of *Picnic on the Grass*, he represents rationalist, atheist, anti-Christian thought. Theirs is a falsely scientific system which seeks to impose on the world a fixed a priori conception of life with its own rules and norms. It is a doctrinal thought which serves the interests of the wealthy. Séverin is a bourgeois (he sleeps with his secretary, but he will not marry her). And naturally he is also a friend of the notary Joly.

Although Cordelier's work disturbs Joly and scandalizes Séverin, they are both really interested in it so far as it justifies their own bourgeois ideology and rationalizes the rule of the wealthy. If Cordelier proves the materiality of the soul, he shows at the same time that there is nothing more interesting and worthwhile than making this discovery. Since only the selfish pursuit of personal gain is likely to bring the soul to fruition (the soul only being worthy of attention once it has reached a certain value, unless it is accounted for as is), this quest becomes the goal of all existence. Individualism appears as the only solution. Unfortunately, the angel gives birth to a beast. The soul turns out to be nothing more than the projection of the most loathsome, destructive ego, the polar opposite of the sort of force which leads to development of the individual through creation. Even more unfortunately, when this science of the soul is put solely at the disposition of the rich and the powerful, it sows misery among the poor and weak (the little girl, the prostitutes, all of Opale's victims).

Renoir has never attacked the bourgeois ethos of profit contained in Christian thought and in its enemy and offspring, rationalist thought, with more rigorous logic than he has in this film.

It is no surprise to find *Le Testament du Dr. Cordelier* following such films as *La Petite Marchande d'Allumettes*, *Night at the Crossroads*, *The Rules of the Game*, *Diary of a Chambermaid*, *The Woman on the Beach*; that is, the films of Renoir's fantastic vein. These films plunge us into a universe dominated by idealism and its denial of reality. It is no coincidence that some of Opale's expressions and gesticulations remind one of Boudu. Boudu was the joyously anarchical dream of Mr. Lestingois, the liberal *petit bourgeois* brought up on Voltaire and Anatole France. Opale is the product, or more precisely, the pathetic residue, of the mortal conception of life, of the severe *grande bourgeoisie*.

JEAN DOUCHET

Le Dejeuner sur l'Herbe (1959)
(Picnic on the Grass, 1960)

DIRECTOR: Jean Renoir

SCREENPLAY: Jean Renoir

DIALOGUE: Jean Renoir

ASSISTANT DIRECTORS: Maurice Beuchey, Francis Morane, Jean-Pierre Spiero, Hedy Naka, Jean de Nesles

SCRIPT GIRLS: Andrée Gauthey and Marinette Pasquet

ARTISTIC CONSULTANT: Jean Serge

TECHNICAL CONSULTANT: Yves-André Hubert

SETS: Marcel-Louis Dieulot, assisted by André Piltant and Pierre Cadiou

COSTUMES: Monique Dunan, assisted by Josiane Landic

DIRECTOR OF PHOTOGRAPHY: Georges Leclerc

COLOR: Eastmancolor

CAMERAMEN: Ribaud, Jean-Louis Picavet, Andreas Winding, Pierre Guéguen

STILL PHOTOGRAPHER: Philippe Rivier

SOUND: Joseph de Bretagne

WARDROBE MISTRESSES: Yvette Bonnay and Y. Maupas

MAKEUP: Yvonne Fortuna, assisted by Fernande Ugi

CHIEF MECHANIC: Marcel Jaffredo

LIGHTING: André Moindrat

ELECTRICIANS: Georges Gandart and Henri Prat

EDITOR: Renée Lichtig, assisted by Françoise London

MUSIC: Joseph Kosma

SHOOTING: July-August 1959 at Francœur studios and on location at Les Colettes and surrounding Cagnes

PRODUCTION: Compagnie Jean Renoir

PRODUCER: Ginette Doynel

DISTRIBUTOR: Consortium Pathé

ORIGINAL LENGTH: 1 hour 32 minutes

FIRST SHOWING: November 11, 1959, at the Marignan and the Français

ACTORS: Paul Meurisse (Etienne); Catherine Rouvel (Nénette); Fernand Sardou (Nino, Etienne's father); Jacqueline Morane (Titine, eldest sister of Nénette); Jean-Pierre Granval (Ritou,

Titine's husband); Robert Chandeau (Laurent); Micheline Gary (Madeleine, Laurent's wife); Frédéric O'Brady (Rudolf); Ghislaine Dumont (Magda, Rudolf's wife); Ingrid Nordine (Marie-Charlotte); André Brunot (the old curate); Hélène Duc (Isabelle, the secretary); Jacques Dannoville (M. Paignant); Marguerite Cassan (Mme. Paignant); Charles Blavette (Gaspard, the old shepherd); Jean Claudio (Rousseau, the steward); Raymond Jourdan (Eustache, the cook); Francis Miege (Barthélemy, the chauffeur); Régine Blaess (Claire, the maid); Pierre Leproux (Bailly); Michel Herbault (Montet); Jacqueline Fontel (Mlle. Michelet, secretary); Paulette Dubost (Mlle. Forestier, the telephone operator); M. You (Chapuis, the foreman); and the four announcers: Dupraz, Lucas, Roland Thierry, Michel Péricart

The year 1959. Two subjects, among others, animate the television talk shows: artificial insemination and Europe, whose birth (in the form of the Common Market) has been acknowledged by a treaty signed recently in Rome. Here are two rather playful subjects to inspire a fantasy based on a completely harebrained tale which invites us not to take it seriously. It is an invitation we will not accept.

Professor Alexis, the illustrious biologist, announces his candidacy for the Presidency of Europe. His success seems assured, since his crusade for a program of artificial insemination to "genetically" elevate the human race has found such an enthusiastic response among simple people of low station, who see it as a sure and unexpected means of bettering their condition. Naturally Professor Alexis is from a wealthy family. He is related to the major chemical fortunes of France and Germany, and his relatives are happily backing his candidacy in hopes of increasing their profits when their cousin institutes his program. And to help secure the cause of European unity on a solid economic foundation—in the same spirit which reigned at the founding of the Common Market—the professor announces his marriage (of both expediency and money) to a lovely German cousin, who is an avid exponent of scouting and the outdoor life.

Paul Meurisse and Catherine Rouvel in *Picnic on the Grass*

But it is summer. The world of industry is on vacation. Employers and employees descend on Provence for their holidays, the former to their sumptuous estates, the latter to the camping sites.

There Antoinette, known as Nénette, a girl from the grape country, who loves children and wants to have a baby, but without the help of a man, rejoices at the professor's arrival. She tries to meet him. But a man as busy as the professor is unapproachable. So Nénette has no choice but to get a job as a servant in his house.

So here she is working at the great ceremony, the picnic on the grass at which the professor and his cousin celebrate their engagement before the international press, which has been brought here for the occasion. It is quite a stuffy ceremony, where all contact with lowly nature is prohibited. Alas, it takes place in the shadow of the ruins of a temple dedicated to Diana, in which an old shepherd roams with his goat. Like a faun or the god Pan, the shepherd plays an air on his flute and a sudden windstorm rises up, sowing disorder and confusion into the meticulously planned ceremony and panic among the guests. The shepherd stops playing, and the storm subsides. It is followed by a soothing heat which awakens the senses and sharpens the appetites. A bacchanal is unleashed. Professor Alexis, looking for his cousin, who is trying to calm her excitement by a salutary promenade, gets lost and comes upon the spectacle of Nénette swimming in the river, in the splendor of her nudity like a bather in a painting by Auguste Renoir or Maillol. Happy to please the professor, Nénette gives herself to him. The professor abandons himself to inebriated sensuality.

The professor is revolutionized. Fleeing society, he takes refuge at the home of his young friend and there discovers the joys of a patriarchal universe in which man, like an idle king, leaves to woman, who is happy to have the privilege, the cares of working and assuring his happiness. A dull life in which time is organized and planned gives way to a savorous existence marked by the leisurely and natural flowing of the hours. "Perhaps happiness just means submission to the laws of nature," Professor Alexis starts to think.

But the family chemical cartel has not given up its mercenary hopes so easily. As the result of a rather vulgar bargain accompanied by blackmail, Nénette runs away. Once again in the hands of society, the professor gets ready to marry his cousin. In the hotel where the marriage is to take place he runs into Nénette working in the kitchen. She tells him that she is expecting his baby. The professor sweeps away all his old ideas and prejudices and brings her to the ceremony to present her as the future first lady of Europe.

Because of the similarity of their titles, *Picnic on the Grass* has often been thought of as a sequel to *A Day in the*

Country. This notion is neither right nor wrong. The two films play the same note but in different chords. They do not have the same resonance. *A Day in the Country* treats the awakening of sensitivity to nature and the emotion which comes with it. *Picnic on the Grass* plunges us into the sensations which grow out of direct contact with nature. It is a sensual film, as hot and carnal as the other is cool and delicate. The first is sentimental and breathtaking. The second sacrifices everything to the ethos of pleasure and gaiety.

It is as if Renoir, annoyed or frightened by the sinister character of technocratic society and its standardized notions of happiness, was seeking through the healthy, vigorous reproach of an almost farcical fantasy to restore a taste for the joys and charms of life. It is not surprising, then, that the veneer of entertainment should cover the most serious of purposes.

In no other film has Renoir more openly presented (for example, the scene of the shepherd in the temple of Diana) the crucial idea which informs all his work: the conflict between the Apollonian world and the Dionysian world, between the fixed framework of existence and the irresistible movement of life, between the theater set built once and for all and the changing, forever moving production which animates it; in short, between order and disorder.

Obviously the Dionysian universe is favored in Renoir's work. Life is always seen as it surges and strains against the bounds of existence. It does not rest until it destroys this framework to replace it with a new order which permits it to complete fulfillment. But once formed, the new order itself has a tendency to become frozen and limiting. The author of *La Marseillaise* and *La Vie Est à Nous* is the film maker of permament revolution (do not forget that part of his *Petit Théâtre* was originally called "It's Revolution"). This fundamental conflict is the point of all Renoir's films: the theatrical representation leaves the stage to invade the audience, the cyclone of disorder explodes order so to regenerate it. Renoir thinks of life as the dynamic of liberty, which can realize itself only by rising up against its obstacles and overcoming them.

When man, such as Professor Alexis, tries to force life into a rigid, immutable frame, it is only right for nature to rise up and defeat him (the scene of the tempest). Man is invited to penetrate nature's secrets. And once he has done it, she gives herself to him both as a lovely spectacle and as a source of physical pleasure. (Alexis's previous inactivity underlines the galvanizing power of nature.) Thus he discovers that the fundamental conflict that rages in his bosom, the conflict symbolized by the tormented olive trees or the buzzing insects, is the very basis of his harmonious unity. The permanent revolution produces equilibrium. He can now set himself to thinking about the notion "that happiness is perhaps nothing more than submission to the laws of nature."

Ten years before the subject became one of the major concerns of our time, Renoir explored the relations of man and his environment. And in the only way possible: politically. In contrasting a cold, industrialized, efficient, technocratic northern Europe to a rural, underdeveloped, semicolonial Mediterranean Europe, he sought to portray the two great currents of Western thought: the materialist philosophy which began with the Greeks and Christian spiritual thought, which was overthrown and replaced by the idealist thought of the rationalists. This second current is illustrated by the often misunderstood dialogue between Professor Alexis and the village priest. Smoke from the factories has a hard time replacing the incense of the churches; these two priests from hostile camps understand each other very well. They serve the same interests: money and those who have it.

It is the idealist religion of progress which Renoir ridicules. He denounces its technocratic science which defiles nature in the interests of men obsessed with profit (cf. the film's portrayal of the "paid vacations"). Far from leading to a better life, it imposes a way of life which benefits only the ruling class. In the only film to date to examine the Europe of the Common Market, Renoir lucidly exposes the falseness of the glowing promises of this "new society."

For Europe to find its harmonious equilibrium, science

must abandon idealism and submit to materialism. Professor Alexis must marry Nénette because she is going to have a natural child.

JEAN DOUCHET

Le Caporal Epinglé (1962)
(The Elusive Corporal, 1963)

DIRECTOR: Jean Renoir
SCREENPLAY: adapted* by Jean Renoir and Guy Lefranc from a novel by Jacques Perret
DIALOGUE: Jean Renoir
CO-DIRECTOR: Guy Lefranc
ASSISTANT DIRECTOR: Marc Maurette
SCRIPT GIRL: Charlotte Lefebvre-Vuattoux
DIRECTOR OF PHOTOGRAPHY: Georges Leclerc
CAMERAMEN: Jean-Louis Picavet and Gilbert Chain
SOUND: Antoine Petitjean
STAGE SET: Eugène Herrly
LIGHTING: André Moindrot
EDITOR: Renée Lichtig
MUSIC: Joseph Kosma
SHOOTING: winter 1961–62
STUDIO: Vienna
LOCATIONS: Vienna and surrounding area, Pont de Tolbiac (Paris)
PRODUCTION: Films du Cyclope
PRODUCER: René G. Vuattoux
EXECUTIVE PRODUCER: Yvonne Tourmayeff
DISTRIBUTOR: Pathé
LENGTH: 1 hour 45 minutes
FIRST SHOWING: May 23, 1962, at the Ermitage, the Français, the Miramar, and the Wepler Pathé; selected for the Berlin Festival

* Charles Spaak earlier collaborated with Renoir on an adaptation, but this was abandoned. Not long after the film's release, Renoir protested cuts made without his consent in the newsreels used in the film to establish a political context in the story of the escape. See France-Soir, May 28, 1962. F.T.

of 1962 and presented in inaugural sessions of the London Film
Festival on October 16, 1962

ACTORS: Jean-Pierre Cassel (the corporal); Claude Brasseur (Pater);
Claude Rich (Ballochet); O. E. Hasse (the drunken traveler);
Jean Carmet (Emile); Jacques Jouanneau (Penchagauche);
Conny Froboess (Erika); Mario David (Caruso); Philippe Cos-
telli (the electrician); Raymond Jourdan (Dupieu); Guy Bedos
(the stutterer); Gérard Darrieu (the cross-eyed man); Sacha
Briquet (the disguised escapee); Lucien Raimbourg (the railway-
station worker); François Darbon (the peasant)

A Renoir film is first appreciated on the level of the senses.
Both film and characters define themselves immediately in
terms of impressions, of which the most important are of heat
and cold. *The Elusive Corporal* is a cold, lucid, abstract film
about characters in search of heat, of fraternity. The black-and-
white photography (except for *Le Testament du Dr. Cordelier*,
it is Renoir's only black-and-white film since *The River*) and
the dreary, gray climate emphasize the point of the film: the
need for the sun and its warmth.

The Elusive Corporal recalls *The Lower Depths* more than
it does *Grand Illusion*, even though it is a story about prisoners
of war. The corporal is a young French soldier taken into cus-
tody after the fall of France. He repeatedly tries to escape and
finally succeeds on his sixth attempt.

Even more than in the film of the Gorki play, the characters are thrown into the lower depths, reduced to the very nadir
of existence. The film is intended as the reflection of a man in
the year 1961 facing the end of a world, ours, and the beginning
of an era of transition and combat. It confronts the collapse of
Western civilization and speaks of the necessity, in the result-
ing chaos, of rethinking our attitudes about life. Liberty is its
sole subject. Renoir has never been more to the point than in
this work.

The film focuses on an existence of intolerable oppression.
The triumph of the Nazi regime, with which the film begins,
marks the devastation of the old orders: society, nation, Western
civilization and its system of values. There remains only capi-

talism stripped of its justification, democracy, and reduced to its most brutal function, the complete exploitation of man (cf. the barking of the German civilian foremen in the work camps). It imposes a new existence from which every glimmer of humanity is banished, as much for the masters as for the slaves. Europe has become an immense stalag; the world (the action takes place almost entirely outdoors) is a prison.

But in such a situation, life rebels. It thirsts for liberty, which is every bit as much a natural need as eating, urinating, etc. And it is an urgent need. The corporal feels it greatly, for without any other reason, this animal impulse leads him to make his first escape attempt with his friends Ballochet and Pater. Naturally they fail, for in the new order which has been imposed on Europe there is no more freedom beyond the barbed wire than there is inside it. Indeed, the character of Ballochet suggests that there may even be less. Ballochet is the only one to retain his belief in the idealist values of the defunct Western civilization. And this belief, far more than his imprisonment, has alienated him. All the other prisoners, except the corporal and Pater, who had no profession in civilian life, cling to the only physical, material values which they retain from their previous lives: their crafts. But Ballochet is ashamed of his former job. His post as an employee of the power company was denigrated in the idealist culture and its illusion of chivalric, Christian heroism which has been instilled in him.

It is the same grand illusion which Renoir has exposed in Nana, Emma Bovary, de Boïeldieu, Christine, Eléna, Cordelier, and many others. But never before has he exposed it with such clarity. With Renoir there are no novelistic heroes any more than there are movie heroes. All individuals, and all characters, have the same importance. To flourish, the individual personality must merge with the collective personality rather than seek to differentiate itself. It must learn, as did Camilla and the corporal, to give itself to others rather than to fence itself off from them. We must be what we are, not what we are led to think that we are. This is the basis of Renoir's cinema and of his direction of actors.

Unhappy with the conditions of his former existence, Bal-lochet adapts easily to his new one. The rigor of the new order becomes easier to accept as it becomes a habit. Captivity, by ensuring a life without problems or strife, allows Ballochet to escape reality, to "shut himself up in his dungeon," to con-struct an *ideal* universe in which he is master. He has taken advantage of the situation to procure himself a comfortable setup. He satisfies his desire to escape by imagination. It is there that he finds his freedom.

In a disciplinary camp after his third escape attempt, physically exhausted and spiritually empty, the corporal lets himself be tempted by Ballochet's easy, selfish, and cowardly solution. But a fortuitous toothache results in his falling in love with the dentist's daughter. After reading him Ronsard's epi-curean poem on the rose, the young German girl tells him that she loves him for attempting to escape, for refusing to be a slave. It is a revelation. His need for liberty finds its expression: live fully lovingly every instant to fully enjoy life.

Thus in the course of his six escape attempts the corporal learns the reason for freedom and the way to acquire it, which involves getting rid of every shackle, of opening oneself to life, of coping with its problems as they arise; but always the ulti-mate goal is to fight without surrender to vanquish oppression and establish an order in which no man is exploited and every-one can freely fulfill himself. Is it any surprise that the film should end in Paris with an idea which a slogan would make famous a few years later: "It's only a beginning . . ."?*

The film's lesson goes beyond the social and the political. It reaches what might well be called a cosmic dimension. Re-noir's vision is founded on a materialist conception, and what he treats here above all is the relation of man and the universe in terms of matter. Matter plays a vital and omnipresent role, both through the oppressive weight of its inertia and the liberat-ing force of its energy. On the one hand, necessity. On the other, chance—chance which the corporal meets continually in his escape attempts and with which he can deal only when he

* A slogan of the student rebels during the uprisings of May 1968. Trans.

has stored up enough internal energy to throw off the oppression which weighs on his body and accede to freedom and grace. From this perspective, freedom is no longer considered as a natural need but rather as a physical element of the energetic dynamics of matter.

This materialist conception affects Renoir's direction. Since *The Rules of the Game*, Renoir's *mise en scène* has obeyed the laws of gravity. It reflects the strange ballet of attraction and repulsion danced by the particles of an atom or the celestial bodies of a galaxy. Just as *The Rules of the Game* can be seen as the light of a dead star, its journey to earth like the dance of a ghost striving to maintain a last illusion of life, so *The Elusive Corporal* might be seen as the symbolic portrayal, according to the theories current in 1960, of a galactic system. This might explain the fascination created by the film's movement, which seems to be controlled by a principle completely independent of the story. It might also explain the scenes in which the camera suddenly and violently pulls back from the characters, as if to re-situate them in the general movement of which they are both agents and objects. Certainly this interpretation is not inconceivable. Many artists have sought to enclose the form of their work within the scientific theories of their time.

Without further insisting on this hypothesis, let us take note, toward the end of the film, of the appearance of the drunk in the train, a sort of incarnation of Dionysius himself, sowing disorder throughout the compartment; then the panic in the train (the bombardment), the ultimate revolt of life, completely intoxicated by itself, against the absurdity of existence. And the camera, from far off, contemplates the chaos before the coming of the new dawn and the soft, warm light of the sun.

JEAN DOUCHET

In the years following the making of The Elusive Corporal, *Renoir wrote two books, a biographical study of his father and a novel,* Les Cahiers du Capitaine Georges. *In 1968 Renoir was filmed directing the French actress Gisèle Braunberger in an extract from Rumer Godden's novel* Breakfast with Nicolaïdes, *which Renoir translated from the English. In 1969 he played himself in a film called* The Christian Licorice Store *by James Frawley, before making* Le Petit Théâtre *for French television.*

La Direction d'Acteur par Jean Renoir (1968)

DIRECTOR: Jean Renoir
DIRECTOR OF PHOTOGRAPHY: Edmond Richard
SOUND: René Forget
EDITOR: Mireille Mauberna
PRODUCER: Roger Fleytoux
PRODUCTION AND DISTRIBUTOR: Films de la Pléiade
LENGTH: 27 minutes
ACTORS: Gisèle Braunberger and Jean Renoir

In this improvised film, shot in half a day, Renoir directs Gisèle Braunberger through a text chosen and translated by him, an extract from *Breakfast with Nicolaïdes*, a novel by Rumer Godden (author of *The River*).

JEAN KRESS

The Christian Licorice Store (1969)

DIRECTOR: James Frawley

Renoir plays himself in this film shot by a young American film maker in 1969, commercially released in 1971. Trans.

Le Petit Théâtre par Jean Renoir (1969)

DIRECTOR: Jean Renoir
SCREENPLAY: Jean Renoir
DIALOGUE: Jean Renoir
MUSIC: Joseph Kosma (for "The Electric Polisher") and Jean Wiener
SHOOTING: June, August, and September 1969 at the Saint-Maurice
    studios and on location in Versailles (Grand Siècle housing
    project) and in the South of France (around Aix-en-Provence
    and St-Rémy)
PRODUCTION: R.A.I., Son et Lumière, O.R.T.F.
PRODUCER: Pierre Long
ACTORS: FIRST SKETCH, "Le Dernier Réveillon" ("The Last New Year's
    Eve"): Nicholas (or Nino) Fornicola (the bum); Minny Monti
    (the female bum); Roger Trapp (Max Vialle); Roland Martin,
    Frédéric Santaya, Pierre Gulda
    SECOND SKETCH, "La Cireuse Electrique" ("The Electric Pol-
    isher"): Pierre Olaf (the husband); Marguerite Cassan (Isa-
    belle); Jacques Dynam (the second husband); Jean-Louis Tris-
    tan (agent); Claude Guillaume and Denis de Gunsburg (the
    young couple)
    THIRD SKETCH, "Quand l'Amour se meurt" ("When Love
    Dies"): Jeanne Moreau (the singer)
    FOURTH SKETCH, "Le Roi d'Yvetot" ("The King of Yvetot"):
    Fernand Sardou (M. Duvallier); Françoise Arnoul (his wife,
    Isabelle); Jean Carmet (Féraud); Andrex (Blanc); Dominique
    Labourier (Colette [or Paulette?], the maid); Roger Frégois
    (Jolly); Edmond Ardisson (César, the tramp)

This film, as a title in which every word counts indicates,
is a work which brings into play Jean Renoir himself, racon-
teur of the theater and of life, each reflecting the other. Introducing the four tales, a Renoir as big as life speaks to us through
a miniature theater and assesses the moral of each fable at its
conclusion.

"Le Dernier Réveillon" ("The Last New Year's Eve") is
played against a set and at a time of the year which are both

naturally and artificially theatrical, since Christmas is the time when society paints itself as a picture of happiness. We see how the poor (the old couple), once only spectators, become participants. Having watched the spectacle of the rich banqueters on the other side of the windows, they inherit the leftovers and have their own final celebration under the bridges. Finally, disappearing into the snow and death, they will leave the stage forever. Again Renoir is paying homage to Andersen, as he did in *La Petite Marchande d'Allumettes.*

"La Cireuse Electrique" ("The Electric Polisher") is an adaptation of an earlier Renoir project entitled "C'est la Révolution" ("It's Revolution"). The idea is to show us first-hand the rise of the spirit of rebellion through a series of situations of the most concrete and trivial, and therefore the most laughable, sort. The theater here is the conjugal stage throughout the life of a woman who, obsessed with taking care of her floor, subjugates her successive husbands to the tyranny of the wax polisher. The last husband rebels, throwing the electric polisher out the window only to see his wife leap out herself to rejoin her machine. This tale is treated as a drama and sung as an opera, i.e., it is hypertheatrified. Thus Renoir contradicts the deliberate modesty of his case. It is as if he were blowing everything a little out of proportion to bring the revolution home to the people who are in the midst of it but don't know it, just as he introduced minutiae into *La Marseillaise* to point up the importance of banal daily life to those whom we always consider to have been consciously living and leading the Revolution of 1789.

Renoir presents "Quand l'Amour Se Meurt" which falls somewhere between the previous two stories, a little more forcefully than the others. It is about a past age which Renoir liked: the beginning of the twentieth century, *la belle époque.* Yet the episode opens and closes abruptly with the simple appearance on stage of the actress and singer Jeanne Moreau, who interprets (à la Marlene Dietrich in *Morocco*) Oscar Crémieux's song, "Quand l'Amour Se Meurt" ("When Love Dies"). With this approach Renoir has gone far beyond any possibilities that a simple narrative would have offered him to present his tale in a manner which is at once modest and grandiose.

"Le Roi d'Yvetot" ("The King of Yvetot") concludes the film. The little steel marble which Renoir tosses onto the stage of his Little Theatre becomes the heavy ball of a game of *pétanque*, and we find ourselves in the midst of a great social game with all its rules and norms. This last story, of all of them the most moral, could have been called "A Tale of Good Manners." In it Renoir shows us how the customs of a society, rather than being blindly denied or respected, can be compromised, circumvented, flexed, and varied if we want the rules of life to embrace the art of living. This accounts for the variations which Renoir contrives on the theme of the eternal triangle. How can the couple consisting of the old man and the young girl adapt to the arrival of a younger lover without clashes? How can the arts of living, of loving, and of growing old encompass the insouciance of youth? We are gripped by these questions up until the moment when the actors come out to greet the audience and we are brought back to the reality of the spectacle and the unreality of the life we have imagined to be taking place there. Unless of course it is the spectacle which is right: art for life's sake. But that was the question in the first place.

Jean Renoir is as little contemporary as usual in this film, since, as usual, he is well ahead of his time. His modernity is all the more extraordinary in that it owes nothing to styles; the styles eventually catch up to him to prove him right. Renoir begins the film with a sketch that is very carefully "dated," in which he calls the poor "poor" (a name they have lost) and restores them to the elevated position on the margins of society which the "disadvantaged" are clamoring for today. To conclude the quartet (after a sketch on a theme which has since become vulgarized under the catchall term "alienation") he advances toward another sort of marginal existence which is not without current repercussions.

Further developing his reflections on entertainment and illusion (*The Golden Coach*) and the art of living (*Picnic on the Grass*), multiplying one by the other, Renoir is always blithely cross-checking and surpassing the aestheticians preoccupied with the theory of the artistic packaging (the placing in a succession of boxes) of the various dimensions of spectacle and life.

The most curious thing about *Le Petit Théâtre* is that it seems to have been made in the spirit of a first work, establishing the foundations for the next. Jean Renoir is our greatest debutant.

MICHEL DELAHAYE

Jean Renoir during the filming of *Le Testament du Dr. Cordelier*

INDEX

●